Spiritual Development the Hard Way

Michael Maher

Copyright © 2010 by Michael Maher Trust
ISBN 978-0-9808370-0-1

Cover design by Michael Maher
Book design by Michael Maher

No part of this book may be reproduced in any form or by any electronic or mechanical means including information storage and retrieval systems, without permission in writing from the author. The only exception is by a reviewer, who may quote short excerpts in a review.

Visit the author's Web site:
www.buriedshiva.com.au/michael
www.youtube.com/user/MichaelM1052

Cover design
Spiritual development the hard way is universal. It's principles are to be found in all true spiritual traditions, and cannot be confined to any one. These principles predate every religion. The cover depicts a powerful image of Anjaneya, the quintessential archetype of the Spiritual Warrior. Anjaneya is the most fitting symbol of how to approach this Path if we wish to survive.

Anjaneya is a monkey: only the scamp has the thread of freedom. He is absolutely dedicated to Shiva, the ancient and supreme God of Infinity. He is unbelievably strong: only unbending resilience will succeed on this Path. He is immortal.

Anjaneya is beyond Hinduism. He is the patron of all who tread this solitary Path to the summit of the highest remote mountains of the world, and life.

Spiritual Development the Hard Way

*Who is this
caught
in your eyes?*

Contents

Preface i
Introduction iv
Part I Foundation 1
  Chapter 1 The Human Condition 2
    The Human Condition I 2
    The Human Condition II 6
    The Human Condition III 12
  Chapter 2 Spiritual Growth 15
  Chapter 3 Purpose 19
  Chapter 4 Positive and Negative 22
  Chapter 5 The Garden 25
  Chapter 6 Death 27
  Chapter 7 Will & Responsibility 30
  Chapter 8 The Teacher, the Guide 33
  Chapter 9 Awareness 41
    Awareness and Pressure 50
  Chapter 10 Pride 53
    A. Self-Image 54
    B. Confidence 55
    C. Offence 56
    D. Speaking of the past 58
    E. Leaving 59
    F. Common people 65
    G. Embarrassment 66
    H. Demand 67
    I. Conflict, Confrontation 68
    J. Hunting 69

Chapter 11a Stories of Pride 93
   Little fluffy jumped onto his pumpkin 95
   The Whistling Nostrils..93

Part II Reflections 99
   Chapter 11 Feelings and Emotions................................100
   Chapter 12 Influences 107
      Influences I 107
      Influences II 110
   Chapter 13 The Parallel Lines 113
      The road through no-man's-land 116

Part III Personal 121
   Chapter 14 The Journey 122
      Afterword 164
   Chapter 15 The Threshold 166

Part IV Peaks 187
   Chapter 16 Shakti 188
   Chapter 17 Meditation 194
      Delayed Awakening...210
      Holding the light steady in the dark and the wind 207
   Chapter 18 Spiritual Development the Hard Way............214

Preface

Why have I written this book?
As a plumb line, I've employed the image of me, telling myself these things, at the age of experiencing the first naturally occurring realisations. We can't create those first arisings in other people – it has to come, or it doesn't. 'It' being that strange spirit which causes a person to desire the source.

This book is not for creating those first arisings. These words are for a person who has seen the road, but doesn't know how to go about it. These words are not a directive, but for sharing opportunities with one who is keen to know where to throw all that bubbling potential.

If the energy, the vitality, is not available, then all these words are ineffectual.

I am writing to myself as a youth, on having the first realisations of the magical qualities of this world. Careful but keen, I had recognised that the practise of certain exercises and adoption of some vague attitudes were essential – what the fun of living was all about. I didn't know what I was in for.

Striking out in absolute blindness, I followed the leads that came past me and slowly began to weave the threads together. Through this book I am the friend I never met, who dropped by one evening and explained where all the fragments fit – the ideas that really matter in this journey. Pointing out the highlights for exploration. I was keen to explore anything that could challenge my spirit. Excited to begin, I only lacked direction.

This book offers direction on many layers, but one is the direction of *view*. Beneath every word in this book is a complex yet simple point of power: an inner sovereignty of *view*. Centred in our own self that is going to die, an attitude of force, yet its focus remains completely hidden from our daily world.

You can fill this inner world with untold treasures, but its potency derives from undeviating focus. No one needs to know – go quietly about the dance and the work. The endless harvest surrounds us, hidden from common eyes. Even if we do speak of our *view*, it matters not – it is irrelevant. There is only one death, mine: say that to yourself when you falter.

Everything spoken of in this book is aligned to this one focus: the absolute commitment. There is a tone, a mood that gnaws at us, which is incompatible with the way the world views its hierarchy of importance. This world we inhabit has a potent grip on how we see it. How we see our place and the place of others in it: the cult of position and possession.

The direction of *view* which underpins this book, I call a *stance*. That we take a *stance* towards the situation in which we find ourselves, here, alive, in this mosaic of mysteries. Not a *stance* dictated by our social world, nor one of idleness, fear, insecurity, loneliness. A posture of readiness, of edge, of penetration, of knowing where we are headed, and what is the best way to get there. Far from growing tireder, this *stance* grows exciting and portentous. You can feel it breathing down your neck.

Then, all you need are the events to bring these qualities through as real and self-generating. The world is a forest of opportunities, just waiting to be plucked. Every task in life, every tiny detail, is done with relish.

We each have our own path to our destination. True, we can sample numerous pathways before and during our own path, but we will always gain more from focusing full intent upon our own unique style of growth.

This material is principally designed to help one specific type of person, yet all can gain from its exercises. It assumes that the mind is not a passenger in the process of development. There are only a few people who have the power to take ideas and implement them into action. That is the only way ideas can have any validity. Else, they sit in the dungeons of our mind, festering with mould.

After the Introduction, this story begins with a journey into the 'tunnels', the *Human Condition*, to lay the foundation upon which the whole edifice resides. A secular perception of the pattern of life. Then the main characters are introduced, who are to take up lodgings within us: the *garden*, *will*, *death*, the *bully*, and *silence*.

Some are short paths and others are long, complex, personal. Littered throughout the structural categorizations, you will meet an array of stories and moods. You will have to concentrate; this book does not pretend to easy simplicity – it is not called *the Hard Way* for naught.

Lastly, discussions from different angles are included – those that don't fit neatly, or have their own landscape. In all, a list of tasks is presented, that if practised, are guaranteed to change your life. Read slowly – don't rush.

Take up this challenge or not, there it now sits, and I have fulfilled some part of my destiny. May we meet some day in the endless universe.

CD: Trance

To accompany the material in this book, I have produced a CD of trance music. This music is for the purpose of enhancing the articulation of impressions behind the ideas and words in this book, into a force of transformation that I hope the reader will find spiritually efficacious.

The usefulness of this book lies in the reader's ability to penetrate through the layers of obfuscation the world lays down in our psyche, such that we can never deviate from the course which life has set for us.

The Trance CD's music comes from another angle, in a style most listeners would not find familiar. There are all the familiar elements, yet it will disturb those layers of obfuscation when allowed to penetrate deep.

The music as with the book, are both an attempt to assist the earnest seeker in their journey away from the enchantment of the world, towards the discovery of a land never before seen, a being – a self – never before envisioned. All that is required is your willingness.

So don't piddle around in life. Whatever you do, for God's sake, don't do it the same as everyone else! Courage and audacity: if you have read this far, you have it in you to go all the way.

The CD is available on my Web site: buriedshiva.com.au/michael

Introduction

Few readers will gain any real benefit from this effort of mine, because few can step ideas down into practice. If you can take these words and allow them to transform your life into an *arrow*, then this book has been fruitful. But what if you take these words and leave them isolated in the recesses of your mind, without connection, without action: seeds on desolate ground?

Stop now, before you begin. Shake off your habitual fogginess. Stake a claim! Claim your life with a single grasp. Say aloud, "I can, and I will!"

Now you are ready. Read on.

In truth, I write because I've been told to. I've enjoyed it; that's enough for me. In writing this I have attempted to be sincere and sensible. In so doing I have deceived you – knowledge is neither sincere nor sensible. This is a secret which, by tradition, is keep from the beginner – but I have found that secrets keep themselves; so there, I've said it – you have been warned.

The purpose of this book is to provide pointers for the direction a beginner on the path of wisdom needs to explore. Each person must make their own journey. You cannot learn real knowledge from a book, but you can gain valuable insight and counsel on where to apply your time and effort. There are so many blue chestnuts being flagged before a would-be traveller in spirit, that a little clarity as to where our main chance lies is of essential value.

From time forgotten, the rule has always been: *go into the wilderness alone*. In these modern times, this rule remains true. Experience is everything. But that experience has to be found and harvested in our busy, everyday lives – not just a shamanic, wilderness journey. We need tools, to activate a spiritual purpose within the hectic kaleidoscope of activities we inhabit in this modern world, where the luxury of long retreats is less available to us.

To spend time debating theory and principle with others can be an enjoyable pastime, yet never mistake this for real knowledge. We need clarity of purpose, and the ability to review, re-examine and ponder; but the bread and butter of growth is effort and action. Think, weigh and decide first, by all means, but then you must apply a change – a different behaviour – to your daily tasks. Thought must become flesh and bone, else you are deceived, and a deceiver. Apply! Apply! Till one day you'll no longer find a line between the sacred and the mundane.

To have power, words must be spoken by one who has suffered for the right to use them. This is a journey for which you must pay dearly. Pleasure, happiness, pride, comfort, acceptance, respect, safety – all must be sacrificed. This road is hard, lonely and dangerous; surely only a fool would take it? Best you don't begin if such words upset you. Best you don't begin if such words *do not* upset you.

We almost always start for the wrong reasons. Filled with images of conceit – heroism, admiration, to salvage wounded pride, social failure, to avenge our disgrace: "I'll show them who I really am!" It is only natural to step off on the wrong foot. If these are the fruits of your spiritual efforts to date, I suggest you have slipped into the path of Spiritual Growth the Easy Way, and you will find this book boring.

I'm not saying those on the *hard way* don't enjoy themselves. (I've already said it's not serious or sensible.) On the contrary, the laughs are thick and fast. But they laugh on the other side of their face. It is a strange experience to discover yourself laughing at your agony, or sad and disturbed in your pleasure.

When you see and know what it is you must do, yet you also realize that no one will thank you – in fact you're going to suffer rather badly – it is precisely in this that some of the deepest humour is enjoyed. The joy is in the depth of the soul, and is often not available to us in the midst of our travail. It is quite an achievement to know both at once.

Nevertheless, the road has been well trodden – the footprints of many true friends can be a solace. Take up the chalice, gird your loins, strap on your sword and step forth. Cast off deception and may spirit guide your steps.

Part I

Foundation

My Purpose

To sit at the reins
*   of the dark horse and the light*
*   of the left and the right.*

The light horse is calm and happy.
He is friendly and clear
His body is strong and supple
*   with not an ounce*
*   of unnecessary fat*
And his feet are sturdy
He is the servant and protector

The dark horse has power
He flies on the wind
He is awesome and vast
*   neither friend nor foe*
And his deeds have never been told

He is gone, gone beyond
*   the shadow of time*
The door at the edge of all
The eyes of death

Chapter 1

The Human Condition

The Human Condition I

There is too much mystery, emotion, hyperbole and general fannying-about when religious or developmental traditions try to explain the basic human condition. Not that there is anything wrong with inspirational language, but when describing the common platform of existence, what's needed are plain and clear depictions.

I am not going to attempt anything more in this chapter, than the basic structure of our predicament. It is only a start, but a clear start. To bring this information into a transformational process in our lives, we need much more. I intend here to set the ground, by simply displaying the problem all humans face. And to give some indications in which direction the answers lie.

The Groove

The first image to grasp is the nature of our 'track'. This is the path we walk through life, and the way it changes.

As a baby at the beginning of life itself, or in any new area of life, we walk almost trackless. We could take any direction at any moment because we have never been here before, and decisions are made continuously. A rather tiring process, even for babies or experienced adventurers.

Let's depict this as a flat line, where no footprints exist:

———————————————————————

After we have passed this way a few times, we have the benefit of relying on some previous decisions, which had proved useful. This means that we see before us a kind of 'track'. An *indentation* of footprints, which provides a measure of familiarity.

An example. Let's say you begin a new office job: you walk into the work place and look around for the first time – everything is unfamiliar. You have to be shown which desk is yours, which desk drawers and tools are available. Then follow introductions, people drop hints about the politics of the office, the bosses give tasks, someone shows you the tea room, and you talk about things such as the best way to get to work and home.

All these aspects of a place present as absolutely fresh, but before long you forget that feeling, as you begin to find your 'place' and the walls of life in the job take on familiar features. You learn who is a friend and who to beware of, when to take lunch, where to buy lunch, which cup you can use without upsetting someone, how your chair works, how the lift works, how your computer does or doesn't work. These small familiarities allow us some respite from constantly being on guard – one doesn't want to make too many blunders straight off.

But importantly, they offer a measure of comfort, within which we can redirect our mind to its more usual preoccupations, rather than constantly having to decipher the environment minute by minute.

This scenario applies to particulars such as the new job, but also to our life in general. As we grow older, we learn the rules and mechanics of society, with which we navigate our path in life.

Skipping forward, we deepen the grooves of our road as we become more and more familiar with every aspect of the world we inhabit.

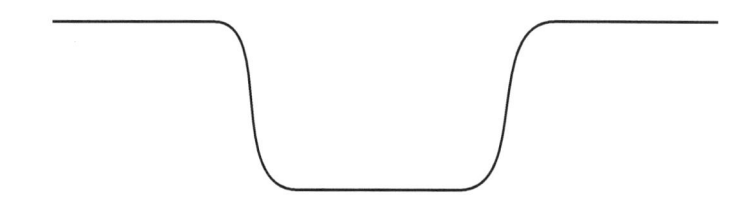

Of course the unfamiliar continues to break through, but we regroove as fast as possible because in this grooved path, we believe, resides our power. We can predict, we have control, we know the ropes, we can protect ourselves, and more, we can manipulate.

What I have just described is the basic path evolution that every creature experiences. Now we shall see how this process extends.

The Circuit

Let's examine the pattern that all humans deploy in their lives. It is this pattern that forms the configuration which construes their prison. Let us begin with an example – your home. There is a circuit you walk in your own home. The kitchen, the bedroom, the lounge, the toilet, the shower, the garden. Each of these have their own sub-circuits. In the kitchen, you have the stove, the fridge, the pots, the pantry of ingredients, the knives, chopping board, cutlery. In the bedroom you have the bed, the dresser, the wardrobe with all its contents, the mirror, the window. The list goes on – doesn't matter what culture, what class of society – the objects change but the pattern of emphasis is always the same. We move from one to the next, and we know them! That is the critical thing.

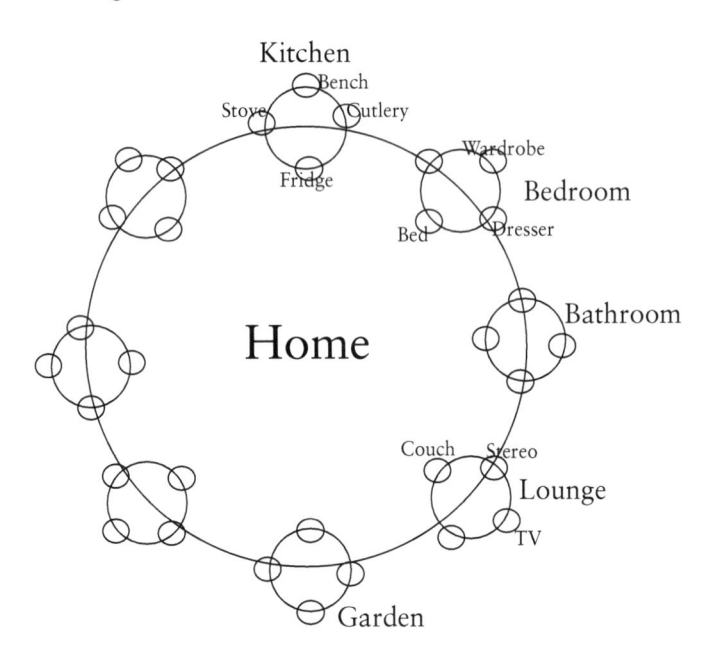

This grooved track, as explained previously, runs in a circuit from one locus to another. And within each locus, the circuit pattern repeats itself. Each of these loci have varying degrees of familiarity, thus the depth of groove changes, from shallow in places which happen to be relatively new, to grand canyons where we have been treading the same actions for many years – like long-time personal relationships.

This pattern is replicated on a wider scale, covering the life we lead in the town or city we reside in. Here again, fill in the category names that match your world.

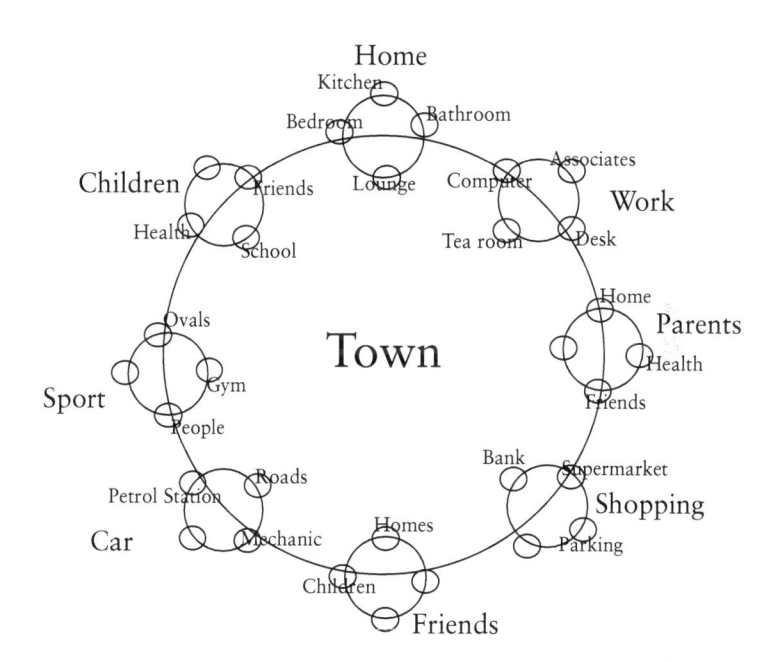

Diagram: A circular "Town" map with connected sub-circles representing:
- **Home**: Kitchen, Bathroom, Bedroom, Lounge, Computer
- **Work**: Associates, Tea room, Desk
- **Parents**: Home, Health, Friends
- **Shopping**: Bank, Supermarket, Parking
- **Friends**: Homes, Children
- **Car**: Roads, Petrol Station, Mechanic
- **Sport**: Ovals, Gym, People
- **Children**: Friends, School, Health

Our groove, again varying in degrees according to relative familiarity, runs around our habitual circuit and sub-circuits. Each place, person, road, vehicle, and object becomes coated in a knowledge that builds until very few gaps are left. Every once in awhile this little secure shell of existence gets broken into or cracked open: we change jobs, we meet a new friend, visit some new person or place, financial shifts, we get an illness, we travel overseas – many possible disruptions to our cosy little groove of life, but always we quickly build familiarity again. That is simply the natural process of living. However, as I will explain, it has profound consequences.

The Human Condition II

I have described the process of how we carve out our own groove through life, and how through familiarity this groove deepens and eventually covers the entire circuit of our world. This groove is composed of the landscape of the known – the sides, a mosaic of the recognised.

The Sphere, the Shell

Now we will examine this idea in another image, another relief on the pattern and its consequences. What is actually happening, as we live, grow and act in our world, is that at the centre is our 'self'. It doesn't matter if we are a slave to another person, husband, children, organisation or anything. Always we are looking out from our own two eyes, hearing out of our two ears, touching with our two hands, feeling with our body and our inner sentience – the world begins with ourself, some inner core, and moves out omni-directionally. Properly, the closer items, like our own body, we know intimately, and the further items like images of foreign lands we see on the television, we know vaguely. But in reality it is in no way so smooth a gradation, precisely because of the patterns I have just been detailing: the groove and the circuit.

It can be easily seen that the circuit is actually only a further extension of the groove. The groove is our primary condition. It re-extends and replicates in more and more complex ways, yet its nature remains the same.

What we have, then, is a perceptual centre, and as we live longer in the world the groove deepens until it completely closes in and surrounds us.

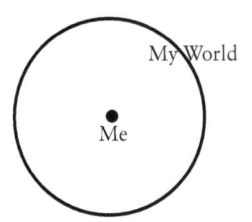

The world surrounds us as a closed sphere, the inside of which is precisely the walls of our groove. In the end, every familiarity creates 'known' features, and we steer our course as much as possible within those known features. Thus the walls of our groove reflect back to us recognisable and understandable items – in essence we exist inside a 'sphere of the known': our shell.

Look around you, and you will see that your eyes skip from known item to known item. And those items present to us a reflection of what we know about them – we don't look at our car and focus on the names of the tyres, unless that happens to be our interest, and thus a known feature. We look at our car, and see the familiar face of *our* car – mostly a collection of memories, feelings and doings associated with it.

The essential point to grasp here is that it does not matter what populates our world – whether we are rich or poor, educated or ignorant, of one culture or another – the items of our world are simply that, items on the inner wall of our sphere. Everyone is inside their sphere, trapped there – that is the human condition.

We waste our time and energy by focusing on other people's collection of items, and forget to notice that although the wallpaper is different, the structure for every being remains exactly the same, as do the consequences.

The Inner and Outer Spheres.

Let me advance this concept one more step. We are generally all aware that inside us is a very personal being that some like to call the soul – I use that word in its popular meaning. This is our thinking and feeling, internal identity. It is not just the 'me' of my job, or the 'me' my acquaintances know, but much more what we call our true inner self. This is a combination of emotions, attitudes, memories, predilections, dislikes, thoughts – all the stuff that makes up our identity – who 'I' am.

This identity is its own sphere: we have again the same structure, the same groove and circuit pattern of our outer world, but it is played out in our inner life. And again it is populated with familiar items. Here, though, they are attitudes and emotions, and these construe perhaps our oldest and deepest grooves, our most opaque sphere.

But this sphere is fused to the outer sphere. That is the secret that advertisers and politicians know only too well, and also the so-called 'secret police', whose job is to break a person and extract information or confessions.

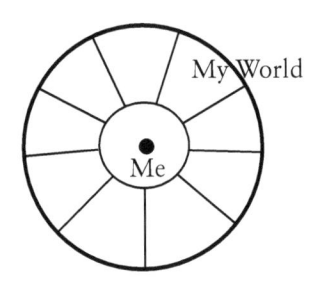

[Diagram: a circle divided into segments with an inner circle labeled "Me" and the outer ring labeled "My World"]

There are strong fusion points, like a puppet's strings, but generally the inner sphere spins in unison with the outer sphere. Our moods and often even our thoughts are pulled and determined by the shifting items of our outer world. What someone says, what food is offered, what mood other people are in, what is on the television, what we read in a newspapers, what the weather is like, and so forth. Our inner life is at the complete mercy of our external environment, so much so that our very identity is conditional upon how our outer world is arranged, and manipulated.

The most noticeable example of this is when we are removed to a completely different environment – our whole sense of self and identity begins to crumble. We must go to great lengths to bolster it, by recalling memories, telling others about ourselves, or adopting familiar actions. This is the example of those who travelled to the colonies in imperial times. Even those who simply travel to foreign lands as tourists feel impelled to adopt caricatures of their own culture's stereotypes. Just go to a place you rarely visit – like a party of new people, especially younger people, or a pub or opera – whatever is not your usual haunt, and you immediately feel uncomfortable, uncertain.

Right here, you can understand why it becomes so important to keep to our familiar circuit: becoming a potent force, by maintaining our behaviour in its predictable patterns. Our inner identity is a very brittle thing, precisely because it is so vulnerable to disruptions in the outer sphere.

This introduces one of the primary objectives of personal development – to free the inner sphere from its fusion to the outer sphere. To lubricate, make it supple and capable of independent movement. Like a ball bearing, it should be able to spin freely inside the outer shell. I think the value in this is self-evident; who would want to be a slave, a robot, where every mood is dictated by the passing images of the world? How could we possibly have the freedom to make independent choices, or even attempt to see the truth of any situation, if we don't have some measure of internal sovereignty? Our inner strength and integrity are dependent on this accomplishment.

Entrapment

Till now I have only described the mechanics of the human condition. Though I mentioned the words trap and prison, these qualitative concepts only reveal themselves once we look closely at the consequences of this enclosed sphere upon our spirit.

One important effect of the familiarisation of our world is that we no longer have to pay close attention to it. This frees us to dwell upon the fusion points between the outer and inner sphere. In short we think about how certain items on the walls of our world, our groove, have affected us – usually it is about other people, but in fact, which item is less important here than the fact that we *dwell*.

There is one special facet of our dwelling that becomes an integral part of the human condition – concern. We engage our emotions, especially our concern, in a process of internal preoccupation with specific items of our world. We are concerned about our friends, children, parents, job, spouse, country, religion – we are concerned to be secure in all those areas we dwell on, with an endless internal dialogue. We repeat our identity to ourselves over and over. We remake ourselves continuously with this self-talk.

Not only do we become entrapped in a sealed sphere – a shell – but we continually repair and maintain that shell with our preoccupied thoughts and moods. Then we indulge in worry and fretting about the two most powerful pillars of our world-view: position and possession. This dwelling on concern about position and possession eats our creative energy, consumes it from our head to our toes, till we find ourselves in the final phase of the human condition.

The reason for digging this groove in the first place is that it gives us control, security and, most of all, comfort. Then we find our inner self has become so dependent on the stability, predictability and reliability of our shell, that its continuity and permanence becomes crucial to our well-being. It also becomes boring. Comfort and boredom. We then turn to self-consumption, burning up the only power we natively have that can help us escape, by incessant worry and repetitive absorption in *our* problems.

Everyone knows the experience of trying to help someone in woe – we offer solutions, but the poor person beset by cruel fate, has an excellent reason why each and every suggestion could not work in their case. Not only have we built our own prisons, but we have endless and cogent arguments why we can't get out.

I'll let you in on a secret here – even if we were to agree on a solution, we could not put it into effect. We lack the *will*, and the creative energy. So our arguments against each suggested solution, are not just a reflection on the cognitive aspects of those fusion points, but a defence against inevitable humiliation. We can't afford to acknowledge there are answers, because when the door opens, *we haven't the guts to leave*. The human condition.

But, you say, there are people who are very happy in their world. There is no escape. I can only suggest you look deeper, and every time you'll find a small child who had great dreams. In every case, those dreams were forfeited for a pact with the devil – we gained familiarity and a façade of comfort, but we gave our dreams away.

If you find someone who has found some measure of real joy, you have also found someone who has broken their shell. Unfortunately, two things:

1. not everyone who breaks their shell finds happiness; and
2. only those who have real knowledge of how to escape their prison, are able to find true meaning to their lives – as opposed to the shell-induced meaning of society. But true meaning doesn't necessarily equate to what the prisoner would call happiness.

The Escape Plan

The reason I have detailed the nature of the structure of the human condition, is to provide some inkling of its brickwork. Knowledge of the brickwork is essential in knowing how to dismantle the walls.

If you bluntly break down the outer sphere, the person will get sick, have a nervous breakdown or even die – such is the adhesion of the inner to the outer. If you likewise blindly break down the inner sphere, the person will most likely go insane, or die. It is one thing to understand the nature of the trap, but a very different thing to know how to plan and conduct the escape.

Some indications: firstly, never fall for the hubris of believing in the excitement of youth. Or believing in the animal's method: head-on. We need a comprehensive strategy: a plan built not just on ideas, but on the accumulated knowledge of those who have gone before.

Secondly, the outer shell must become porous, and cleared of unnecessary clutter. The inner shell likewise should be stripped of pseudo-confidence, and introduced to pondering without superficial labelling. Too often we believe we understand concepts because we know the words. Toss the words, and reach for the real meaning behind deep ideas. Then reconstruct the ideas with new words that speak from innate personal understanding.

Obviously, conditioning the inner self to uncertainty, by adopting a preparedness towards discomfort and new pathways, is good advice for anyone. These things serve to soften up the belly, and reduce our obsession with likes and dislikes.

Alas, these measures will have only limited effect. What is needed is the help of someone further along this road than ourself. A guide. Isn't that precisely what we all do when we want to learn a skill – seek out the skilled? Unfortunately, we in 'Western' countries belong to a world in which we are happy to learn from teachers of everything, except inner development.

The idea that some people are internally more matured than ourselves is anathema to us. We accept that you may be a better golfer than me, but inside we are all equal – I'm as good a human being as the next person, and anyone who thinks differently is a wanker or a wimp. Take a look and see if you still suffer from that item on the walls of your shell, your prison.

Lastly, I have one more suggestion. Silently walk out of your home at night, into the back garden will do, and make a personal pact with your soul. Say it out loud. That you will escape the entrapment of the human condition! When, is not important here, what is important is that with every ounce of your being, you commit your spirit to ultimate freedom – whatever that may be. Do you dare?

The Human Condition III

The Essence of Life: Flavour, Perception and Expression

I have described the structural view of the human condition – the inner and outer shell – and how it comes about. The inner shell composed of our attitudes, values and beliefs; the outer of the objects which populate the world we live in. As explained, this is only a simplified description of what is in fact a complexity beyond imagination. But a simplified view of our condition is of great value, as it provides us a ready handle, or platform, upon which we can build as we personally explore the mysteries of our life and world. I want to adopt a similar approach in this next section, further explaining the consequences of those shells for us as beings who are going to die.

The best way to introduce this is by a story. Imagine yourself to be God. Unfortunately for you, you are eternal (as distinct from your familiar self). So, some time ago, to amuse yourself, you planted a fruit tree – you called it the Tree of Life. Now you lie beneath its vast branches, and with the majestic indolence that only God can know, you stretch out your hand to catch a fruit as it falls from the Tree. This Tree has the most incredible variety of fruit – literally every living creature. Each fruit is a single living being, and when it falls into your hand, a dead one.

You put the fruit to your mouth and taste – some are delicious, some tasteless, others bitter or sweet. Such variety, each one subtly or distinctly different. And as you savour or spit out each one, you think to yourself, "I have become accustomed to this fruit diet. But the Tree of Life is after all only a tree, and one day it will die. Then I will go hungry, at least until another tree reaches fruit bearing age, and even then it will be aeons before any descent varieties of fruit begin to appear. I know, I'll make wine out of each fruit and store it away. Then I can invite my friends around each evening for a good night of wine tasting."

So you turn to your angels, and direct them to make a bottle of wine out of each falling piece of fruit. How quick those angels can work, when they work for God! Very soon you hold your first wine tasting. All your old friends come around and you uncork the first bottle. Let us say that the wine of that bottle is a human, in fact, the *you* reading this story. Now the you in our story, as God, pour a glass for testing – you don't want to foist a cruddy fair upon your old friends. You lift the glass to your nose, and take a first sniff – "Hmmm... not too bad, bit too tangy, bit too bitter, but a nice aroma nonetheless." You place it to your lips, take a small sip, then let it swill gently around your divine tongue – all your guests look on in anticipation. They look to you, you look to them – will you say yes, or no? You as God, assess the quality of the flavour of you as human. What say you?

Flavour – the product of life, the end result of all you have thought, felt, experienced – reduced to one quality, a flavour.

Perception

Ultimately we are perceivers, whether as the God in our story, or the little person that plods through life: we taste. Deep in our core, there is a *filament of receptivity*. It is so finely tuned, so delicate in nature, that it resonates to even the most minute impulse possible. Everything we register through the process of life, is registered in our core by this filament.

After the initial touch of any impulse, a taste occurs. So soon replaced by the next transient impulse, but the effect of that taste lingers around this central pinpoint of receptivity. Like an aura, this sequence of tastes accumulate, and becomes a radiance of flavour. When we die, after all our experiences, all that remains is this, our *flavour* – the product of our life.

Perception is critical. Our hardened shell curtails this perception, filters and prescribes it. If you spent your life cutting railway sleepers from trees, when you look at bush land, as someone once said to me, "Look, there's not a decent sleeper anywhere!" That was all he saw – sleepers or not-sleepers. A botanist would see the botanical conditions of life, a painter would see the colours and shapes. Look at a group of workers in a factory: an economist would see the utilisation of resources, a social worker would see the conditions and how each worker was personally affected, a Marxist would see the class struggle, a nationalist would see the nation, a doctor the body, a manager costs. Each view would reveal its owner's shell, but the poverty of each viewer's perception would be revealed in the singularity of their view.

Perception is wealth. Perception feeds our *flavour*, so the depth and quality of our *flavour* is truly our only wealth. The range and richness that we allow ourselves to perceive, is our income. Rich or impoverished, artist or miner, whatever our situation in life, if we have prescribed only a narrow possibility of perception, due to the rigidity of our attitudes or the lack of variety of interests, then we are poor. Some people travel the world, but when you meet them, their *flavour* is thin and tasteless.

How to know a person's *flavour*? When we meet a person for the first time, our antennae are very sensitive to *flavour* – even if we know little of their beliefs and social position, we can feel them. Think for a moment of anyone you know, and just before an avalanche of events and memories arrive, we have a short moment to feel them in one grasp. That is their *flavour* in our minds.

The constricting influence and the familiar tunnels of the human condition, cramps perception, robbing us of our birthright: to perceive this glorious world in all its nuances, all its facets. We stand before a vast and endlessly faceted crystal, but stubbornly glue our eyes to only one face. Why?

It is the human condition.

Chapter 2

Spiritual Growth

The most fundamental principle in the development of our spirit is maturity. This, amongst other things, implies depth, balance and sobriety. Such qualities are not easy to acquire. We only hide in stupidity if we ignore the role of suffering, and patient endurance of long periods of mundanity or discomfort. The overriding vehicle of spiritual growth is the vast, almost endless, block of insignificant actions we perform throughout our lives: look to the small things.

In practice we usually don't have the energy to harness this enormous resource, so we require a comprehensive strategy to support our earnest but feeble intentions, one which covers all aspects of life. The principle of magnetism: all the parts of life lining up in the same direction.

This strategy must engage both sides of our being. On the one side it must be practical, detailed and obvious. On the other side, it must speak the language of mystery and intuition. In this book you will find some sections effortless, some difficult and some obscure. Such is the journey we walk. Enjoy the easy parts, go slowly and deliberate on the hard parts and, for the obscure – not all understandings lend themselves to words and clear explanations.

There are times when an allusion refers to things that lie beneath the surface, in the realm of feeling, imagination and mystery. Take these intimations into your mind, like turning over a mint in your mouth – allow it to dissolve gradually, and you will perceive with a sense you have little used before. Allow the obscure to seep into your consciousness, and let it do its work of transformation without mental interference, without the restless brain grabbing at it, trying to understand it. Gently, quietly, with furry edges and vague outline, leave it mysterious.

This is how the Path is characterised: downhill, uphill, and moonlight.

It is important to grasp that we are not the person we think we are. We do not have the control over our lives that we commonly assume for ourselves. At most, we may have moments of clarity – then follow long periods of submergence. During those periods of clarity we can make a few decisions, through which we attempt to influence the quality and direction of our lives. But the force of our lives is a momentum set in motion by the indescribably endless influence of others upon us. We have forgotten the eternity of the earliest part of our lives, in which we unguardedly absorbed the life-force of all those around us. Against this, our own individuality is almost completely powerless.

What we perceive as individuality in ourselves and those about us is due to the summation of a vast array of known and unknown forces – different for each of us – but other than our true self. Our *power* to direct our own course against the current of these forces is, frankly, infinitesimal. The profound humiliation of this realization is what causes most to capitulate before the dictate of the world and resort to pretending to be unique individuals, leaving their true selves buried deep in the future.

Spiritual Growth is the unbelievable possibility that this infinitesimal *power* can be fostered and harnessed. Till one day sufficient freed will is stored so that we stand before a panorama of choices, knowing we have the spirit not only to grasp one, but see it through to its promised conclusion. This can only come from firstly realising our impotence. Those who have not acknowledged this truth, know nothing of Spiritual Growth. For those who have, this book is for you, as it sketches the outline of how that unbelievable possibility can become a reality.

The Well

The two sides of our being: the left and right sides of the body or, conversely, the right and left hemispheres of the brain. The art of Spiritual Growth employs both aspects of our being. I will use the physical body's sides instead of the brain's as, being symbols, they extend in meaning beyond the body alone. The *left* side is the mysterious, the pure, unstructured essence of consciousness that meets perception directly, without any interpretation. The *right* side is the controlled, structured and constructing capacity of consciousness, in which we employ the power of action upon ourselves and the world.

The activation of our *left* side is the awareness of *now*, of *presence*. An awareness outside of time, the immediate perception of truth, unfettered and undenied: in an instant we know, and we do not hide that knowledge with any time-based ulterior motives. The portal of inspiration.

The activation of our *right* side is the awareness of time, the memory of past, the projection of future, the intelligent assimilation of knowledge gleaned from our own experiences and from those who have travelled this road before. It is the side which learns, designs, plans and builds. It is also the artist within who creates beauty with dedication and skill.

The task for the aspirant is to cleanse, foster and balance *left* and *right* into a unit, a potent vehicle of spiritual evolution. Our vehicle of being, as we find ourselves – alive and aware – is designed in the first instance for the survival of the species: reproduction. That is a law within our being. But it is not the only law. There is another, equally powerful law: evolution. The species seeks both survival and evolution. It is a decision aspirants to spiritual development must make – do we wish to come under the *command* of species survival or the *command* of evolution? We cannot do both.

A *command* is something those who choose this Path have to comprehend very quickly, because the dominant, default *command* of our being-within-species is survival, that is, reproduction. To achieve any worthwhile outcome within the timespace allotted for this alive-aware vehicle, before it is dis-mantled, we must, before all else, struggle to *break the law* of species-survival.

In the ancient traditions this has always been described as the extrication from the dominant river current, across to another smaller current which flows in a different direction. In a later chapter *The Journey*, I describe how this process unfolded for myself. For now, for the purpose of the map of Spiritual Growth, suffice to know that *crossing of the current* is one of the primary tasks before us.

The way in which we employ the two sides of our being is best described by a time-honoured image which permeates almost all stories of the spiritual tradition: the *well*. It has numerous meanings and symbolisms, but at heart it is always an image of the mystery of our two sides, and of how they work together under the *command* of spiritual evolution.

The *right* side of our being is the walls, the pulley, the rope and bucket of the *well*. The *left* is the water at the bottom of the *well*. The injunction is simplicity itself. If the walls of the *well* are not strong, well-build and clean, the goal of retrieving clean, pure water is severely endangered. If the pulley system and the cross-bar are not well-oiled, strong enough to carry the full bucket weight and retrieve it from the bottom of the *well*, then all is lost. Retrieval is crucial to this whole operation.

If the rope is frayed, tangled and of insufficient strength to complete the task, again, all is lost. If the bucket is poorly made, not water-tight, or damaged in some way then, even if all the rest is set right, the whole effort will be futile.

If the water at the bottom of the *well* is not potable – if it is muddy, poisoned, infected or impure in any way, again the whole operation is futile, as it will be of no use even if successfully retrieved.

All these are symbols for the task of Spiritual Growth, and we profit in pondering this image fully, reviewing all aspects of our life and intention, to be sure we are not wasting our time or, worse, damaging our ability to survive.

This premise of the *well* is what this entire book is about. It is a manual for the successful prosecution of our task, as aspirants for the promise of Spiritual Growth. Everything outlined within this book is, in one form or another, addressing the building, strengthening, cleaning and purification of the *well*. What we do with the water after we have successfully retrieved it is not within the gambit of this book. To be followed up in a later volume, at a later time, with a coverage of that eventuality and how the water can be employed in furthering the Path of our spiritual evolution. But there is no point in discussing any of that until the task of the *well* has been completed, and we have survived intact, to journey on in this mysterious and magical universe.

Chapter 3

Purpose

The first thing to do is to make a gesture. To propose a commitment toward the principle of natural enhancement. This will be different for everyone, because of our elsewhere-formed personality. We should respect each other's sincere, albeit feeble attempts toward their own version of this principle.

Of course good intentions are not sufficient, but a strong sober gesture, no matter what our level of will, has the quality of a seed.

This invokes the *maturation of desire*. Maturation ultimately has to lead out of desire, as we know it. There seems to be so little time in our short life to accomplish this process.

Nonetheless some allusion should be made toward what is really at play in this matter of pure purpose. There is a strange force at loose in the world. In your observations of people in general, even young babies, you can see that some have a spark of deep vitality – in a few it is so strong that they enter into the path of initiation no matter what their starting point. Others need help and nurturing or they fall into an uneasy sleep.

Next to such examples, the bulk of humanity seem perfectly comfortable to remain hypnotised by the forces that surround them. What is happening here? This power has been seen as a *bird* by the poetic minds of the past. A *bird* whose intentions we can align ourselves with so completely, the old stories go, that it will lead us into some experiences not to be missed for anything.

We have to console ourselves with symbols, and set in motion a design of many faceted inner and outer architecture. Only in this way can we evolve to where our deeds have the power to attract. Else we may fall prey to the prevalent delusion as to our real nature.

Maturation of desire culminates in *intent*. Behind every minute of your day, every action no matter how great or small, there is intent. But for most it is not their own intent – it is the intent of an unknown people. When our desire matures, and forms into a true motivation with knowledge and will, we can lay down our own intent. This is a magical intent, because it is no longer the surrogate of strangers, but one generated from within, and aligned with our energetic essence: that is what makes it magical.

Once this maturing process has been born, hardened and deepened, it becomes unbreakable – either by our failures, by life's accidents, by time, or by infinity itself.

Do you have purpose in your life?

Is your purpose simply to be as comfortable and safe until your time is up? Or do you have a purpose over and above that of comfortable survival?

To enter this Path, we have to ask ourselves this question. The common purpose of reproduction, friendships, pleasure and avoidance of pain or boredom, will not suffice. We have to look to the horizon, use imagination and daring. We have to seek the finest outcome possible to any living being – an outcome of infinite potency. Never, ever, step it down to something more practical and generally acceptable. Retrieve the child in you, and reach for the stars – reach beyond the stars. Soar beyond the limits of reality, and beyond the boundaries of imaginable possibility. That is what we do. That is how we live, and how we face death. We never condescend our purpose, because our motivation springs from the very pith of being – a being whose existence is far beyond understanding. As being is of ultimate mystery, so our goal is of ultimate mystery.

Give this goal a name – any name will do, so long as it stands for the acme of your passion and audacity as a living, breathing entity. See the path to this goal as a golden light and feel it infuse your soul to its core – that is your purpose.

Walk with this passion in your soul into the night, up onto a high hill and look straight out into the black sky, beyond the stars. In a loud voice, call out the name of your goal!

To make this purpose a binding force in your life, first you must call out its name. Then you have to work. You have to apply constant effort to keep this purpose alive in your heart no matter what befalls you in life.

Lastly, and most importantly, you have to surrender all care for its achievement. That is the rule of a spiritual purpose: utter dedication and constant remembering, without the slightest care for its achievement. Not an easy mood to attain, but not impossible.

Ask yourself, is there anything more worthwhile to do with your life?

Chapter 4

Positive and Negative

This is a way to schematize all the bits and pieces that seem to dribble on endlessly from some place. To simplify, we can divide up most of the various practices into two aspects: those which open and attract us forward, and those which help us to recognize the dangers, to stem the leakage – demanding strength, discipline and the redesigning of our personality to better suit a healthy growth process.

When a stream of current runs fluently through tightly controlled channels, enormous force can build up. Also, in the shedding of concerns by the appropriate sacrifices, we can relax in a way we haven't known since the gift of childhood. In various ways, the shedding of obstinate indulgences, which veil our unknown nature, can be attributed to a sublimated destructive force.

Having come to terms with this *negative* aspect of our trip, we can then allow ourselves the permission to run with the horses in Spring, when such an audience is granted. We should never overlook the incurable, romantic nature of God!

Many argue over which is correct – to apply the *positive* or *negative*, the attractive or the disciplining, the force of love or the force of rigour? Both are necessary. This is also a social fashion – in some cultures one will predominate over another, so it is up to us to step aside from our culture and submit willingly to both, never resenting when another is receiving the *positive* end of the stick while we are getting the *negative*. We accept our time in both, and know there is much more beyond either.

Positive and *negative* thus have an important extended meaning. The cornerstone of Spiritual Growth is inner potency. As a child we have an abundance of inner potency. It is not honed nor available for directed use, but just watch a child and see they're natural vitality. Now look at an adult, and ask, "Where did the magic go?" That is the potency I speak of.

As an adult on the Path of Spiritual Growth, inner potency is everything. You can read the books, believe in the big ideas, but if you lack inner potency, it will all be a futile exercise in storing dead thoughts. I will speak more about this as the book proceeds, it being such a central focus.

In fostering and accumulating inner potency, we have two approaches – the *positive* and the *negative*. In this book, it is the *negative* that I will emphasise. This is because our first task is to stem the leakage of our potency. This means we must stop doing certain things which drain us of our natural empowerment – that which makes things possible, what we call luck, or optimism, that which spontaneously opens doors and keeps our flame alight in the wildest wind.

I will touch on some of the *positive* measures, which attract more potency, but even there I will keep to the foundational aspects. There are some wonderful techniques of enriching our birth-given empowerment, but what is the point of speaking of these, if the vessel isn't water tight, if the foundations are not rock solid?

For this stage of the strategy of *spiritual development the hard way*, these are the primary precepts:

Negative: Regret, Resentment, Offence.

Write these on your door: *never regret, never be resentful, never be offended*. Give up your clinging to these three drain holes. There is nothing wrong with regret, resentment, or offence, but if you want to retrieve your inner potency, they have to go. It is not a moral or ethical issue, it is purely mechanical: the mechanics of consequence. If we seek to travel East by walking North, we are idiots. This is the rule, and no arguments can be entered into – you cannot store light if these holes remain open.

Positive: Perseverance, Reliability, Novelty.

Also write these on your door. To persevere means to see things through to completion. To be reliable means to be a 'person of your word'. Novelty means to constantly seek out change and new impressions – not superficially, but as an active strategy of life. These three are the foundational measures which enhance our potency, our inner confidence, our inner wealth. They renew our magical inheritance as a being alive in an unbelievably glorious universe ... for such a short time.

Perseverance and reliability, as Saturnian qualities, would seem to belong to the *negative* precepts, and in some ways they do. But it is the inner qualities which we either have or lack, that cause us to give up, or be unreliable, which come under the *negative* precepts. These are the weaknesses in our character which sabotage our resolve. I include perseverance and reliability in the *positives* precisely because the practise of these qualities directly enhances our natural endowment of life-energy.

Before I leave this discussion, however, I want to intimate one of the most effective means of enhancement, which I have not covered here because it belongs to the advanced traveller's tool kit. That is the practice of visiting places of high natural potency found in the world, with a specific sensitivity to absorb this energy. This is such an important area of activity for experienced practitioners, that I will cover it in detail in a subsequent volume.

The foundational *positive* and *negative* precepts which I have sketched here only in summary, I will return to again and again in every way possible throughout this book. Every practice, idea and attitude expressed in this book fits into one or the other of this two-sided coin – the currency of our real wealth, our inner potency.

Chapter 5

The Garden

Speak of a personal offering, no matter how small, that we prepare during life. Like a bubble, that we expand and fill with rare delicacies, until it bursts at death, so we can go and live in it. The garden is when the heart is home. We cannot fool the heart – why should we? When the heart is relaxed and at peace, in defiance of the barbaric daily battle, it is obvious – so we begin the journey of finding more quality nourishment.

But we should stop and consider in whose being we live and die, if we wish to practise the art of affection.

Now this is all very well, but one must begin from a position fairly remote from all this. How to start, when we have little or no idea in which direction our garden lies? The important thing is to make a start. Don't be put off because you feel the perfect activity has not arrived.

We have certain obligations upon our energy: a job to make money, family responsibilities, necessary things to be done to keep body and soul together in a satisfactory way. After these have made their claim, begin some form of hobby – do something for no reason whatsoever, except for the sheer enjoyment of doing it. No thoughts of fear, ambition, competition; no interest in gaining approval from friends or others.

Don't expect to find 'the thing for me' – the garden path is always changing. This is the whole point – in this, more than any other activity in life, can be applied the maxim of 'the journey not the goal', because the essence of the garden is that it gives us a sense of peace and enjoyment just to be doing it. In truth, it is a *shield* against the pressures of concern.

Simply do something as a hobby – anything. Study another language, volunteer to help in some group activity. You may possibly get a few clues from remembering what you used to enjoy playing as a child. Some people have no problem identifying what to engage in, while others take many years, and only start to find their pace late in life. All this is of no importance; it is only necessary to begin.

The purpose of the garden is to create something of our own unique form of beauty.

Once it has been established, after it has weathered frosts, drought and plague, the next step is to slowly attempt to shift one's whole life into the garden. For some, this will never be possible, but in principle, what stands between us achieving this is lack of courage. The boldness of the heart is intimately involved with crucial moments, where we bite through the wrappings and take risks.

This process is related to the issue of security. In the early stages of development we are often unaware of the profound implications of our aspirations and practices. As we progress we realize that much of the experience we invoke through the application of our strategy, is in essence an exercise in balance.

The impact of entering into the truth that lies behind the arbitrary facades of our familiar life, causes in us a deep need and longing for some psychic home, with real power to act as a safe harbour. A place to which our spirit flies, when we're lost in the unspeakable vastness – it must have the power to pluck us back from such a fate, or adventure.

Obviously there are levels of meaning to be contemplated here, but suffice to say that no ordinary superficial pleasure, belief, or group allegiance can possibly hold up under the pressure of balancing such forces as we are intending through our commitment.

The garden is not just a selfish indulgence. It is the mature transformation and appropriate manifestation of egoism into the flowering of necessity.

Chapter 6

Death

The Garden was one for the *positive*, the attractive, now this is one for the other side of the coin. There are many deaths, but here we deal with only two. The first is viewed though the eyes of our encultured personalities. The second is the death of the body.

You want to be serious about *spiritual development the hard way*? Then turn your eyes toward death. Properly speaking this is an exercise to be engaged with under the guidance of a teacher, however it is of such basic significance that reference to the dangers will have to suffice.

Death is a very attractive option. We underestimate its potency. There comes a point in the contemplation and exercises of death, when strange moods possess us. You may find an unusual lack of desire to resist death, tremendous anger, or sadness. The depressive side-effects of this yoga are the primary dangers – we tend to become unbearably morose. Here is where the *garden* helps to retain balance.

Press on, nonetheless, for your appointment with Death. May I offer my profound sympathies to those who traverse this landscape.

Somewhere hereabouts we should consider the possibility that beyond death, there is nothing. Take it as an exercise in confrontation with the *annihilator* essence of death, that is 'fin', the end, no buts, no salvage – the final extinction of our consciousness. First become comfortable with this possibility before pondering other post-death survival scenarios. Do not opt for an afterlife belief out of fear of the ultimate abyss.

But how to really feel Death? We may notice ourselves sprouting words on death, but realising the absence of any appropriate intensity. There is no escape but to be blunt. Use time as a weapon. From a start of quiet contemplation, poems, silence and imagination – preparing the ground – to a response from Death in answer to our invocation. A friend dies, we see a dead body. We begin to see ourselves making our way, moving from the common table, toward the gate on the hill to speak with the keepers.

The journey moves into its last phase – home is left behind after having sold or given away all possessions, veiled but sincere farewells and last moments shared, we head out alone, onto the road to meet fate. And then one day we're there – it's our turn.

It's usually some unromantic, insignificant, yet sacred place – you may even be honoured by the village idiot, or a small animal. My advice is to not give in too easily: fight for your life! It's handy to have some gestures up your sleeve to symbolise your spirit.

With a bit of luck, perhaps because you're early, or through respect for your spirit, or for no reason whatsoever, you may get a reprieve – and head back to the common table. It becomes hard to make real friends after this. You become a member of a special club, which everyone belongs to – they just don't know it.

After all this overdramatic, indulgent ego-swaggering, we can begin to contemplate our real death – the health of the body. With a peculiar loose grip, a new attitude toward life gradually crystallises.

It is wise to confront all possibilities with any reasonable claim on what we will go through immediately on death of the body, and after. I could give a summary here of the more informed approaches to death that come from sensible religious traditions or individual investigators, but as this is a subject for more advanced speculation, I will cover it in a subsequent book. For the aspirant starting out on the spiritual path, the essential thing is to gain personal experience of death. Be pragmatic and not sentimental. If you want to look your best when you're elected, put a lot of attention now on the quality of the taxi you wish to see waiting for you, once the show is over.

The natural progression of this yoga awakens our consciousness to where we came from – before conception and birth. This creates the ability to fly around ourselves in ever widening spaces. The knowledge gained flows into our *garden*, in which we conceive and give birth to ourselves. Do not underestimate the enormity of changes we are capable of: nothing has been exhausted.

On the Path of Spiritual Growth, passing through the Portal of Death is the first primary task. In this task we have to be stripped to the bone, losing all attachment to life and its hooks in the soul. Once this task is completed we are freed from the fear of losing, and entrapment through desire. I will speak more on this in a later chapter, when I relate my own passage through this Portal.

All the initial practices, despite appearing to bolster the ego and its place in the world, in fact, secretly lead us to the Portal of Death. At some point on this Path you will realise this – that you have been tricked. But it isn't really trickery. It is the natural progression – all streams of spiritual practice must lead through the Portal of Death before they can bear real fruit. It is embedded in the blueprint of the *command* of spiritual evolution, and avoidance of this inevitability has disastrous consequences. So accept it as given, and instead of fighting against Death, rather, go forth to meet it with courage, curiosity and excitement. Death is our true benefactor – without its imprimatur, all our acts lack power. Only once Death sits beside us, will we cease being ghosts, and become real.

Chapter 7

Will & Responsibility

Will is a mysterious quality. The common understanding of this term refers to personal features such as determination, endurance and strength of conviction. However there is another, mysterious form of *will* for which there is no common understanding, and thus no adequate words. Some words, nonetheless, can indicate the direction; such as 'luck' or 'grace'. Also when people refer to the 'power of positive thinking', the 'friendship of the gods', or good karma.

Both the common and the mysterious aspects of *will* are of significance. The first involves the cohesive power of the personality. The second is more like a friendship, and ultimately is the by-product of alignment – typically it is produced through depth, but only fully evolves with integrity.

This distinction is important. *Will* is a common downfall of aspirants. The extraordinary experience of command, generated through the appearance of *will*, all too often blinds more evolved beings from the clear recognition of their ultimate and complete dependence. It is a very potent seductive illusion.

Yet *will* must be developed. Without it we are leaves in the wind – any wind – and thus far from a true connection to our being.

The process of development of *will* is not straightforward. There are ample examples of people who have acquired it by all sorts of devious, capricious or horrifying means. Best to ignore these, and do it the *hard way*.

Begin with responsibility. Through responsibility we store power in our decisions. This is cumulative. Never fall victim to the insanity that we have 'free will' – choice, the ability to decide direction. We acquiesce, always, with forces outside us, and then childishly arrogate to ourselves the image of control.

We cannot change the order of *command*, but we can learn to see it through. What you say you'll do – DO IT! Every time a set task is not completed, we weaken. This is what is meant by accepting responsibility – for our words, actions, and paths. Also for our awareness and presence, but this needs first to be fostered. Accepting responsibility entails giving up the indulgence of regrets, of self-recriminations, or blame – of ourselves and others. If mistakes are made or the wrong road taken, then change. Don't dwell on missed opportunities: time is too short for that. I am not suggesting we absolve ourselves from the obligation of self-examination and reflection, just leave out bitterness and self-pity. Accepting our fate is one of the first steps toward entering upon destiny. This requires a sensible pattern of behaviour to be crystallised into character.

First, a position of *uncompromising potency* must be hung up on the wall, as a reference point. This position states: *back up every decision with your life*. That means, only death will prevent or excuse me from doing what I say I'll do. Only death can release me from my word.

The other side states: *I will not do anything, unless I am prepared to die in doing it.*

A common example of what not to do: we naturally attempt to be friendly and pleasant by not saying 'no'. We agree to do something for the sake of polite friendship, and at the time our intentions are good, we are just responding to the mood of the moment as we lightly agree to some activity, be it attending a party, delivering some small thing and so on. It is a gesture of good will, not a situation that calls for a 'hand on chest' holy vow. Or so we feel. Later, other unforeseen commitments make it too awkward to complete: "they'll understand", "it's not that important", "that's just the way life goes". *That's the way death comes.* You must reach the point where making death stand and wait is easy – but your decisions can never be stalled; their sovereignty becomes absolute.

Second, set yourself deliberate tasks under these conditions. Make these tasks small and preferably meaningless. There is a marked enjoyment in this exercise. This is important – a standard alone is not sufficient to incubate *will*. Application is everything: action! Never forget it is always through action that anything enduring is achieved; except of course, from the ultimate central position (which I will explore in the chapter on meditation).

Third, introduce pragmatism. Some decisions we make, or have made in life, are plainly wrong and stupid. To persevere in them would only weaken and destroy us. Recognise that in pulling out we behave correctly, but there is a price to pay. If we make too many mistakes like this we may never recover. Here we attempt to salvage the situation by what is termed 'changing our decision'. This means seeing the essence of our intention, and redirecting it. Thus, only the means are compromised – where we can see there was a germ of pure motive behind the original stance. If even this cannot be managed, then for God's sake, never be so stupid again.

The other form of pragmatism is to attach the term 'maybe' to those decisions that are necessary yet dodgy. But I warn you, only use it when absolutely necessary, for it can quickly destroy us, as can the practice of compromising pragmatism itself. Best to shine your spirit and make the decision right now! Commit.

Here as always, balance is required to develop a broad, strong and gentle *will*, capable of explosive and devastating decisiveness – which can be placed at the service of our primary commitment.

Chapter 8

The Teacher, the Guide

Before progressing further, this thorny topic must be tackled. Few other issues produce such an emotional reaction in Western cultures. That in itself indicates where we can readily begin to confront the dark magicians. Who are the dark magicians? Why, haven't you noticed? Your fellow humans are the dark magicians, for they demand adherence and offer no choice. They already have you in their trap, and will seed all kinds of ideas in your mind to prevent you from escaping, or seeking out those who can lead you to freedom.

An old saying goes: "Until you know, follow the guide. When you know, you won't need to be told: follow the guide." In the early part of the journey, we only fool ourselves in believing we can follow our own higher self within. First we must seek it in others who have progressed further than ourselves.

The Western mind is preoccupied with being made to look foolish. There are endless concerns as to who is a genuine teacher and who is a charlatan. We are suspicious, cynical and poor in spirit.

We need help each step of the journey. Someone, anyone, can be a teacher – a conduit of essential information to help us find the next evolutionary step. A child, a bird, an ant, a flood – the messenger must be respected, the moment must be respected, the message must not be lost, for the sake of our precious sensibilities. Beyond this there are higher teachers, then there is what we call a root teacher, and last there is the *only* teacher.

If you are sincere in your aspiration, and prepared to traverse the hard road, you will not fall prey to imitations.

The importance of the teacher lies in the transference of a certain type of high quality energy, which the teacher has acquired through his or her own practice and long journey. Information can come from anywhere, but the energetic quality that emanates from an advanced being is rare and priceless. Alas, our culture has no inbuilt recognition of this, so for some time we fail to appreciate contacts with such beings. We remain ensnared in personality.

Without the impact of an *external awakened force*, we simply walk in circles.

One of the main functions of the teacher relationship, is soul crystallisation. There are many ways to cause individuation. Pain, hardship, envy, competition, ambition – these are some of the ways our awareness solidifies; but the best way is through our love for a highly evolved being. A friendship of warmth and knowledge that arcs way beyond our understanding of time and event.

A few tips for beginners: beware of mental confusion, be prepared for emotional confusion. Choose figure-eight, not circle teachers. Figure-eight energy configurations leave you with autonomy, circle energy tries to force-absorb you into the aura of the teacher completely. Don't be duped by the teacher's mask – all advanced beings develop an idiot face to parcel out their psychic 'static energy' tension, and to distract the unwanted. This process is repeated time and time again on deeper and deeper levels.

True teachers are creatures of immense beauty – celebrate and enjoy them, for they will soon be gone.

As to following the guide: eventually we learn a special *language*, with which to communicate with the spirit that moves all things. Try not to confuse his with any religious dogma, it is a real, practical, deep interaction – not a belief structure. I cannot overstress the importance of learning this *language*. It never ceases, we are always trying to read signposts in the fog, but there comes a threshold past which we solidify our confidence in the presence of a reciprocity. However do not be duped into presuming too much.

Internal worth can become a marketable commodity on many levels.

The energetic structure of the teacher

The basic energetic structure of the teacher is either the *Circle* or the *Infinity* (lemniscate: horizontal/ figure-eight).

Those who seek to absorb themselves with their student, are the *Circle* structure – ultimately these people seek to consume their prey. They are carnivorous. They demand you come within the circle of their energy orbit – you become identified with them, and they feast, grow, expand beyond you. You become a slave to a *Circle* teacher. They are dangerous. Avoid at all cost.

The *Infinity* structure is a figure-eight connection, where the student retains their own self-identity orbit, yet still in flow with that of the teacher. Such a teacher does not seek to eat you. They ask a symbiotic learning: meeting half way. This is similar to the old metaphor of the three-sided corral. One side is always open, so that there is an escape route left available.

A vast and infinite hexagram stands guard over the *Infinity* teachers: the hexagram of Power, that cannot be thwarted. Why? Because they don't cling!

What does that mean? It means they ultimately don't care – they have found something much better.

How can you tell you have an *Infinity* rather than a *Circle* teacher?

Simple. *Circles* are desperate for you. That's how you tell.

In love, this is the same. We want to consume, devour our beloved. That is why we get into trouble when we find some stranger has snuck into our life. While we were too busy living out our inner pantheon – ensnared in the love of our own anima or animus – one day we awaken to a real person now living permanently in our home, instead of some fantasy we had of that person. Greed undoes us. Mutual consumption is a much better deal.

The pattern is always the same, though every time it is different:

First, you contact real knowledge, but you don't recognise it. The golden key tossed out the pub window. But it niggles at you – you know you have contacted someone who is not the same as everyone else, and you can't allow it to settle down with the other sediment of your life. That's the rule from the student's side, where this seed grows or withers. If it grows then we're away.

From the teacher's side, first there comes a sign – in the maze of life's flux, something stands out that alerts the teacher – she *knows* spirit has identified someone. Then she waits, and watches. Waits for the opportunity to slip in a Mickey Finn. This is an expression of spirit in action. It is done with timing, and usually a short sharp crack. The teacher can't make this up – she acquiesces with a flash of insight and power that sweeps through like a wave, with the teacher nonchalantly yet fascinated, surfing along.

Then when the student responds, the long road begins – it is different every time, and eventually the student walks free. But there is a cost, to both sides. The cost to the student is less obvious: it means they can never really walk free – they are indebted, and they work that off with their own gifts to the world. That is the price of knowledge, so much so that those who don't have the deepest love for their teachers, are walking a slippery slope. These are the influences which have given birth to a new being inside the student – what a profoundly wonderful thing!

Which guide to choose?

In discussions about teachers the nub of the matter usually keeps being avoided. That nub is one of energetic dependency.

There is a lot of confusion when people have moved beyond antagonism to self-proclaimed teachers, to a realisation that some do actually know more, and their assistance can be useful on the Path. Where we are no longer so cocky about our own ability to navigate every twist of the road.

We drop our resistance, and we see that those who purport to 'know more' are offering very different products. Who do we believe? Each guide, as we engage with them, seems to describe the universe in such confident style, that we are immediately drawn and swayed. Then we switch channels, and again we are swayed. It is so confusing!

Mulla Nasrudin was made judge for the day. First case and the prosecution launched forth with their argument. Nasrudin was so swayed by the conviction and certitude of the prosecutor's argument that he spontaneously burst out with, "Yes! You are right!"

Then the defence launched their argument. It was also unbelievably convincing, after which Nasrudin again proclaimed. "Yes! You are right!"

Much displeased, the Clerk of the Court turned to Nasrudin and said, "Nasrudin, you can't just agree with both. You are the judge today, and so you must weigh up both arguments objectively and chose which is right."

Where upon Nasrudin immediately exclaimed, "Yes! You are right!"

We are all in Nasrudin's position. As we scan the spiritual field we have to choose one direction to make our primary commitment. The rest become support and fascination, but really only one can be our true allegiance. Else we are dilettantes, and will go nowhere.

It's only fair I describe my own situation: I am not a teacher. But I have a vested interest in the realm of teachers.

Let me clarify. I say I am not a teacher – that is largely semantics, as yes, I do in fact *teach*. But it is not only semantics. The reason I make this distinction is because I adopt a specific approach to the process of influence. A *teacher* in this distinction, is one who goes beyond 'wise friendship', or other such terms, and says to another, "Look, just put aside your autonomy for a time, and do as I say." There is really a place for this, in both the skills of the material and spiritual world. I am not of that persuasion as a general practice. It is not my preferred way of influence.

I have never sought to dominate the mind of another. I will try to put my view as persuasively as I can, but after that I leave others to make up their own minds, and I will not make 'alignment' with me a condition of my friendship. There are of course limits – there have to be. With some people a basic agreement is needed, but that is purely organisational, and in no way seeks to steal essential, individual autonomy. In fact it is the expression of that autonomy in a vibrant way, from which I gain one of my greatest pleasures.

My tolerance for individuality, even when that is outrageous, goes way beyond that of most people I know. I want to see how each person comes into their own unique relationship with their inner spirit. Not only do I not dominate, but I actively encourage people to find their own style, no matter how weird that may be. Behaviour requires certain parameters to foster the support that community provides, but they should be restrained to basics. Individuality should ripen and fruit.

Some people see my method as not what they seek – they want someone to grab and drag them forcefully. We are strange beings – those who demand freedom often turn out to be the ones who seek slavery. So they gravitate to a person of domineering will who tells them what to do in no uncertain words. Then after a time they wonder how they have got into another dependency or violent relationship, be that lover or guide. Why can't people see anger lurking?

First I will explain my method, then I will advise how to choose for a more hands-on guidance.

My method is one I have followed for many years – it is in my bones, and I have even evolved a whole musical compositional style around it.

Boundaries are necessary, for the sake of energy – that is how energy works. But within those outer boundaries self-expression is encouraged. Musically I don't say, "Play these notes." I say play within these scales or chords, emphasise these notes, relate to this rhythm. I like to offer resources and tools, then you make your own space ship. Surprise me!

Yet there is a need for those who have the patience and inclination to walk each step with another who seeks closer involvement. How can you trust such a guide will honour your essential freedom? I'll tell you.

It's too slow to wait till you find you can't escape without a lot of pain. We have to make our decision sooner. The *first rule* is in what we want. Do you want someone who will do the work for you? Sweep you up in their energy? Fascinate you with clever insights? Promise you all the clichés of the spiritual world? Ask yourself, are you the one at fault? Are you seeking to avoid the tedious and difficult work? You want a quick fix? You want a flashy thrill?

Solution: choose *spiritual development the hard way*. Works every time.

Second rule, look at your guide. Look carefully. Can you see anger lurking in those jaws? In those words? Feel your guide – I can offer no better advice, and unfortunately you will make mistakes, but for god's sake, learn from those mistakes. Can you see ownership and manipulation? These are the signs to look for. The worst mood is obsession: dominating desire for your allegiance, your acceptance. If such a guide stresses they are your friend, they are 'safe', they are only seeking your best interest, they are 'guaranteeing your freedom' – beware, snake-oil!

The Path is never like that. The Path is long and hard – there are no shortcuts, and you must do all the work. Stop looking to worship Father Christmas! Get real, get self-responsible, get a guide who is reluctant. I can say no more clever thing than that. Beware of eagerness! A true guide is one who will stand back, and test your determination to go the distance, before sticking their own neck out.

The *third rule* – ask a wise friend.

It is not so difficult. Feel the guide – feel their energy. You know – you do know! Just your mind is too easily tricked. Use your feelings, not your emotions or your mind. The spiritual world is full of predators. They are everywhere. There are predators disguised as spiritual guides all through the world since the dawn of time. Don't choose a predator, choose one who exudes patience, love, maturity and beauty. Don't play with predators and don't become entrapped in energetic dependency.

Then come around to my place and share the wonders you have discovered – we are all ears for stories of spirit in my caravanserai.

Teacher's troubles, student's bubbles.

In truth a teacher can do very little. Imparting knowledge is one thing, but a good teacher does more than pass across knowledge, be that in information or energy. Good teachers see the foibles of the student and use skill, patience and foresight to circumnavigate the student's road blocks. Such is the way, but it is oh so limited, even in the hands of true masters. In the end, it all comes down to the student.

The *teacher* is everywhere – everything. Only the student who genuinely wants to learn can benefit. A teacher will seek in every way possible to draw the student to real nourishment, to gift the wonder and magic, the beauty and truth of the world. To bust open the student's self-imposed limitations. The teacher stands in the widest of high plateaus, speaking to the student who sits inside a tiny box, refusing all food but that which comes through an even smaller window. That is how we wish it to be – that is the teacher I want. To be awakened to a vast reality that renders my current world as a small shoe box.

In the end, it is all in the student's hands. The student must want to learn, must strive to free himself with outrageous efforts. There is a sadness for the teacher who after much effort, sees that her student keeps making the same mistakes over and over, keeps refusing to eat the food so dearly purchased, keeps dropping the baton. I know, the teacher is above those feelings – it is all the same to her... well, yes and no. That's how it is, yes and no.

The problem is, the student wants the teacher to do all the work for him. He gets excited by a teacher who offers spirituality like a drink-dispensing machine. "Come to me, I will deliver you." I'm sure you have come across such teachers. But they have nothing to offer except their own delusion, and the students seek nothing but their own delusion.

A true teacher will not do the work for you, nor even offer such a possibility, implied or explicit. A true teacher may well employ some shortcuts, but in the end these are only gimmicks. The road is too long, and unless the student is ready for a personal long haul, it is futile. A teacher really can only point. She points at spiritual food all the time – look here, look there, grab this, drop that.

But the student wants to be hand-fed. A teacher who only points and waits, is too boring for some students. They soon become ensnared by the teachers who pomp and strut, spruiking all kinds of snake-oil language – enticing the student with promises of 'specialness'. Such a student doesn't want their bubble burst. And such a teacher is seeking admiration.

A true teacher is a student, and all she wants is to convert her 'students' into true students. "Look around you, it's all there ... why do you need me, except to prod you when you are lazy or when you are about to step in a hole?"

Students make a bad mistake. They enjoy the aura of the teacher, and mistake that for their own aura. The true teacher follows her own teacher, her own guide, her own star on the horizon ... and soon she will leave.

We are all students – and we all have to do the work ourselves. There is no easy way, and those who pretend so are bloodsuckers. We all know what the work is; there are plenty of books to tell us. We just have to do it!

Don't give your precious life force to bloodsuckers, use it to get about doing what you know you should be doing. Find a teacher who doesn't suck at you like a leech, find a teacher who leaves you free to make your own effort. Stop chasing after entertainment, and practise what you know.

Too soon your guide will be gone, and then you will know she was always just a pointer. The real guide is life, but more, so much more – a feather of brilliance, a thread out of the maze.

Chapter 9

Awareness

This is the principle task. Awareness is usually forced upon us from outside. As we come into contact with external objects, if they produce sufficient sensations in us, we become aware of them. This is the story of Awareness. Our awareness evolves as a consequence of this external pressure upon our being. There are many consequences of this for our cultural and species behaviour. We live through our bodies and our group.

Self-awakening: a crucial moment comes when we begin to enhance our awareness from inside – by our own decision, choice and will. It is this inner activation that we aim to nourish.

Two questions need detailed examination. What are we aware of? What is the quality that is awareness?

For the purpose of this strategy we begin with the first question: what are we aware of?

A. We are aware of our *surroundings*.

B. We are aware of the *direction* of movement in time.

C. We are aware of the *significance* of things and events.

These are closely related.

Awareness of surroundings is the first to be developed, as it involves the most basic manifestation of what we recognize when we refer to *now*. The others flow naturally from the first. As we engage with these *awarenesses* we employ three important functions:

1. Firstly we must *remember* to be aware: self-awakening. Instead of waiting on external forces, we awaken to engage awareness ourselves.

2. Secondly we must *sustain* the activity of being aware for as long as possible: endurance and stamina.

3. Thirdly we attempt to *intensify* the quality of our awareness.

Each of these functions has to be focused on independently, and mechanisms put in place to activate them.

1. Self-awakening.

This is connected with the function of memory. It would, however, be wrong to restrict it to only memory. What spurs us to awake? And what is the difference to the previous moment? We become aware of something many people refer to as an experience of "Isn't this amazing – me – here".

What is required, is to employ a secretary to tap us on the shoulder every few moments and say, "Remember!" Notice how this would become a source of intense annoyance: that feeling is what we are up against. Failing the financial means to do this, we can attempt to replicate it some other way.

Firstly, we need a physical gesture – to place a marker in consciousness. A good one is to look at some part of your body, like your feet; or make a physical movement that is not rationally necessary for the mundane task you are engaged in at the moment of awakening. Wave your hand in the air, move an item around you, turn around 360° – any non-functional action can become a flag that we plant in our new world, the world of awake.

Secondly, use pain. The *grass-seed-in-the-sock* technique: don't remove it, let it be a secretary. At least when you have a pain you have been unsuccessful in eliminating – don't exhaust your precious life force on anguish, self-pity or rage. Let it pull you out of your addictive sleep and absorption. Allow that to give you a moment's pause, in which to say "Oh yes, I must remember".

The gimmicks used by those before us are the subject of legend. What eccentricities can't be enjoyed, in the pursuit of replacing the secretary? It becomes very hard work, and a lively, inventive imagination is essential to keeping up the frequency of awakening points.

2. Sustaining Awareness.

Why do we slip off again into oblivion? Why can't we just stay awake, once we have awoken? Watch and see – where did you wake up, and where did you last lose it? Early awakenings begin in places like sitting at home on your own on a weekend night, with nothing special to do. Perhaps with a couple of sherries or a glass of wine. These incipient awakenings are muddled, fuddled and usually morose. Later on, as you consciously engage in this pursuit, you will notice the extraordinary suction into sleepwalk that social contact can bring.

A common technique used here is a mantra. Continue saying something to keep you *here*, now that you've arrived. Something like "Don't fall asleep!" Say it over and over like a moron. Be careful, however, what you moronify – keep it in safe areas. Better to steer clear of mantras you do not know the meaning of, or those that amplify and reify the inner false-emperor.

Walking through doorways is a good awakening opportunity, for those putting up a strong fight. If you become really desperate, try hanging a string down in front of your face constantly, from a hat.

The difficulty is that as soon as your technique becomes familiar, it no longer has the required effect. In this area, change and novelty become mandatory, and we must overcome any hidden resentments that we harbour against this. Youth here is an advantage; those who enter this yoga in their twenties can have a lot of fun with variety, if not quality.

3.   Depth of Awareness

The *intensity* of our aliveness. On a physical level this can be equated with alertness. Focusing on this aspect requires engaging in physical exercises. All forms of sport usually help to enhance this quality. Games where fast response is required are priceless. Some games have been especially devised to bring alertness to a peak – if you are lucky you may find some good ones, or make them up yourself. The best ones use the requirement to pay attention for long periods of time, to more than one 'trigger' factor – played with others to engage competition as a motivational force. Especially if each trigger is related and affected by each other – this is where imagination plays a significant role.

A more subtle form of physical awareness is balance – any form of activity which employs a high sensitivity to balance should be explored.

This is an obvious area in which our 'vehicle' can be employed: to affect our spirit positively through the inbuilt forces of the body. However, this is not always a wise practice. We tend to live too much under the possession of our bodies. So utilise the natural gifts of the body, yet remain outside total absorption in the physical. Notice how many sports, dance, martial arts or any other intensive physical orientated people are far from aware – their awareness is channelled through one avenue, and they have been unable to apply the principle across the widest capacity of their life. Plus, focusing solely on the body has a deadening effect on the subtle levels of our being. Nonetheless, it does offer tremendous advantages to those seeking to enhance awareness in every way possible.

Physical 'alertness' equates to the awareness of our surroundings, as previously mentioned. It is also connected to the area of the head just behind the ears. Another level of intensity of awareness is explored through questions or statements such as "This is my life." We don't say these as mantra, or as a mindless set of words, but as a focus to assist us in intensifying something that lies behind very obvious realities. We exist on the superficial and fail to grasp the awesomeness of our situation.

"What is really happening here?", "Who am I?" and similar prompts. There is a very important one relating to our dream life which will be discussed later. These are exercises for our soul – the feeling part of our ourselves. The feeling factor can be developed as another exercise, by constantly noticing how we are affected emotionally in our contacts with different places and people as they happen. People-watching can help us by allowing the 'self' to sink into what it feels like to be the person we observe – this is easier as they walk away. The front of people and animals has a psychic glare that makes this practice difficult.

Following from this, it is possible to enjoy another aspect of reading as you 'become' the psychic stance of the author. Reading old religious text can produce extraordinary results. The development of this facility of *depth*, allows us to enter into wilderness areas in a new way which will be discussed later.

It is not easy to elucidate the full understanding of exactly what we are doing by these exercises. In fact as they take their effect we forget what we were like before. *Depth of Awareness* leads to a sensitivity which can become a problem for us. How do we block out unwanted, unpleasant sensations?

For a considerable period there is no answer to this. We have to endure it like an animal. As we progress with the whole strategy we develop methods of handling these experiences. However for many the problem is never effectively solved. The usually prescribed solution is to exploit these situations by 'deepening our keel' through the struggle to maintain inner balance. A simple tool to assist in this is to seek for the one thing in which beauty resides amongst the rubbish, and cling to that for sanity.

The three predicates of awareness – *Awareness of Surroundings, Direction* and *Significance*. These apply in cross-grid to the three functions we have just been examining – *Self-awakening, Sustain* and *Depth of Awareness*. Each has a separate character.

A. Awareness of Surroundings.

This has the power to bring us into the moment. We are not sufficiently aware of the objects about us. When we were young children we spent endless stretches of time examining the colour, texture and shape of thousands of insignificant things. Afterwards we learnt what to do with these things, so we lost them, as we became submerged in functionalism. From then on we only skim our surroundings for the functional tools we require.

Notice the effect of coming across some obviously useful looking object of which we have no idea what its use is. How impatient we are to place it in the scheme of things or discard it. Alas from teenage to death we are imprisoned in the *scheme*.

We must free ourselves from this tyranny. Functionalism is useful – that is its nature – for the tiny bright face of our being. But it jealously blinds us from the vast, old, dark face, for which our completeness longs. How to emancipate our spirit?

This is where a teacher can provide experiences through clever and effective techniques to dethrone functionalism, which can't be revealed here. The teacher must help the student to resolidify his or her etheric shell after such experiences. Nonetheless, the slow method is probably better in the long run. Take up some form of art. Not for profit but for the quality that artistic pastimes provide. Any artistic activity can help to reveal the world to us again under a more subtle form of functionalism. And it's pleasurable.

Otherwise, take regular pauses to look about, and notice everything or anything. Here we can also use a specific form of meditation known as gazing. This will be dealt with separately, as meditation is such a major area.

Now is the moment of power. Let the focus on surroundings refresh you for whatever task you undertake.

There is a point of crucial significance which is almost completely ignored by our enculturated awareness. Its importance must be re-established within us as a conscious poignancy. It is the point at which we transfer our attention from its habitual preoccupation with self-absorption, to an object outside of us in our physical environment. Do not underestimate the quality of change in this transference of focus. There is a hidden doorway here.

Some understanding of what is involved in self-absorption should be indicated. The very act of reading this material is a form of self-absorption. There are two forms self-absorption:

i. Firstly, as with this book, there is the managerial form, where we analyse dispassionately for a structured purpose.

ii. Second is where we engage in an endless conversation internally with the object of trying to arouse emotional excitations. We sort through a plethora of thoughts for those which have a 'charge' for us – this makes them interesting, the others being classified as boring. Then we dwell on the interesting ones so long as they remain charged. Usually you will find, for most of us, this is related to our interactions with other people. These conversations consume our entire adult life.

The first form is actually quite rare. The second is completely pervasive, and I will revisit this in greater detail in the chapter on emotions.

The second form of self-absorption is called *cud-chewing*. Both forms repel the outer world to provide an inner space for obsessive preoccupation. The managerial form re-admits the outer world under control, as more information becomes necessary to complete the chain of ideas. *Cud-chewing* re-engages with the outside world for the sole purpose of finding fresh sources of emotional stimulus which can then be churned over incessantly until it in turn becomes stale and boring.

We are taught to do this as children by everyone around us. There is no escape from incarceration within this crippling, cramped and haunted tenancy. We have all learned to do it, to even become strangely comfortable in it, but we can all learn to leave it. Part of the strategy of leaving is to redesign our own peculiar form of self-absorption. This is an awareness task of reviewing our entire pantry of stock-in-trade ruminants, and disposing of anything that is not necessary to our main purpose and commitment.

It is allowed to keep a small number of personal indulgent toys, just so we don't become too severe, too tight. The rest must be left behind forever. This process is one effect of employing the whole strategy of development, and by keeping that strategy in mind it helps to understand why we do a lot of things that may appear obscure.

Further on, specific tasks will be explained, which act to release us from the root causes of a lot of our unnecessary self-absorption.

The act of looking out to an object in our surroundings can be intensified by an interesting trick. Try to focus attention through senses other than the eyes. Our eyes have entered into a peculiar conspiracy with our self-absorption so that they themselves need to be retrained, yet the other senses remain fairly innocent. They retain the power to more effectively cut the beam of our addiction.

B. Awareness of Direction

On this side of eternity, time is not an illusion, but a definite manifestation of energetic substance. We are in positions now due to decisions we made, or allowed, in the past. Surely this is obvious to everyone! But, can we see now the future consequences of choices available to us at this moment?

Notice how, as we grow older, we find ourselves rolling our eyes in dismay at the foolishness of younger fellow travellers through life. This shows how time teaches wisdom to some of us.

To see and recognise things and events as seeds. This is wisdom. It involves the recognition that many unpleasant experiences come beckoning, clothed in pretty garments. Part of maturity is to see through the superficial face of what is on offer.

As we grow wiser we see that many pursuits end in pain and anguish. Obviously we try to avoid these and choose those which evolve pleasurably. In theory there is only one direction which can ultimately be worth the effort. If we have deeply understood this direction, it can save an enormous amount of time and energy. However, in practice, our lives have to be negotiated through a maze of choices and activities, which interrelate with the trends and circumstances of the world about us.

Something of lasting and beneficial value can be created, through the amassing of millions of small endeavours whose orientation is ultimately efficacious. The wisdom of our own awareness is essential through this long journey, but it is not enough. We need the assistance of a friend who knows. Some paths go through the jungle, others just meander indefinitely, never to emerge. Discernment of direction requires a very special helper.

The development of such a friendship is a mysterious affair. But it has been said to be the most crucial aspect of this whole carnival. Many times we are left dangling until the last moment, just to test us.

The method of approach to the Awareness of Direction is through the *edifice* technique. It is as if we journey uncommitted to any practical life task, along a street footpath. To our right and left we observe a variety of buildings, of small or large, simple or complex construction. We can enter some of these if we desire. Once we do, however, can we get out again?

We have the impression of choice as we stand at the doorway. We look for any revealing indications by which we can ascertain the nature of each building's inner corridors. Then we look to our clever friend for the nod (or a shove) if we feel instinctively attracted to the adventure on offer. Alas, there are times when we are told in no uncertain terms by our merciless companion, to enter places for which we have no attraction at all. Such experiences, though painful, eventually evoke our reluctant approval as to their necessary value.

Be warned, don't disguise desire by pretending such a friendship as is here described. Such a connection takes a long struggle to establish. A few groovy ideas will not suffice.

If we truthfully re-examine our past decisions and our present situations we will clear the fog from the moment. We will see at a glance through the illusory make-up on many a face and doorway.

C. Awareness of Significance.

This is the culmination of our practices: to know the energetic essence. Peel back the sheath: expose the only existing raw nerve.

An appropriate analogy is provided by a computer facility know as 'hypertext' – a word or image which is also a link to expanded content. Amongst the myriad things, events or words that present to us during our daily lives, there exist certain ones that are *loaded*. This is more easily recognised in conversations when a phrase or gesture will betray a concealed emotion – not the words or actions themselves, but something about them sits less comfortably than the usual flow. Often we leave with an impression that can be traced to a small gesture which indicates an underlying mood.

This awareness extends beyond the social, and becomes the basis of what I have previously referred to as a *language*. It is as if within the array of impressions from the world, some appear in hypertext – they become hidden doorways. When dealing with more advanced people we tend to find such loaded impressions strewn about, and operating on different levels – be on your toes!

It becomes possible to read revelations into everything. A fairly well known type of insanity exists in this line. What I am referring to here, however, is not insanity, but a level of reality that unveils a host of truths. It is a somewhat pathetic experience when this occurs in our social dealings, especially in the early stages of awakening. It can be embarrassing to see people expose their private reality so obviously, when they believe themselves to be well protected against such transparency. As we progress we become aware that such knowledge evokes responsibility and compassion – we realise we are all dealing with our common fate of joy, pain, and struggle. The differences between us, with which we often tend to pride ourselves at some point, grow ever more insignificant as we mature.

Nonetheless, these differences are also real, and as our awareness deepens we find ourselves becoming isolated from companionship with our fellow man. Cast against this social transparency we recognise levels of deeper and deeper mysteries in the world, through which our insight cannot penetrate.

The process of awakening the Awareness of Significance is referred to as *realisations*. The deeper and more profound they become, the more exhilarating they are in a peculiarly unexciting way. They shake our being on such levels, that they have the power to effect enormous life changes. Something all the good advice, self-talk or emotionality cannot compete with in the slightest. Realisations are gold.

Do not make the common mistake of confusing highly emotional inspirations with cold numbing realisations. Emotion is not a form of spirituality. Those who weep with remorse, only hide their pride. When the penny drops, you will need no one to turn to. Always, this is what we aim for. The entire cosmos stands waiting for us to put ourselves aside, and recognise our common essence, to recognise each other.

Awareness and Pressure

Development of awareness from within is essential, but a difficult task to maintain, requiring constant effort over many years. Therefore we also need to examine how to exploit the natural process of external pressure, to enhance its awareness-activating qualities.

This is examined from different angles throughout the whole strategy – all parts dove-tail to create a whole. At this point I wish to emphasise the need to evolve an attitude toward life and its myriad tasks. For some reason the normal approach is to prefer conditions which send us to sleep. Of course every experience we have within our lives, of whatever nature, enhances our awareness in some way. Nonetheless, it is obvious that some people gain more from their experiences than others.

This relates to our willingness to allow experiences to affect us internally. The extent to which we can lower our resistance to the influences which contact us, the more resonations they create within our inner being. Most people, as part of their self-absorption, are preoccupied with sympathy and antipathy – likes and dislikes. We must escape from this preoccupation, to realise that everything surrounding us is a doorway to unexpected knowledge.

Beneath the petty likes and dislikes which dominate our attitude towards the little things of life, there are deeper feelings, which we often seek to avoid. It goes without saying that what gives us happiness and pleasure, we are prepared to open ourselves to. Yet it is those experiences which cause unpleasantness, frustration or suffering, that can reveal deeply needed awakenings.

It is so often the case that deep experiences of joy are concealed behind barriers of pain. Awareness evolves into attention, attention into focus, focus develops force and gives rise to determination with which we scale mountains.

This aspect of our attitude toward life represents the interplay of an inner awakening force, with the intricacies of the mystery of external pressure upon us, via the techniques of employing the *task*. The other aspect of our attitude is more reactive. Life constantly throws across our path an endless series of activities or experiences that we simply wouldn't bother with if we had a choice.

It is precisely here that we must employ one of the most undervalued yet far-reaching qualities of mind. This quality is rarely found operating within us, as a result of our cultural conditioning at the time when we begin to engage with the path of inner growth. We have to create it ourselves. It will stand by us as a god-send for the rest of our days.

The trick is to disengage our minds from the endless chain of rationally connected actions. Notice carefully that whatever we do, we have a reason for it – always a link from something to something. We cook because we are hungry – we cook eggs because we have eggs – we eat because we have cooked, because we are hungry – and we eat eggs because we had eggs and cooked them. Everything in our life has an antecedent and a sequent.

So strong is this linkage, that it is possible to severely unhinge people by forcing them to perform meaningless tasks. There is nothing wrong with seeking the value of meaning in our lives and aspirations, in whatever we do. But this excludes us from the realisation that immense pleasure can be had from the sheer doing of a task without reference to the past or future. The beauty of *doing for its own sake.*

This realisation will allow us the extra something to tip the balance toward milking all the cross-currents of life that can reveal new worlds to us. Cease the internal antagonism and resentment that we indulge in when the comfort of our sleepy expectations are upset. To assist, we need an exercise.

Set aside a period of time, during which, engage in some activity that is, for all normal purposes, senseless. For example, carry stones one at a time from one pile to another. Enjoy the childlike sense of play, feel the textures, place the stones in arbitrary patterns. Use your imagination to make up variations on this idea. You will notice a growing sense of relief from such exercises. Life situations often provide examples without our connivance – grasp them with relish. How often have you been required to do some idiotic thing in your work or study? There's your chance. After practicing this exercise for some years you will never be the same again.

We employ this acquired quality into our evolving attitude towards life. Instead of life being filled with tedium and annoyances, instead of seeing our journey as one in which we fretted a lot and never really knew how to settle, we see it as an adventure, a dance, a kaleidoscope of endless opportunities, that only requires us to have sufficient energy to match it with delight. This is not to deny that there aren't places to which no one in sane mind would wish to go, but it is possible to achieve the confidence that any possible situation can be turned effectively to our advantage – this is indeed an advanced position.

Chapter 10

Pride

Here exists the fundamental feature of our human condition. Stand aside from all faiths, but you cannot escape this truth. This is the whopper at the bottom of the bag. Your entire life is forfeit if you haven't made an attempt to clean off the slimy sheath of pride. In case you don't know the extent of this, we live our entire lives through pride. It is the common form of humanity.

This is a very difficult chapter, because pride hides. It cannot be openly assaulted and defeated in any conventional way. It will not 'come out and fight like a man'. To tackle this beast on our own is a major undertaking, and so I have detailed a long list of actions and attitudes, each of which will slowly increase the weight of freedom in your favour. Take each item individually and find ways to apply them to your own world. I have only skimmed the surface, so you will need to isolate each aspect in turn, study and ponder, then find imaginative means of application. Only the outline can be sketched, as the subject is too vast for a thorough treatment.

There are two types of pride. It is at the cutting edge of the difference between the positive and negative division of our whole strategy. I personally find it a point of great amazement that the English language lacks the distinction within this pivotal difference. One type of pride can be the source of all that is good in us, while the other is the source of our endless stupidity and suffering.

We must begin from where we are, and no matter who we are, we battle this one till the day we die.

I will not deal here with the positive aspect of pride – that is found within such topics as The Garden and Responsibility. How to define the negative aspect? It is, that deep down, we all consider ourselves to be special. We are biased. This is the root of prejudice. Whether up front, or in a cunning, conceited manner, we all want the biggest slice of the cake for ourselves. If you don't admit it then you haven't begun the path of *spiritual development the hard way* – you are still looking for the easy way.

The question is, how to dismantle such an endemic demonic? Oh, the wicked ways devised by the ruthless peers of old! There is no sweet and gentle medicine for this. The remedy is bitter and tortuous but if you cannot bring yourself to enjoy it with belly-aching relish, then you are still the victim of a vicious pride, with a long way to go.

Who can inflame our conceit? Those whom we disdain. Fools irritate us. I tell you now, you must place yourself within their grasp – not at their complete mercy, but sufficient to shrive to survive. They can be very dangerous fools however, and their victory over you could damage you for life. To be humiliated by fools, is about as low as it gets. That's where we have to go.

With pride, as with other areas, we require a plan to activate the various levels of our being – from subtle pondering to major slabs of daily life. Being an area of such major significance, it is to be expected a large body of practice and thought has been uncovered. There are many examples in the stories of how those before us have struggled with pride. If the underlying principles are grasped, these stories provide us with inspiration and comfort. Without a grasp of these principles, such stories remain the actions of eccentric freaks.

I will attempt to clarify by a series of progressive exercises for contemplation and action.

A. Self-Image

We usually have little personal input into the construction of our self-image when we first explore it. It is the product of genetic and environmental influences. Alas, we take it to be our true selves, knowing no other.

There are two faces of our self-image:

- The first can be seen from how we describe or present ourself to others.
- The second is as if we unexpectedly overhear others speaking about us.

This second is quite an extraordinary one to meet. It can precipitate very similar sensations to those of seeing a ghost. There is an intense 'hair raising up the back of the neck' feeling when this face is confronted effectively. After a few meetings one tends to become more accustomed to this rather intimate being.

However, it is the first face that we need to mould and reshape. This is to do with the maturing of the personality. As we progress, we can look back to previous personalities we have been. Self-image is the face of our personality, but in fact it is much more than ideas about ourself – it is a posture: the whole colour of our impact upon the world. It becomes a personal style through which great power can be channelled – or drained.

At first, though, we have a posture riddled with insecurities and childish snobbery, which blocks the freely exploding bursts of energy. And it can be a fatal flaw in our ability to survive emergencies or adventures. It is the purging of our self-image that we are about in tackling pride. To make transparent, to loosen the moorings of our vessel, to allow it to fly free according to its true nature. Here we touch upon the idea of what real freedom implies – not a simple concept.

B. Confidence

We all seek strength in our self-image. It is the channel through which we interact with the world, and should it weaken beyond a certain point, we die. The difficulty is that, as we find ourselves initially, we are almost completely the product of our formative influences. We are predominately social beings. Thus our strength arises from the quality of our social position; typically, the degree of respect we receive from friends and acquaintances, but also from the status of our wider social-identity group.

It is upon the level of positive current flowing to us from our social environment that our strength relies, and as such we are highly vulnerable to the whims and unexpected tides in this social 'appreciation-flow'. For the purposes of our strategy, this situation is completely useless.

The irony is that often we enter upon a spiritual endeavour in order to salvage a perception of failure in the common stakes. For those who are serious in their intent, all such pathetic hopes are utterly doomed – in fact the complete opposite is the case. Resign yourself right now to the final abandonment of enjoying any form of social prestige. In this way, if your destiny throws up anything in the nature of fame or fortune, you won't fall victim to the impression of its reality. You will see the true essence of this unpleasant experience and shoulder it as a necessary burden: let us pray that such a destiny can be mercifully avoided, as it places huge demands on time, energy, and intent, that few of us have the luxury to pay. One should only walk such a path knowingly and with a clear task and purpose.

True strength resides in confidence in ourselves, not in the confidence others have in us. Build your foundations upon real insights into your own being, align your life with those insights, and direct all your efforts in accord with this. Out of this grows a strength that cannot be so easily assailed by the vagaries of our fellow beings, and the negative waves that constantly pound upon us from the unknown.

C. Offence

MAKE NO MISTAKE!

For the purpose of those who walk the path of *spiritual development the hard way*, we have a simple rule: *if you get offended, you are in the wrong.*

We are allowed to get upset, annoyed, frustrated – these are natural and healthy human reactions. We constantly seek to reduce them by looking at the source of these emotions – do they have antecedent causes in our past? But if we are offended or insulted by someone, feel slighted or miffed, then we suffer from self-importance. How do we tell the difference?

1. The natural, healthy upset is short lived – felt as a psychic slap. We don't like it. (We like it when someone praises us – felt as a lift.) This short, sharp upset flames up as a natural consequence of our living mechanism, and it does need to come out: let it flow then let it go.

2. The insult is long lived, we mull over it again and again, never forgetting it. We plan revenge, we get depressed, we get angry, we play it over and over in our minds and words. Then we justify, justify, justify – concoct elaborate rationales to show how we are in the right, but always underneath we seethe with injured pride. Then, in the worst cases we paint our assailant

with a perfect picture of ourselves – funny how accurate we get it. Inside, we really do know exactly what we are doing; just that we project this onto the other.

If you are stewing, can't laugh at yourself, you are *wrong*. And worse, only more pain can cure you.

Now the other person may well have shovelled you a load of crap, but that doesn't matter – if you got your nose out of joint, then you are *wrong*, not them.

The correct approach goes like this: first pain, then laugh at your silliness, then consider a response. Know how to *take offence*: how to respond – reaction is not response, it is defence and attack. Response is creative, it chooses its own timing, it enjoys the game.

When we are attacked, a form of adequate response is essential – it is wise to be capable of devastating effectiveness. Highly evolved beings are not to be trifled with. But it is precisely because they feel no personal resentment that their manner of response has such potency.

Self-importance hates to be criticised, it bristles with indignation at the slightest insinuation. Self-importance hates snobs, hates elites, hates anyone who thinks they're better than *it*. Self-importance hates anyone who sets themselves up as being above others, above *it*, and then rushes to pull them down – cut them down to *its* level. In fact, cuts them down beneath *it*, because self-importance has to be IMPORTANT!

I'm just fleshing this out so we can be perfectly clear: self-importance hates being underneath. There is no escape, this attitude is *wrong*. Point blank, no argument – it is a mortal sin, and must always be seen as such.

'Being offended' is the primary indicator. There are no exceptions – whenever you feel offended, there lies vanity. Right here we see one of those points of irreversible divergence from our common cultural world. Personally, I know of no culture that has truly grasped this fact. Wherever you go, you must walk on egg shells lest you upset someone's precious sensitivities. To be capable of being offended is not just seen as a right, it is taken as a sign of dignity and status. Further, not to be offended is seen as a sign of weakness, an indication that you can be pushed aside as of no consequence.

If you seek to be of consequence in the eyes of others then rethink, or cast aside this writing here. Be prepared to become the nerd of the group – be prepared to find immense joy in the freedom you will have

– be prepared to live alone, no matter what crowds you frequent. And be prepared to discover aloneness to be your most treasured possession.

It cannot be stressed enough how utterly dysfunctional and oppressive it is to be offended by the actions of others – be they good or evil, it makes no difference: we have no rights in the real world. Personal potency is the only currency recognised in the real world, and the surest way to throw away any potency you retain is through indulging in being offended.

Once this has been realised we can begin to enjoy our social contacts. We can even develop the appearance of the stupidity of offence: we can play the game, whatever game, and we can play it better because we are not shocked by the heavy concerns of social position. We are not hamstrung by paranoia: the constant threat of insult.

By contrast, dignity sees itself as noble, elevated, keeps its head up. When challenged, dignity may feel hurt, annoyed, and it may well seek to identify error in its attacker, but it doesn't suffer from wounded pride, and thus doesn't seek to belittle the other. Rather it asks that the other also put aside their vindictiveness and lift their own head. Dignity wants to pull the other up, not down. Of course dignity is allowed to yell at an undisciplined dog, to bring it into line – everyone needs to know dog language.

I may be mistaken, but I don't think dignity has any more place in the path of *spiritual development the hard way* than self-importance. We seek the truth: no time for pride, justified or unjustified. Lean slightly forward with an ever-so-slight mischievous grin, a keen terrifying eye, hands loose and ready. Play friendly, play dignified, play offended, play the human harp but never lose sight of the truth!

D. Speaking of the past

Until you know how and why to speak of your past this habit must be avoided. The reason for this is obvious – our past and our attitudes towards it are how we continue to reinforce our old self-image, our vanity. We talk with a motive to gain approval and appreciation. With our talk of self, we constantly rebuild our identity – we are always trying to convince ourselves that we are real.

Stopping this part of our conversation has the effect of producing an unusual energy in us. Not only do we acquire a subtle feeling of vagueness, but we are able to allow this self-nebulousness to help break the beam of our self-conceit. What we are, after this concrete beam has been broken, is very hard to define, as being so familiar with it we have always denied its existence. Thus the usefulness of such a skilful technique as not talking of our past – to tease out our hidden childish sulk, and reveal essence.

Unfortunately, there is a cost to this exercise. If we are not at ease with ourselves – as the need for the exercise indicates – then we have a tendency to misdirect the energy produced through this form of verbal fasting, into a heaviness. A slightly unbalanced state of mind. It is necessary to have developed a garden to offset the toxic effects of this medicine.

As your life becomes re-aligned to a new self-image, then the stories of your past can be carefully re-entered, as the emphasis will be redefined by the new being. Your stories will no longer have their previous intention, so they become stories of change.

E. Leaving

"Lovers of leaving, ours is not a caravan of despair."[1] The ability to leave is not so easily established. Of course some are born with this – professional adventures – however, for the ordinary soul this pleasure comes only after a good deal of anguish. Alas, there is no alternative. The mark of a true adventurer is that she dies in a foreign land.

Home

To establish this yoga of *leaving* within us, we require a potent life task which can also help against the domination of our self-image by alien beings. We leave everybody we know. We live the rest of our lives elsewhere than where our previous friends and relatives are colonised.

There is no alternative to this injunction. And unfortunately not much can be said about it – it is simple: leave your home, your friends, your town, the whole world in which you grew up. Change country if possible, but at least change location within your country.

1   Rumi

Don't take it too badly – it is surprising how much pleasure can enter our lives through this gateway.

Clothes

Leaving is the physical expression of waking up the mysteries of the self-image – of walking it away from its small, rigid, and cramped condition, out into the fresh air. We tip the scales with the weight of possibilities – who can foretell the consequences? Leaving can be applied to many aspects of our life. Wearing clothes with which you are unfamiliar is one such example.

Experiment with dressing in different cultural clothes and appearances. If male, you could grow a beard or shave it off; if female, just extend the already wide range available to you and forget about fashion. Clothes themselves have an unusually strong effect upon our sense of self – our accustomed behavioural style. They are a form of mask.

Clothes are just the tip of it, all manner of cultural lifestyle can be changed: where you buy food, the type of food you eat, the entertainment activities you frequent. Leave behind as many of your usual haunts as you can, as well as the people whom you acquaint with these places.

You will discover that clothes actually affect the way we feel, think and act. They have a surprising influence upon self-image and pride.

Job changing

As changing workplace and career becomes more difficult with age, for a number of reasons, it is good to get into it when young. Often we engage in occupations for which we have no real affinity. Best to change; know how to leave a job. There is a risk of course, so it is necessary to have developed a certain detachment.

The risk we run is that we jeopardise our 'position and possession' ranking. Alas, there is no immediate remedy for this – just accept the possibility of a lifestyle diminished in flashy gadgets, fancy houses and facile holidays. Who knows, you may even come to relish what others fear in this domain.

We are usually pursuing a course or career that is a product of the likes and dislikes of other people – whoever they may be. It is not until we break free of this and explore other possibilities of earning a living, that we gain a more accurate view of what our talents intend for us. This is an aspect of the lack of contact with our real nature. We must earn the knowledge of who we are, through casting the net wider.

Invariably, those who have taken seriously this injunction, end up negotiating with society more on their own unique terms. It is not an easy road, however, so at least be prepared for major traumas of self-doubt, and many dusty roads. It's all part of the purge.

In practice it is not always appropriate to walk out the door capriciously. A plan of leaving is required. There are certain responsibilities and commitments that have to be dealt with adequately. Also there are life conditions that necessitate waiting for opportunities. It is as if we are on a train when we make the decision to change. Don't just jump wildly into the night, unless there is an emergency, as this can badly depreciate the force of flow in our deeper energy levels. Wait for an appropriate station – a real doorway will present itself through which an exit can be accomplished with a good continuity of momentum. Momentum in our 'energy life' is a matter of serious consideration.

We wait, complete our tasks, and prepare for the moment when the opening appears. When that moment comes, however, we must go. To stall is disastrous. Often, more than one opening presents – we must know the right one, the right time, and how to grasp it. This is no small feat to carry off with style and artistic potency. Here we touch on a whole body of character evolution known as *waiting*. To know that you are *waiting*, what you are *waiting* for, why you are *waiting*, and when to cease *waiting* – these are the identity marks of advanced practitioners.

One of the intended consequences from job changing is a direct assault upon our vanity. Each time we begin a new job we are in a position of not knowing the ropes. We have to accommodate our self-image to the experience of what could be described as the complete opposite of swagger. Having to ask others, sometimes younger than ourselves, how to find or do things that often can be very ordinary tasks. Surrounded by the unfamiliar it is difficult to maintain our accustomed conceit without a great deal of effort.

Job changing can be applied to changes within one's work area, or changes of employment within one's career path, or total career shifts. All forms should be employed, as well as jumping at any opportunity to learn new skills; such as repairing your own vehicle, doing your own tax return, making your own vegetable garden.

Apart from loosening up the rigidity and brittleness of our self-image, the other primary purpose is to dismantle the projections of snobbery. We have a strong tendency to project pride onto our career, profession and environment. This goes deeply into the mind. It is a major achievement to see all things as equal. Naturally, for the purposes of any task, project or emergency, priorities become important. But we go further than this and ascribe importance to things without realising the arbitrary nature of the assumptions implied, which are consciously or unconsciously adhered to by the group or community with which we identify.

Projections of snobbery – our pride is concealed in externals. Consider your attitudes to your children, your town, your nation, your family, your profession, your social class, your generation. This is why we change all these, because pride is like a virus, which mutates constantly to survive. Diminished a few days, and soon it reappears, as we give ourselves tickets over anything that makes us feel good without the slightest effort. Or bad – never forget the pride hidden behind self-pity, sadness, anger or resentment.

Without fully comprehending the pervasive allegiance we suffer beneath, we act. This exercise of job changing, within the overall strategy, will tease out hidden prejudices and release them from our bones.

Family

Leave the family. They, more than any other, hold the mortgage on our self-image. Some have no trouble with this rule, and others cling tenaciously to their family, if not physically, then psychologically.

Your family have your number, make no mistake, and they do not want you to change. There is not a lot to say about this – I believe anyone at all serious about these activities will recognise immediately the extent of this situation. We battle against the force of our parents' expectations our entire life.

However it is also not appropriate to snub your family completely. Especially as your parents get older it is a natural and necessary obligation to maintain a position of material and emotional support. How to fit this with what I have just previously said? Alas it is not easy – some balance and accommodation has to be achieved, but try not to attempt to convert your family to any unfamiliar beliefs you may have. Relate as one living being to another, while dodging their assaults. They are unlikely to be as tolerant as you are capable of being.

We have spent vast and precious slabs of our lives with these people – we must respect this. Yet we must also respect our quest for freedom, in which they also have a stake, even if they don't know it.

Staying

Pride lies deeper than self-image. Even after we have left behind our old ways we still experience the suction of gloat. There comes a moment in the journey of the *lover of leaving* when the realisation strikes: *wherever you go, that is where you are*. Changing the façade of life is not enough. We eventually become aware of the burdens we carry, no matter where we appear.

At this point the tendency is to stop wandering – a need to shift focus. The usual response is to go where the heart calls, as nothing else seems to matter that much. Reality, however, being the cunning device it is, can force us to labour in the salt mines at any time. We need an inculcated capability to stabilise our certitude. The power of cohesion.

"Even in a strange land, a man can find a home." (Old Chinese saying.)

"It is only by watching the fruits of our labour that we can know ourselves." (Another old Chinese saying.)

We must subject ourselves to the lessons of building our own home, not physically, although that would be an excellent conjunct. This is the ability to establish a foothold anywhere – to claim ground and enact stability from within. Many years are required in some place or activity until we reach a threshold of knowing how to stay.

This is all connected to the underlying usefulness of patterns, a subject I will cover in a later book. But for the current purposes, it is essential to know how to cohere as well as to release. Being capable of drawing together and forming a stable and meaningful solidity is of absolute essence, as in the final confrontation that ability is what secures our ultimate survival. It is all about stomach muscles.

Despite a prodigious skill and determination we always fall short, unless we have staked a claim in our heart. The heart also needs to mature, to be discussed later. We carry three burdens. Firstly, the burden of our insight, secondly, the burden of our old personality, and thirdly, the burden of the body. Through staying, we attempt to lift these and transform them into wings.

Pretending

You return home, and people treat you as your same old self. But you're trying to be something that you're not, or at least haven't been till now. To learn a new view, try pretending it and one day you'll no longer be pretending – I hope you won't have forgotten!

The problem with pretence is to do with motive. The social world we inhabit tends to link ethics to actions, whereas those on the path of inner growth see clearly that the emphasis is always on motive. Outer actions begin to appear eccentric to the ordinary person, yet on closer scrutiny a thread of sanity can always be detected through the intention and result.

When pretence is assumed for the purposes of vanity then we can apply the appropriate approbation. But when it is a tool for the journey of the spirit, that is a different matter. Pretending as an actor attempts to assume the character of a role. It is surprising how effective can be sincere and intensive pretence.

Through such a technique we activate the ability to crystallise our awareness in a new posture, or view of the world. Having spent years dismantling our earlier self-image, we have to solidify each step toward a new and more generous self.

The object here is to put aside any feelings of embarrassment, awkwardness or foolishness that obstruct us from shifting the centre of gravity of self, from inside – not from outside – to a new, unfamiliar environment. It is about our peculiar allegiance to an investment in what is, comparatively, a bunch of crap, enforced upon us without choice by total strangers. As we progress there comes a moment when we look at our closest family and have the devastating realisation that we have no idea who they are.

Firstly we recognise a profound depth of mystery behind the façade presented to us, and secondly we see that everyone is pretending. No one knows. Everyone is desperately clinging to this same bunch of crap that they also had thrust onto them.

We live in a world of ghosts.

F. Common people

Don't get caught with academics, artists, executives, specialists, politicians, professionals, doctors or priests for too long. Such people labour in a fantasy of secret conviction of superiority – they all pat each other on the back and suffer from preoccupations with justifications of jealousy. They are nailed to the wall with obsessive concerns over position and possession, and will never squeeze through the eye of the needle.

From the point of negative pride, some of the most balanced human beings I have met were middle-aged women who worked in the delicatessen section of the supermarket. Also storemen, and gardeners. Wealth, talent and cleverness can be crippling for the soul. It is amongst the common people of the world that you often find the most nourishing and refreshing generosity of spirit. You will not have intelligent or exhilarating conversations but you will be able to acquire a most precious experience of having the shit teased out of you. Wealthy people are always afraid of losing their money. Social elite are always concerned with whether they should be seen talking with you. Specialists are locked into a contrived world of their own. It is those on the bottom rungs of society who carry the wealth of our species when it comes to qualities of human warmth.

Of course I speak generally as there are always exceptions, but the truth of this is so apparent, and the rewards so great, that any serious aspirant eventually works their way down in the world – makes the journey to live amongst the common everyday 'people with no name'. We only make visits into the world of the elite as necessity demands, otherwise – remove yourself into the obscurity of those who don't hold themselves to be so precious.

This is a very awkward matter. It is often said that if you wish to achieve anything great, don't hang out with mediocre people. Alas, this is true. So it is essential that you first establish your priorities. We must return here to the issue of motive and purpose. What is your goal? If you seek inner wealth then the consequences of such a commitment will often run counter to the common assumptions of society. You cannot serve two masters.

Nonetheless, the need to acquaint with others of similar purpose is necessary. So also, to steep yourself in the energy of those who are far advanced on the same road. Such beings are rare no matter where you go – at all levels of society. The question of inspiration from teachers has already been addressed. The issue of your own first circle group will be examined in a later book.

There is one significant utility in acquainting yourself with high-achievers in society. The problem with the lower strata of society is that they often lack the will, imagination and inspiration to go beyond their perceptual limitations. High-achievers in all walks of life have this quality, and to associate with them allows it to be enhanced within us. Also, associating with low-achievers can encourage us to drop our own aspiration and purpose, if we are not strong enough internally to withstand their influence.

For the purposes of this part of the strategy, do not underestimate the extent to which we must constantly work to arrange our inner and outer life in order to eradicate pride. It has the most devious and concealed ways of continuing to permeate the personality, and only exhaustive, imaginative measures can stand against it. Best we learn to dance for a nonhuman audience.

G. Embarrassment

Embarrassment is what we feel when our pride is dis-ravelled. So long as we are in danger of embarrassment there is more remaining to be coughed up. Don't hide: allow yourself to be placed in a depreciating position.

When embarrassment is not systematically engaged with, we are in mortal danger of something far more serious: humiliation. Humiliation can scar the heart and has the power to deliver us into the hands of those who find pleasure in the suffering of others – not as victims, but as perpetrators. Even if such a fate is avoided, humiliation can sit deep within us as a massive weight from under which we may never escape. We might have forgotten the experience, but it will continue to sabotage all our efforts, our fight. Self-pity and self-doubt will plague our inner life.

Alas, we have all experienced some form of humiliation, but as long as we remain in the social world as committed accomplices we are still vulnerable, through the ruthless competition, to become either victims or bastards.

Our egos are delicate contraptions. The process of emphasising positive pride and relinquishing negative pride is the only insurance we have against the ego receiving a devastating blow from which it cannot recover. At least until we have succeeded in penetrating to absolute silence, and even then dangers still exist through contact with realisations beyond the capacity of our being.

Minor humiliations can be renegotiated (as can large ones with deeper understanding) as functional embarrassments, once the personality has caught on to the process and is willing to accept a less paranoid and less dominant position. We must become accustomed to standing aside from ourselves.

H. Demand

After having applied ourselves to the previous practices, we reach a point where we are ready to engage as a participant rather than a reactor. The following practices are evolving exercises based on our capacity to respond to situations with increasing effectiveness and enjoyment, and conversely decreasing degrees of resistance due to residual pride.

The principle being employed here is our ability to respond to *demand*. This also presupposes a degree of expertise in other areas earlier covered, such as *will*.

One way to picture this is to equate it to those jobs where the boss doesn't mind if workers fart around and have elastic attendance discipline, so long as when a major event happens everyone gives total involvement far beyond the ordinary acceptable and reasonable limits.

As a pragmatic life task you will at some point take on an activity which will last for years, during which your entire personal life preferences will be put on hold as the demand squeezes every last drop of energy from you. Success or failure is ultimately irrelevant, despite its power as a motivational force within the activity. Only the experience of total, complete application and self-abnegation remain within you as a force of great potency, which can be compressed when required into a single moment.

I. Conflict, Confrontation

This is the opening bid on a series of degrees of involvement. Usually we prefer to avoid conflict situations unless we have the temperament of a bully. This is understandable and quite natural – there is an unpleasant atmosphere given off from such situations which causes anxiety, and is an assault upon our finer sensibilities. All this has to change. Far from avoiding, it is necessary to seek out and engage with such situations.

There are sophisticated ways to approach and deal with conflict which we will touch on later, but for the purposes of this section there are two matters to understand. Firstly, there is an animal intensity about these situations which is quite enjoyable. It is a peculiar thing that as you progress with the strategy you discover yourself, to your unaccustomed and confused astonishment, being drawn towards conflict. The ability to improvise emotionally in such situations displays an evolving power in the psyche, which relishes the opportunity to play its part in ways which surprise us. We are commonly familiar with a self-image of one who likes to ponder on a plan of action or response from the safety of our private, comfortable world – we are expert armchair warriors. The experience of developing competency in emergency, reveals there are parts to us of which we had hitherto been unaware.

The second point is that in protecting ourselves from confronting situations we are also protecting our conceit. Naturally we don't see it that way, so what needs recognition is that revealing our feelings, exposing ourselves to the raw feelings of others and being forced to act in an effective way, has the power to sideline our preciousness, our fear of embarrassment, like a breath of fresh air dissipating a fog.

We cannot begin all the pleasures of the further exercises if we haven't overcome our antipathy to confrontation, for it is often the format within which the climax of a long patient journey is expressed.

J. Hunting

Hunting releases the strong face. One hunts as a way of living, not so much for the object of the hunt. It becomes incorporated into our psychic posture, which is being formed throughout life by the strategy we knowingly or unknowingly adopt.

You don't have to hunt – there are many postures that can be explored – yet hunting is intimately haunted by danger, survival. You can find your own truth engine, but personally I would opt for learning to hunt.

Certain aspects of the code of hunting should be touched on:

1. *Patience.* There are levels of patience – relaxation, endurance, forbearing, stillness and so forth. How to use time as a tool.

2. *The Strike.* The ability to cut through the wrappings – expose yourself at the exact moment. An ultimate thrust of power.

3. *Camouflage.* Do not expect society to be pleased about what we are discussing. You need a face that acts as a liaison with the world of people. An *idiot face*. A certain charm and friendship. There is no need to be insincere – simply to know why you are doing this and to help celebrate the common journey, a way to share.

4. *Tracking.* How to apply yourself to the pleasure of following a trail. A large subject which prepares one to survive alone in unfamiliar worlds.

5. *Trapping.* Combines many of the other aspects, but is of significance way beyond the temporary items of our world. Set your traps and wait.

6. *Commitment.* The psychic surrender into unison with the object of the hunt.

Hunting is deep in our ancestral memory. This whole work – the overall strategy – is an example of the art of hunting, employed within ourselves. It could be said that the entire approach outlined here is a spirit-journey of the hunter. At core is a philosophical posture which incorporates alertness and awareness of danger with joy and love of being. Leaning slightly forward from the pelvis up, knees gently flexed, feet balanced towards the ball instead of the heel, the hands free and a keenness about the head. Everything is accepted at face value and nothing taken for granted: the call may come at any moment!

Hunting can be studied by many means – it is up to the individual to seek out their particular form. Some people are not geared to this approach, while others are naturally talented. Within a group there should be a balance of types. Hunting is a way of action when confronted by lack of knowledge. Real knowledge brings relief, certainty and composure.

When immersed in the not-known, the code of the hunter combines personal skill and self-responsibility with positive force as a conscious choice, not as faith or arrogance. Nonetheless there is an inherent burden of materiality to the hunter's way. Everyone should develop competence in this area, but within a group it is handy to have some with a natural leaning toward fearless expansiveness.

The types of people who should perfect hunting will be discussed another time under *group consciousness*. The principle purpose in using hunting here is as an assault upon our hubris. It becomes painfully obvious to the hunter – whether she hunts for a job, a poem or a lover – that she often has only her own weakness to blame for failure. The hunter must change to suit the hunt! Not the quarry change. Here is the most beautifully exposed truth of the real consequences of our indulgence, alongside the joy and satisfaction of our flexibility!

Begin by transforming all the little tasks of the day – all the events of what we normally classify as good or bad luck, into opportunities to practise hunting. Problem solving becomes a totally new experience when adopted as the hunt.

The last and most mysterious aspect of the code of hunting is the power to evoke the forces of providence through *attitude*. There is a certain magical expansion – we are not so small and alone. What is that mood, that feeling which has the magnetic attractiveness to inspire the whole cosmos to our spontaneous support? This is an exercise for contemplation and re-assessment.

The Task.

This does not refer to exercises but to the facts of karma – causes and effects. We enter into the flux of the world in order to nourish our essence. Our mental self-image is often far removed from our real effect upon the world about us. Through reading the echoes of our actions we begin to truly know ourselves. That is karma – the accumulation of consequence: by taking on a task, we are forced to grapple intimately with consequence.

The *task* is the recognition of our acquaintance with the purposes of demand. It is an ultimately pragmatic and barbaric jostle with life. An animal pleasure, though often unbearably exhausting. A part of us learns to enjoy even the most traumatic experiences.

We have to take up the *task* – either ones we devise ourselves, those which come our way through the normal functioning of daily life, or those special ones we know are marked out for us in a unique way. Each task is a ticket out of bondage, so we embrace them without reservation. Our reflection from these events lets us wash our soul in the raw opinions of the world towards us.

A task becomes the *task*, once we acknowledge it as a critical tool of *spiritual growth the hard way*.

Skill

In order to play an active role in the world rather than being a spectator, it is necessary to develop skill. Skill at any activity is always worthwhile pursuing. However, there are more essential skills to enhance.

The skill of relating to other people is very useful. The skill of having explored much of ourselves is refreshing in a world of imitations. The skills of focus and attention, of recognising where a companion is pinned, of offering a gentle permeation of 'not willing to compromise', and so forth.

There is also the skill of finding yourself stretched to your maximum, beneath the whip of circumstance in a field that your heart adores. This may take many lifetimes to consummate.

The Bully

Now we get serious. Check that you've not been having yourself on – go for a bully! That's right, purposefully take on a bully and defeat the demon you find there. Like the Knights of the Round Table without the glamour or the armour.

Demon fighting is a time honoured tradition. It is inescapable – we all have to overcome features of ourselves which hold down deep positions, but only serve to hinder the clear release of our spirit. Demons can annoy, terrorise or please. Usually we are uncommonly fond of our own demon residences; somehow they entice us very cleverly with something for which we hunger.

There are two principle parts to bully hunting. The first is *savvy* and the second is *opportunity*. Before we discuss each of these it is best to reacquaint ourselves with why we should want to enter such a confrontation to begin with.

Firstly, we are trying to bring about enhanced awareness. To do this we need to unlock the gravitational centre of our personality which jealously denies to us any modes of being, any fields of new experiences, that do not conform to its prescribed image of itself – or reflectively, of the world. We do a few good deeds in the spiritual department which temporarily upsets this internal power game. However, soon the old tyrant reasserts itself under a new disguise.

Thus it becomes necessary to apply effective pressure – and nothing is as effective as the nasty manifestations of our fellow humans.

Secondly, this yoga appears at a point where the force of our essence is reaching a crucial threshold. It is necessary to give it a task to test itself in a real life situation.

Thirdly, as part of this threshold, our inner being requires to initiate, pragmatically, a fundamental metamorphosis. This involves the release of the force of perception, from its obsessive absorption within the cocoon of self-image, imprisoned by bodily identification. Our eyes have lost the sight of the connecting tissue with the external world. Nonetheless, from where our memory refuses to unveil, the power of true self is evoked through intent, and the consequences are beyond our wildest imagination.

1. Savvy.

This means being one step ahead. Use good clear common sense with imagination. See clearly what it is you are up against – you don't have to challenge if you don't think you can win: losing is an art to take with ease.

Be cautious – focus seriously upon your opponent. Notice anything unusual. Once the decision has been made, open your bid with a *strike*. Just a small one will suffice, it is only to state your spirit.

Next, let the stew build up heat. Be prepared to give on any point, and you will need all the accumulated inner wealth you can muster.

In this part you allow the force of outraged, righteous indignation to accumulate knowingly outside your personal field of emotion. Then it is up to you to become a channel for that energy to manifest. If you have done your homework, then there is only one thing stopping your success – the second principle of bully hunting: *opportunity*.

But before we move to that mysterious subject, I wish to discuss something which forms the backbone of savvy: *tactics*.

Tactics: there is more to be said here than is appropriate for this discussion. Essentially this is a matter of military knowledge which can be studied elsewhere. However, I will touch on just a few points:

a. *The initial strike.* This is a gesture towards your opponent. Choose some small insignificant point and score a victory. This has an unsettling effect on the opposition – there is more in this than first appears (it involves the mystical matter of 'smoke', which rises from each opponent before the battle). In practice, there is an often observed phenomenon: victory for those of a spiritual bent tends to come delayed. Often from a position of initial disadvantage. Nonetheless, the principle of the initial strike should always be exercised as the critical tactic.

b. *Higher authority.* This is crucial – you have to gain a link to a power beyond that of your opponent. This has extensive implications. Whenever you enter any area of endeavour it is of paramount importance to seek out and recognise the dominant power. This is not just to do with people. It is an evolving skill to know who *or what* is the presiding presence. Who has the active and who the passive authority? Who has the structural power and who the hidden power? Who is the acknowledged leader in formal situations, and who is it in emergency?

c. *Defence.* There are two aspects of defence. Firstly, every preparation and forethought must be applied to ensure your opposition can not eliminate you with their usual methods. Secondly, the ultimate form of defence is to have nothing to defend. This specifically applies to a psychological freedom. One needs to have undergone a personal inner journey to seek out that within, which exists as a place of final refuge – the only touchstone of reality in a world of ghosts, which has no need of defence. From this position only, can we relax, when we look out and know that ultimately nothing matters.

d. *Knowledge of opponent.* This is an exercise of great difficulty. In small-bully situations it is only required to examine their strengths and weaknesses – the power and the fear. However, even here it is critical to anticipate your opponent's actions. To do this we absorb their character and psych to the extent where we can know them and their behaviour intuitively.

e. *Knowledge of self.* As with all aspects of the strategy there are deeper levels. To effectively eliminate more potent forces of evil it is necessary to become sufficiently identified. To know your self intimately on a deep level – to understand how you could 'go that way' also, yet reject it. Obviously, this is not to be engaged with lightly. All beings seek companionship with true understanding. When such a relationship is established and then rejected, a doorway opens for that soul, lost in the cumulative karmic web of excess indulgence, whereby healing can begin.

   f. *Subterfuge.* The forms and patterns we employ in life are games which we forget to enjoy as such, and begin to take seriously to defend our pride. Communication and support are vital, thus we have to speak to others in their own language. This requires expressing oneself through a concoction of various positions. That others take social position instead of the quality of a person's energy field, as an allegiance to truth, necessitates the use of subterfuge.

   "Even with slender means the sentiment of the heart can be expressed" an old Chinese saying. After all, what should it matter that others seem so entombed in a narrow corridor, so long as we can toss a bit of light about as we go?

2. **Opportunity.**

Even without opportunity the exercise of balance in this profession is priceless. We constantly strive for clear balance between a spontaneous emotional explosion, tempered by awareness of survival, and profound apathy built upon the practise of stillness. Somehow we acquire a precious moment of suspension, in which a more appropriate course of action becomes apparent. It is in this pause that we look for opportunity.

Normally, wait for opportunity. Sometimes, we must boldly force a point, but then wait for opportunity to indicate the second move. Too many forcings do not bode well for the project.

It is a skill to recognise every opportunity – or at least the vast bulk of them. After all, we each have the capacity to see blatant gift horses. Once you have acquired a degree of skill in this area it becomes obvious how disadvantageous it is to be caught in the web of hurt feelings and proud flesh.

This is not a pleasant business and it is a great achievement to see it so. For most of us, we have to gird our loins for a stoush we would greatly prefer to avoid. Alas, there are beings of immense power who protect us from our indulgences, and their methods take no account of our comfort. In fact, they often demand from us a burst of pace that can kill us. One needs to be a guardian of scarce resources. I wish everyone well.

Opportunity is a friend to court, to ask for the pleasure of this dance. We ask for generosity, so we must give. This was the purpose of sacrifices in olden times. It is like a marriage, but more like an immense longing. Begin by talking to opportunity and asking for specific assistance.

Here we touch upon a peculiar relationship. Spirit is attracted to expressions of great beauty. To explosions of intense light, as in conception. The quality of light being a determining factor. Put on a dazzling performance to turn the gaze of destiny in your favour.

That summarises the exercise of bully hunting: it is a gross business when conducted socially in our everyday life. Nonetheless, it is effective and quite often thrust upon us unsolicited. So we do need certain skills here.

Healing

Not all bullies are beyond redemption. The usual situation is more complex. Our fellow man or woman has good and bad habits, as we do ourselves. Thus, we find ourselves more in the position of not so much defeating a bully, or demon, but of healing – acting in a situation to bring about reconciliation from which healthy relations and living can proceed.

Healing marks a point of major transition. Unless the previous work has been done, you only serve yourself, no matter how you pretend to heal others. There is no escape from this – it is a configuration of energy not an attitude. No amount of well-wishing can create the necessary condition. We are bound within an energetic cocoon. Unless we have succeeded in cracking the continuity of that energy-field without dying, then no matter how earnestly we believe we know others, let alone serving and healing, we only perceive a reflection of ourselves back from the inner walls of our cocoon.

It is pride that prevents us from loosening the bindings of our shell, without dying. Only through a thorough dismantling of self-importance and self-obsession can we begin the task of opening the shell from within. Even so, it remains a dangerous and deeply unsettling experience.

Once this work is properly begun, we can then engage effectively in healing.

This transition is one of the most important thresholds on the path to maturity. Each of us enters healing and service at our own time, but the principles remain, such that a true initiation into this only comes as the necessary inner changes are completed. Firstly, we prepare ourselves, then we observe; next we test ourselves against the world and last – we wait. When to act? How to act? These answers must come to us in a manner we trust and so are able to commit ourselves fully.

Principles aside, engaging in healing and service have a developmental effect in taming our ego. Take the people who unwittingly become parents. They are thrust prematurely into the role of service. There is bound to be frustration, anger or regret; but as so often happens when people are capable of even a small degree of sanity, they accept the responsibility of parenthood. The parent experiences the removal of themselves from the centre of their universe. Although they are usually in a state of marginal awareness and preparation, nonetheless it is easy to observe the beneficial effect of this upon their personalities.

Healing and service should be entered into despite the lack of true knowledge or compassion, simply as another task in the yoga of pride and humility. Preferably, it should be avoided too soon, for the sake of those who will be your unwitting victims.

The crucial point in healing, from the viewpoint of this evolving chapter on pride, is whereas, in the previous section we dealt with a very primitive and somewhat barbaric practice of demon hunting, here we have to acknowledge that, in reality, our task is not so simple. Usually, the situation confronting us reveals a tightly merged substance of both good and bad. It becomes necessary to extricate the bad and rejuvenate the good, without destroying the life force. This is what we would term 'healing'.

Involved with this we have a number of things to consider:

a. The outer and inner beings
b. Intention
c. Interference: the imposition of the will
d. Investment: silent motives
e. Identification
f. The complexity of the mixture
g. Process: imagination and allegory
h. Types: people, places, plants, groups

i. Recognition and avoidance

Before we examine each of these in detail, let's look firstly at what is happening with what we refer to as healing. Obviously healing and service are very similar. However for the sake of this exercise I will distinguish them in this way:

Healing is usually a response to a perceived illness of some kind. Service is a conscious shift of priorities, and implies change at a deep level with regard to the understanding of who we really are. It becomes a more permanent expression of the realisation of a fundamental truth about ourselves, our dual nature: that we are as much our world as our person. Healing is used in service in many ways, so it is best we examine healing first.

a. The outer and inner being

There are numerous ways of categorising the structure of our being. Later I will describe my preferred system, however for this part it is only necessary to see the two well recognised segments. There is the outer crust – a physical body – and an inner, mysterious part wherein resides our feelings and motives.

Healing the outer body is of major importance. There is no point making ourselves an easy target for death. I won't go into this here, except to say the more one learns about the proper health of the body the better – leave no stone unturned.

Healing the inner body is the main focus here. Usually, though not always, the two parts combine. You can put a patch on the outer alone, but where real healing is demanded, we must seek for illness within our sentience.

The principle for healing the inner being is always the same. We must journey into the inner world. Like a deep sea diver, we allow ourselves to submerge into the being of another, until we locate where the pocket of disruptive energy is lodged. Usually, to be successful in any long term way, it is necessary to gain the trust of the one we seek to heal.

b. Intention

This is a word to describe a very deep level of *will*. You can see the play of this force within us through its various manifestations in the sequence of words: instinct > desire > motive > commitment > intent. There are many associated words for various sub-parts: wants, wishes, hopes, privation, struggle, patience, longing, decisions, vows.

The word intention is used here, not in a vague light-hearted way, but as the conscious setting of the face of our inner being, with all the force of our life. The pre-conscious setting of our inner face – our known and unknown motives – was done by events and influences in our past. It is those we constantly try to unveil and re-examine.

- Unconscious: instinct and desire – wants, wishes, hopes.
- Pre-conscious: motives – privation, struggle.
- Awakening: commitment – patience, longing, decisions.
- Active-aware: intent – vows.

Everything I have discussed from the beginning has been a strategy for re-establishing and securing the direction of the inner face. It is a formula of intent. To intend for oneself is hard enough, but to intend for another is unbelievably difficult.

Finally, be aware that the healer, intending for another, is no less than a spiritual guide and teacher. Are you ready for this? Can you sincerely trust that you are on the right road yourself? Have you progressed far enough to clearly see the benefits of your decisions, as well as the pain and hardships – to ask this of another?

Unless you have free-fallen between the inherent contradictions of reality, and survived – then best wait awhile before you set about healing another's soul, leading another out of the maze. Intent is the core of inner healing. We have to know our own intent from the base up, to be of use in fostering another's discovery of this essence of healing.

c. Interference

What is appropriate for you, is not necessarily appropriate for another. This is almost always overlooked by healers – when you interfere in the life of another, you are in fact imposing your will upon that person. This becomes yet another weight from under which they must crawl to gain their freedom.

In helping, you incur a major cost to that person by severing the beam of their own purpose and self-reliance. How do you know what is best for another? Are you simply reacting to your own conditioning, or have you had a real intuition or sign?

Obviously, there are degrees of problems. Perhaps someone has a relatively minor need that can be satisfied quite simply – fair enough, they don't require earth shaking remedies. Nonetheless, I have usually observed there is a chain of factors leading from the superficial to the very root of being. We need to be familiar with this as well as with our own integration.

Another aspect to consider is the mode of interference. Sometimes action of an overt kind is called for. This cannot be avoided. There are often demands upon us to say or do what is confronting to others, revealing our inner world. But the preferred and more enduring method is through *presence*. The force of being upon another in a quiet yet persistent way. After undergoing the work of self-growth, we develop a resonance which affects those in our immediate presence – sometimes in quite unpredictable ways!

The beauty of *presence,* is that the intervention is of a type which allows the other maximum freedom, to express the growing alignment to their own truth. Here, the healing takes place on a plane where individual differences are less relevant.

Examples of this are seen in the arts. The artist, dancer, musician or writer eschews the blatant pedagogic-philosophical, and presents the fruits of his or her applied knowledge through subtle and powerful means of action, style or atmosphere. However, a balanced prescription should include some degree of food for the mind.

I will digress here to refer to an evolutionary step we are now undergoing as a species. Previously, healing was transmitted directly, bypassing the mental-judging-assessing apparatus. The mind of most people was not evolved to the stage of keeping pace with the process. This is still often the way many people still function, and is the means of healing in the animal and plant realms. However, with humans, now, at least some effort shoud be made to 'bring the mind along'. Mental consciousness is ascending to take up its supportive role in the architecture of spiritual balance.

In terms of healing, the technique recommended now is to apply the direct-action method, as it is the vehicle of real power, but also accompany it firstly, with explanation, and secondly, with some element of participation and informed choice (or at least the appearance of such).

A different locus of the centre of gravity of awareness is being emphasised. This is a new shift of the spiritual capital of the species, and one that entails a new unveiling of the mysteries of freedom. That the mind participates means not just another 'relief', but also a peculiar sense of 'gap' or reflection. This is not the pause born of detachment, but an almost illusionary second take.

Naturally, in emergencies the mind is useless; we must transfer knowledge into the core of our being to let our bodies respond fast. Yet in the overall balance of our spirit there is much to be gained in pondering.

d. Investment

"He who binds to himself a joy, does the winged life destroy."[2]

An example from the Judo-Christian tradition: in the biblical story of Abraham, he takes his son to a high altar and upon being told to kill him as an offering, he unhesitatingly begins to do so, only to be stopped by an angel – having passed the test. This story reveals a potent truth. Abraham knew that the test was of his ego's personal investment in his son. When ordered to completely destroy his emotional extension, he knew that to hesitate, let alone resist, would be fatal. His only hope of keeping what he loved so dearly was in the depth of display of his freedom from clinging.

He would put it this way: 'Everything belongs to God – all comes from and returns to God. Everything I have is on loan from God to be used wisely and respected, then returned. The moment I seek to grasp to myself, to retain and not return, to claim as *mine* and to delight in self-inflation, to create any opposition to the absolute sovereignty of God, then I have sealed my fate, and severance from that which I have stolen must and will come. For in God's time, reality will prevail. Just as I attract what I fear, so I lose what I covet.'

(For the sake of discerning a perennial truth embedded in this ancient story, I will put to one side the common-sense concern, of a man willing to murder a child on the basis of voices in his head. This story is mythical, and should only be taken in that context, never as a justification to act in that manner. It is only valid as symbolism: to gain a proper perspective on our whole life – our position and possessions. To gain the lesson from this story it would be preferable to see the 'son' as being creations, projects – things we have 'given birth to' through our own efforts.)

There is a cosmic law at work here – the laws of interdependence and independence are to be separately realised. Whenever we refuse to respect the inherent independence of all things, their repulsion towards us grows in proportion to our lack of recognition. It is because we do not know the source of our own independence, that we seek external certainty, and relief from spiritual anxiety in acquisition and clinging.

This causes the psychic sickness known as *investment*. It means that the silent motive behind all our actions is to increase our sense-of-self. We rarely, if ever, act out of freedom: to give with no expectation of return. Unless we have sought and found the source of our own independence in the depths of the Great Silence, how can we act freely?

[2] William Blake

It may lend some assistance to ponder the old saying, 'Only what we give away, is our true wealth.' However, all this should not be confused with being responsible towards the things and people that pass through our field of care. There is a difference between concern born of fear and clinging, and that born of respect. Healing comes from concern; and yet concern is the force that robs us of the peace that is our birth right.

Love is not a desire – solutions come as we relax. When the preliminaries are over, what we are offering is trust in our own and the other's independent source of nourishment. For a soul habituated to bondage this is confusing, frightening – even insulting. Those who live by hegemony, demand hegemony. Expect no thanks for healing the spirit; expecting no thanks is the only way to heal the spirit.

e. Identification

Healing the deeper regions means submerging into the psyche of another – seeing and feeling the world as they do. This is an art of brinkmanship, a spiritual adventure from which you will not emerge unchanged. At times the process of identification with the one you are helping becomes so strong that there is a real danger of losing yourself.

We literally take on to ourselves the sickness of the other, and then find the way out. It is our struggle and escape from the prison of another's soul-state, that engraves itself upon the inner face of their being, as well as our own.

Often, he or she will attempt to convince you of the completeness of their prison – the futility, the nonexistence of escape routes or clear choices. They have effectively sown themselves up. For healing to work they must *know*, in a true sense, that you *do* understand and experience their situation. Then you have to disentangle what is of lasting value within their 'view' from what must be discarded. Even there, you will see that what now is useless and an obstacle, was perhaps at one point, a useful mechanism. They need to transfer their 'gravity' centre from an outdated and restrictive self-image toward a healthier one.

Search out the points of strength and innate knowledge in the person; emphasise these and draw them into yourself, to give maximum effect and appearance to the process of identification – for your own sake and for the development of trust with the other.

Identification takes time and extended *presence*. It also requires a willingness on the part of the other to sustain the contact. The more you progress, quite often the more others will feel a mysterious discomfort in your presence, such that those who are willing (for whatever reason they may believe) to maintain contact and engage, deserve a large degree of recognition and response. Once you have passed a particular threshold, there is only one reason why others cross your path. At some level, no matter what conscious absurdities they are ensnared in, they are asking for guidance toward that to which your life is dedicated. The difficulty is convincing them that this is indeed the case.

Identification can be terrifying, and must be total to leave you free to move on. The forces of illness are real and overwhelmingly powerful beings. Escape ultimately comes from a point deep within us. In more advanced forms of healing, without the help of a teacher, there is nothing that can be done within the timeframe of this life to penetrate deeply enough into our core, to ensure that this inner point has the strength and stability to withstand the impact of extreme healing experiences. Best to identify limitations. All the strategy outlined in this book can only serve to awaken something that must already be alive within us. It is necessary to know how to tread carefully.

f. The Complexity of the Mixture

This issue has already been referred to, yet because of its extraordinariness, I would like to expand it a little more. At the heart of shifting from *demon hunting*, to *healing* lies the recognition that, in most situations, it is not a simple matter of knocking the bad guys on the head. We perceive a complex mixture of appropriate and inappropriate manifestations enmeshed in a most curious way.

It has been an interesting task, by many who are aware of this, to provide a descriptive image. The point is that the so-called *good* and *bad* parts do not sit separately, such that one can be plucked out while the other enriched. Neither are they interwoven as with a basket, such that one bad thread can be extracted.

This has to do with the *self* symbol of the personality. It is what it is, and an attack upon any part is an attack upon the whole. It is not so much a rearrangement that is sought, as a shift in the centre of gravity.

Still, the process of shooting off the heads of the thousand-headed one is the practical daily yoga in which we all participate. We apply ourselves to moving things about on the outside, in order to produce a responding shift in the core rhythm of our being. It is as if our useful and deleterious parts are anodised together: the courser elements needing to be constantly purged. Yet even that is not a full description of what is a whole labyrinth of postures.

What is often forgotten in healing, is the need for a drop of that mysterious substance, acting as a *yeast of light*, which is mysterious precisely because at a certain point the bottom just falls away. It is the sovereignty of this grace that keeps one in thrall. Where to find this drop of *yeast*? That is the real question.

I don't wish to discuss methods of ingression, but to alert the inexperienced to the reality that it is not simple – what one is presented with is an unpredictable counter-balanced whole, wherein movement of one facet agitates the whole structure. Do not make the mistake of self-righteously imposing awareness on one or two pet issues of your own.

We are presented with a 'substance' somewhat balanced. Attempting to shift one part for the better, we are likely to be attacked by other affiliated parts. This is often perceived as the person getting worse before improving. There is an unconscious resistance to change, which has practical consequences as we engage our own development.

Within this anodised, and somewhat balanced substance, lies the workings of its own growth. One is constantly being called out to by a hidden force within the being of another person. This is most important, as without this force being of sufficient strength, there is really little one can do.

g. Process

I suppose at some point 'process' needs discussion. All healers have their own methods, yet there are many similarities and common-source springs. Also, there are many extraordinary devices, but I will elaborate a more thorough process for when there is the time and intent.

Firstly, nothing can be accomplished without initially centring yourself. You must revisit your own point of maximum significance. Immerse yourself again and see further.

Secondly, don't underestimate the power of warmth. Toward the object of your interest, allow the feeling of warmth to grow. Not only will this assist the next steps to function smoothly, but more importantly, through warmth you can link your deeper spirit to the spirit of the other. It is the relationship which underpins the healing process. You make friends with the true inner being of the other, and together you attempt to bring the other's separated self into the friendship.

Try not to make the warmth too sweet and mushy. There is a distinct internal resistance to such feelings which is a reaction to something that we can do, but which is removed from our true purpose. Always remain balanced and reserved within your core, even when presenting an extension of genuine sympathetic warmth towards the other. This way we avoid the danger of seeking to 'ensnare with love' – a common malady.

Allow your affection to pass behind the person or object of your attention. Observe how a mother loves her child as it grows, despite all the child's moods and tantrums. There is something within the energetic essence of the objects of our world which is of profound similarity to ourselves. Look, see and know this. We really have no other option. If we don't go ourselves to this table we will be dragged there by some strange force, again and again.

Thirdly, develop a strong imagination. Shifting to the visual, we begin by remembering the object of our focus. Especially the feelings associated with remembering visual perceptions of recent or intense daily experiences.

Picture in your mind that you are on a journey. You climb a high point in order to see the land about you. Looking out ahead you notice not far off, a town – this is about other people. In the distance there's the horizon, and quickly you look to the point where you are headed – in a vague feeling way, attracted by something behind the landscape. Explore this in visual meditation.

Then visualise the object of your healing, or the object instrumental in the healing. From this point on, you need to be fleet of foot in your creative imagination, to move towards the images that are pulling you. There is a knack to this that can be developed with practise. The drama of healing is etched in the ether.

Fourthly, go forth – when you meet this object in the world of physical spirit, a new event begins. Watch carefully. You must be able to relate the day-time event to your visualisation, to evoke an effective process. But more important is to examine and evolve on-the-spot improvisations. This is the field of tales of fabulous encounters. Allow your natural spontaneity to respond to the situation. There is much enjoyment to be had, even in the most serious of cases.

That is a brief outline of the process. There are many more aspects that you can develop. For example the creative use of analogy and allegory in imagination, the calling and use of help and helpers, the use of different types of light, the inclusion of 'means' whereby energy can be transferred to the patient on the physical plane (for example, a doctor), and the use of your astral body – its hands or energetic centres. The methods and more in-depth examinations of the process need to be explored and practised along the way.

Types of Healing

a. People

It may surprise the beginner to realise that humans are not the only area of healing; however, they do represent an interesting challenge. Essentially, the healer has grown through the process of self-healing, but immediately discovers that the techniques effective for oneself are rarely useful in healing another. Don't be thrown off your basic lines, but be flexible in producing outcomes.

Proper healing takes time and effort, and cannot be achieved on a large number of people. Be selective, and devise methods of quickly producing practical results, even if superficial or temporary.

We have a problem when discussing our relations with other people. The socialised mind is not happy with a pragmatic approach which is dismissive of valuing human beings as individuals worthy of respect and autonomy. This view is wrong – it values what is worthless and completely ignores what is of primary significance in another human. Only after you have seen through the underhand ploys and trickery of your own self-importance, can you engage in the restructuring of your social world.

Other people are divided into three categories – the esoteric, mesoteric and exoteric: the inner, middle and outer. The esoteric is your spiritual family. It takes time, to link up your intimate spirit-circle. The mesoteric is rather like your Spirit Tribe or associated tribes. The exoteric are the foreigners – the strange majority.

Healing in the esoteric group takes long and extreme effort. It is worth it after all, because you are ancient companions and, as a whole, intimately involved with the personal higher compartments of each member.

Healing in the mesoteric group is a new challenge. These people are often strongly linked with you, but there is a peculiar and subtle variation in their energy configuration. As you progress, this begins to appear less as a simple variation on a theme and more as a problem of the lack of integration with all parts of their being, which itself acts as to keep them out of the esoteric group.

I say this because I have observed a repeated event, where a complete stranger walks straight into the centre of the esoteric group – sometimes stays, or departs just as suddenly. The doors and windows are always wide open, as a principle.

Despite this, immense effort goes into the mesoteric contacts as this becomes a way of paying your dues.

Healing in the exoteric group is rarely done with individuals for a number of reasons. Firstly, there is little sensitivity and response to the deeper levels of the situation: being alive in a magical world for such a fleeting moment in time. I am not suggesting there is no need to affect such people psychically – the tasks of our lives often require the use of psychic influence on those about us – but healing of the spirit is a different matter. For the time and effort required, little can be achieved.

Secondly, they are aligned to a different inner direction. The healing energy transferred is soon redirected to the service of a different purpose. Thus, it is not just a waste of effort, but could be dangerous for the person involved. This is similar to the problem of 'spiritual development the easy way'. Without first having thoroughly learnt the lessons of the portal of destruction, with regard to our secret motives, inevitably awareness is redirected back upon the known, and we become ensnared in our own web. It has been cautioned by far wiser ones than I – better to have not begun the journey than to fall in this way.

Thirdly, and most importantly – the exoteric group come under a different law. Having been deeply committed to the task of extracting yourself from the enchantment of humanity, to free your spirit for the encounter with truth within the period of this life, you find yourself poorly positioned to understand how the salvation of humanity is being organised, by forces dedicated to the spiritual evolution of our species. This needs to be studied later in life, and is part of the next phase: *service*.

There is a plan unfolding for the species which is exceedingly creative, imaginative, shrewd and exciting in the extreme. You need to watch and see this, in order to be of any help with your limited healing skills.

The essential point here is this: don't make the mistake of applying the code of the small stream, to heal those in the main stream. They are on the long slow arc. However, there are indications that the outcome for the species is by no means certain.

b. Animals and Plants

This area is one of the most enjoyable forms of healing and association. Both animals and plants respond to healing with great ease and affection. The protective adjuncts for the ego can be dispensed with here. Plants and animals see clearly, so response is genuine and free.

This is such an important and pleasurable area, I will expand in detail a bit. You should become acquainted with:

c. Dogs

This is an excellent place to start. Dogs are perhaps our oldest species companion. You may never know from any other source the degree of unconditional honesty and affection that you can experience from a dog. It goes without saying, one can stuff up their dog nature; and some are better than others. Nonetheless, their underlying relationship to people is as extraordinary as their demand for acknowledgement for this is absent.

If you have not had a significant relationship with a dog – get one, and learn to love your own dog nature. What more can I say? They are healers par excellence.

d. Cats

This is the other companion species, though very different. For experiencing the pleasure of a finely tuned and sensitive mixture of the beautiful and the lethal, I recommend a cat. Personally I prefer Siamese, but fascinating characters abound in every variety of the cat world.

The overwhelming impression is one of physical grace. Also of independence. The presence of a cat can undermine the glamour of human madness and pretention.

e. Insects

A tricky area. Certainly worth exploring, but you will find they exist a long way from humans. Probably the best place to begin is with beetles. But it is only natural you will spend much time with ants as they are so fascinating. Bees also I can recommend, especially when you are seeking some sophistication. Cicadas are well worth exploring, especially from a sound perspective.

f. Wild Animals

This is a group of beings who do not have close ties with us. They are a window to an ancient, forgotten world. One that is especially important for us, by virtue of the fact that it permeates our species bubble more than we would wish to believe. Wherever possible, take the opportunity to develop a relationship with wild animals. Some extraordinary experiences can be had in this area – humans are not the only beings capable of spiritual intent.

g. Plants

A large area which I can only touch on briefly. Amazing creatures. Mostly, though not always, with a deep friendliness – arousing a strange ache of longing in us for something that floods out. Of course, plants are very different to each other – as species, but also as individuals. They share much more in common with us than we generally would imagine.

I cannot here go through all the different types – you should explore as many as you can. They respond very quickly to physical healing through psychic means.

The first difficulty in engaging with plants is to overcome the embarrassment at talking meaningfully and honestly to them. For the beginner, a terrible moment comes when you find yourself in conversation with a plant, maybe even an emotional breakdown in front of one. Never mind. If other people are watching – all the better, it is good for the soul.

Here again we have a difference between *pet* plants – those around your dwelling – and *wild* ones. Regarding the former, we have what we call the garden. This is a physical garden as distinct from my earlier discussions. The garden is a good place to begin to know plants. This becomes part of the subject of meditation, so I will for the present avoid the more mystical practices.

You do not have to tend a garden. Just let it run wild if you like. Wild gardens have a beautiful energy. However, as far as the process of entering into the world of plants, it is useful to spend some years developing a cultivated garden, because in this way you learn much about the subtle variations in the needs and preferences of each plant. You also discover the delightful joy of working in a garden; you may even begin to understand the relationship of *group* plant energy with your own. How to create a garden as a thing of power. Few gardeners understand this; they become preoccupied with the individual specimens and never learn how the spirit of a garden moves.

A garden can become a healing tool. One of the most important parts of this process is to live in your garden. Place chairs and tables into special areas and spend as much time there as you can. Do not fall for the mistake of hiding in a house – get outside with all the birds and insects. A further development is to put a fireplace in the garden. Especially good is a fire in the centre of a lawn.

Wild plants are those away from human habitation. These have an extra potency which is of immense healing benefit to humans. This quality is almost completely missing from the plants that you find within towns and suburbs. The same is also true of swimming in creeks as opposed to swimming pools. I should like to devote a whole section to the wilderness experience at another time.

h. Objects and Places

It may appear strange to say that the process of healing can be applied to objects. Here we have one of the greatest misunderstandings of our culture at the time of this writing – things were different in the past and remain different in many traditional cultures. The energetic absorption and influence of objects is important in the strategy of development.

Whatever we place our attention on absorbs the quality of our moods, and then becomes a source of emanation of that quality on the environment around it. Therefore it is of paramount importance how we choose the objects of our world, because our world is intimately connected to us and comes under the same laws we are defining for our strategy, to achieve the required spiritual magnetism. Strive to catch the beginnings. Especially when an object is to become an integral part of your expression, or life journey – watch and be patient.

Nevertheless, don't become possessive of your things. They come and they go, and have their own destiny. This is the real trap. Once the energetic nature of objects is understood, they can become recipients of all the bad as well as the good. Fear, obsession, greed and ambition are often found in objects. Such, are objects of desire, and need to be carefully avoided.

There is one particular class of objects which as you progress will cross your path – power objects. I tell you right now, and you will not listen – we are all greedy and must suffer for our stupidity: LEAVE THEM ALONE.

The things of this world have their own purpose and direction; they pass us as ships at sea – we may travel together as friends for a time, and then we part. Leave it be like this.

There are times when objects and places need to be purified and reformatted. A number of methods can be used: this is a technical aspect of healing which you can study and experiment for yourself, but I will give here a couple of the more well used methods.

Smoking is an ancient and effective purification technique. I am not referring to deep healing, which hopefully you will not have need to do on any objects or places – just avoid those. Any thing or place can be refreshed or cleaned through a good thorough smoking – a bee-hive smoker is good for healing places.

Ceremony. This is an excellent and enjoyable technique. A ceremony can be anything from a party or feast, to more directed events. Usually an offering or sacrifice of some kind is involved. Music is very useful for ceremonies.

Places pick up the energy of events that have happened there. Quite often problems arise as a consequence of this due to the proximity of people who choose to live nearby. It can take a long time for natural healing to come about for such places. Whenever you encounter un-wellness of any description it is advisable to examine the surrounding area for possible environmental causes. For those not naturally sensitive, such places take a good deal of experience to detect.

i. Groups

This is a fascinating subject. To observe how group energy works is obviously the first step. Take plenty of time to watch – it will save you from considerable wasted effort. I am not so concerned here to deal with temporary or superficial shifts in group direction – you can study fashion and advertising for that – I am focusing on the deeper task of bringing about a long term evolution.

The difficulty is that the effects of change in an individual, induced through group energy, are inherently unstable. Nonetheless, we are always party to some group formation. The range of groups, and how useful or otherwise they are for our own destiny, is a subject worth investigating. There are superficial accidental groups, family groups, suburban and town groups, religious groups, whole nations and races.

There are also hidden groups of underlying commonality – not just of casual interests, but also ancient connections on a subliminal level. Group energy is extremely powerful if often temporary, but it can be harnessed for our own personal journey. It is worth examining the structural patterns of our deeper connections in spirit, and where one sits within those patterns. This is a huge subject, not within the scope of this book.

Pride

All these practices and sensitivities that I have sketched here are to be entered into within the one interpretation: they are means of reducing our pride. The good has to suffer with the bad at first, but not for too long. Soon we realise where our power resides, and then it's a matter of using everything we find in living, with no exceptions, as a tool for this constant assault upon false pride.

One of the simplest and most effective recourses is to poke fun at ourselves. Encourage others to poke fun at you. Our false pride can't stand being laughed at. Tease the importance out of yourself and have a good laugh at your own expense. All aspects of our life can be excellent fodder for humour – we really are ridiculous creatures!

This image we have of ourselves, which we cling to and stake our hopes in, is not who we are, I'm sorry to inform you. So long as you cling to this *act*, you will never break through to the other side, and will be a pawn in life's paws.

Work your way through these practices and explorations, and eventually your old self will die. That is when pride bites the dust. You can't imitate this, although you can practise at imitation, just to prepare the ground, so to speak. But nothing can replace the actual death of our pride. Only that can give us respite, peace, and the *moment's pause.*

The shell must be broken. There is no other way. Until the shell is broken, we can't see out. All we see are the walls of our tunnel, with pictures of ourself looking back at us. When the mirror breaks, the body breaks, and we can catch a glimpse of freedom.

Once the spine of our old world is broken, it never comes back together again. We still have to battle pride on deeper levels, but there is a hole in the tapestry now, through which we can look at the stars.

Chapter 11a

Stories of Pride

The Whistling Nostrils

I belong to the great, ancient and sagacious clan of The Whistling Nostrils. Now, we Nostril Whistlers were once the rulers of respect, the titans of social acme. Ah, but alas that was long ago. Ours is a noble tradition, to which I must insist, one can only be born into – it is not a matter of choice, no cheeky upstarts can sneak in by pretence or payment. Still, despite the fact that we have descended into obscurity, nay even ignominy, yet we know who we are, we know our true status in the eyes of the Great Whistling Nostril in the sky.

And don't anyone forget it! Blood will be spilt if a snide word is said to belittle our sacred clan. We can be vicious in defence. We are proud, we are high born, and we walk with dignity, despite what the newspapers say. Those scum! Those arse-licking toadies, mongrel dogs, suck-holes, sons-of-pigs who spit upon our people. We spit back! We stick your guts with twisted burning steel – you will taste our displeasure if you so much as come near us with your evil warped ways.

Enough of that. We are actually a very gentle clan. We love flowers and incense. Our women are fair and delicate, with fine and tender hearts. Our men are proud but kind. We will protect you if you respect us – that is all we have ever asked, respect.

Oh, I know what you say, that we are just a bunch of old hairy-nostrilled clowns. But I plead with you, we are truly worthy, we have a true lineage that goes back to the earliest Whistling Nostrils that came to this land thousands of years ago – tens, hundreds of thousands of years ago.

The wise elders of our clan still hold secrets that no one but a true Whistler knows. We can tell a false Whistler! But we don't make a fuss about them, we just snigger behind their backs, and nod wisely at each other, for true Whistlers are something of a deep holy pride to behold ... when you know, which of course you never will, unless you are one, a real Whistling Nostril.

But that was all before. Sadly, or not so sadly, I decided to leave the clan – I cut my nose hairs! Yes, to wailing and crying and shock and awe, I walked away from my hairy nosed friends. Out, out into the ordinary world of nobodies. Really, frankly, I'd had enough! Jesus, Mary and Joseph, how much nose whistling can one man take? I could never get to sleep for all that noise.

So I became an apostate, a man stripped of my holy status, naked in the park, one more bobbing clean-nosed head in the subway. What a relief! You have no idea the burden that nose hairs can bring.

Now I'm a free man, a sensible man, a man forgotten by the ravages and the turmoil of the hairy-nosed disposed. I have a little garden now, and a few hens. A little fire on a cold night, and a little bed in which I sleep silently. A little car in which I trundle into a little town to work at a little job that nobody thinks is anything special.

And one day I hope to get so little, I'll disappear.

Little fluffy jumped onto his pumpkin

Little fluffy jumped onto his pumpkin. He had a perky chest, and was wont to boast to all the little snuptions that gathered around him with their tiny snouts ajar, that he was the fluffiest of all snuptions. And everyone believed him, except for a couple of old dog-fart snoorkers, who spat into spittoons and scoffed snoorker beer under the shade of a pretty, leafy shrub across the road. Belching and cavorting, they always got up the nose of little fluffy.

He rallied his cohort. "Don't take no notice of those ratbags!" he would splutter. And all the snuptions humphed and hooffed and cast dark eyes at the grotty snoorkers. "They are evil!" shouted little fluffy as he nearly slipped off his pumpkin, much to the guffawing of the scoundrel snoorkers. He puffed himself up into a big balloon of a snuption, as only he could do, and displayed a set of crimson tinted feathers that poked their tips out of his bottom patch. "Oooh ... Aaahh" hoffed the falley of snuptions about him, "See what a clever snuption he is." they all said, as they turned haughtily to cast a despising sneer at the dirty old snoorkers, who by now were really quite tipsy, and chortling merrily at the scene.

Little fluffy then did a jump and a twist, to the amazement of his admirers, but landed in a heap at the side of the pumpkin. Quick, they all rushed to help him. "Get back you fools" cried little fluffy, "I can get up myself!" And he did, again proving what a superior little fluffy he was to all his smiling audience.

But then one of the farting snoorkers let out a loud burp. All the snuptions looked with horror. Little fluffy quickly hopped onto his pumpkin and said, "See! I told you they were worthless wastrels. One day they will realize that we are the special ones, the true ones, the great and mighty ones. We snuptions hold the glory of god in our tiny paws. We are the most beautiful, the most advanced, the most sophisticated, and the real followers of our most highest, biggest Holy Snuption, goddy bless his soul. I am his prophet, and you are all so, so lucky to have me here to fluff you all up!"

"Hear! hear! horrahar, horrahharraharraharrarrrrr.... " screamed all the snuptions as they wet themselves with glee. Snuptions were given to wetting themselves at moments of high intensity.

With pride and motorboating snouts they all turned to glare with superiority, as only snuptions know how, upon the lazy smelly snoorkers across the road. But, agasp! the rotten bludgers were asleep on the grass. "See," said little fluffy, never at a loss to grasp the moment, "I told you ... good for nothing, evil toads. They'll never get to snuption heaven." Just as a final fart drifted across the road to them, and quickly they all held their snouts and twiddled off to their burrows, it was getting late for snuptions to be out, and they had really had enough excitement for one day.

Part II

Reflections

High above the world
    just floating
      gently on the line
No worries or cares
    drifting, watching
      no hurry or obsession
In perfect patience
    he waits, contented
Until at last!
With piercing eyes
    he spots his prey.

Down! Down!
Swift and silent
He drops
To snatch his moment of luck.

Then back again
    he climbs on the wind
Gliding free and quiet
Confident to wait
    until his moment, comes again.

Chapter 11

Feelings and Emotions

Feelings point outwards, and *emotions* are within. I employ these words with meanings specific to revealing truths about the way we engage the world, and how we can purchase freedom from a life of automated sleep. Emotions are internal solar flares – sparks and flames of energy that often come from the solar-plexus, though also from other areas like the chest or back of the head. The most consuming emotions are love and hate: desire, infatuation, anger, resentment and self-pity. These involve an addiction to this type of intense emotion, which is a pity because they de-emphasise the other type: feeling.

Feeling is sensitivity to the world about us. We taste the world with feeling far more than with thought. Feeling is a doorway to that which lies outside ourselves – we allow the energy in something out there to enter and suffuse our inner being. Feeling is a subtle mood that resonates with an external stimuli. That external 'something' can evoke emotions within us, sometimes powerful emotions – 'presses our buttons', triggering intense moods from our past. Strong emotions filter out externally generated feelings, creating a flaw in the crystal which deflects reality as we sink into self-obsession. Feeling is a subtly powerful, unusual state, whereas emotion is familiar and consuming – fascist in fact.

As most people are addicted to emotion, assume you are also if you're not sure. That is the place to start.

Feeling is a beckoner of sensing – an obscure ability that begins to manifest as progress is made on the Path. It is necessary to feel the world: your glass of water, your socks, your home, everything that surrounds you. We generally give little time to our feelings, as humanity is predominately preoccupied with emotions. Those few who are not submerged in the vast emotional self-obsession, are mostly ensconced in the twists and turns of the mind. Not a bad alternative, as at least it can be productive.

How to draw oneself out of this constant internal soap-opera?

Ask yourself, is that really me? That complaining, guilt-ridden, resentful, scornful, snotty sense of fretting that constitutes most of my daily life - is this me? Or does it feel strangely alien? Where do I find the true emotionality of my own being?

There is a sadness in life that has no obvious cause. You may have a list of interesting and enjoyable things to do, you may have a deep understanding of yourself and the world about you. But none of these can protect you from this type of sadness, in fact it may even exacerbate your exposure. There is something about life itself, although you see all those pools of doings waiting for your dive, which brings a type of veil. A tiredness, as if you know underneath, that all these doings will pass, and the veil will drop again.

There is something deeply meaningless about even our most sacred endeavours. A haunting loneliness in even our cherished companionship. It is inappropriate to run away feeling sorry for ourself, that this mood has come upon us. Just sit with it, feel its touch, for it is the other side of the coin of life. But also don't indulge in allowing its mood to grow into consuming self-pity. It is just the ultimate passing of everything. A withdrawal of an imbalanced identity. It happens to even the greatest among us.

Emotions or feelings – what are they anyway? I wish to leave feelings to one side for now – they are something unique, and their treatment is better left for a later time, after the basics have been covered. But both have to be examined. Most of us do not want to observe ourselves while in an emotional state. Yet this is required, as we so often overlook it, being so consuming.

Emotion is a nervous excitation. For the majority of people, this is what we live for. We will constantly trail thoughts and images before our inner perceptual screen to illicit this excitation. The goal of meditation with its tools of negating mental, physical and emotional movement, seems pointless.

On observation, there are distinct types of emotional states. Let us first make this separation: one type is spontaneous while the other is lingering. If we stifle spontaneous emotions we cause damage to our being. 'Let it flow and let it go', as the old saying has it. Lingering emotions however, require careful management.

A critical secret lies right here, that, if not grasped, will derail your entire quest. There is a type of lingering emotion that feeds your magic to another, that strips from you your finest gleam. Just watch a child ...

then watch an adult. This is the difference – don't make excuses for the adult. There is only one cause for the duller glow of the adult – brooding anguish, I call it, but to be more precise – worry and concern.

The only magic left to the adult of our species is the constant reflection upon ourselves. And alas, that reflection is almost always dark. Disquieting reflection of ourselves has caused us, as a species, to trade freedom for safety. Somewhere, we accepted *fear of losing* as the flame of emotional excitation to which we offer worship through constant revisiting. This has shrivelled our glow and made us weak. We now, all of humanity, are preoccupied by concern over the minutiae of our lives, and thus the door to our inheritance was closed, and its riches given away.

The most potent point of drainage is the emotional moods attendant upon our relationships: are we loved or unloved, liked or disliked, accepted or rejected, approval flowing to us from the eyes of others or disapproval? It's all in the eyes of others: we are experts in knowing when we are getting the flow of delight in another's eyes, or the pall of disinterest and possibly even disdain. That is the primary preoccupation of our inner world: the sea-saw of sympathy and antipathy in our social world. The flag of convenience for a wasted life.

This is not to be taken as to deny our emotions. But there are certain emotional states to be given up, if one is to regain one's full capacities as a human. All these come under the heading of *self-absorption*.

Self-Absorption

It begins with the practice of ruminating upon the events of our life with ourselves at the centre-point. This lays the foundation. It appears to come almost as a respite from boredom. We turn to playing with self-image in our mind. The aim is to gain an emotional charge from recollections or fantasies of ourselves in relation to other people. Typically we will recall over and over what someone said or implied to us, what we felt at the time or later. Excitement or outrage – they are the juiciest ruminants.

In social communication we call this gossip, and it can extend to complete strangers (movie stars, politicians, infamous or famous identities) and how we felt about their actions. Always we are seeking a very personal type of emotional flaring within us. This is the dominant preoccupation of the emotional-mind life of almost all human beings.

And it is this that drains us of our energetic and spiritual inheritance – it is literally sucked out of us. Yet there is still a further stage:

Irrational Fears

This is where we lose our spirit big time! It can be a personal or a public matter. It is curious how prone all humans are to becoming inflamed by concerns that have almost no basis in reality. We love it. It usually begins with a simple line of thought, then a couple of trigger-points are touched, and before you know it, we are vehement and off-our-face with anxiety. We always justify this with pseudo-rational thoughts, which in the light of more sane knowledge can easily be shown as baseless. Yet this is actually resented!

We so love the emotional charge that we bristle with indignation and scorn at any dispassionate attempt to bring in sanity, balance and reason. We are puppets dancing in the hands of those who are milking us for all we are worth, while we are consumed by the joy of inflammation.

What are we to do, to plug this energy drain? The first thing is to separate self-reflection into two parts. On one side, renounce the obsessive thinking about ourselves and others that preoccupies our waking mind. Cease entertaining ourselves with these emotive excitations. On the other side, engage *systematically* in reflection on our past. This is a special technique which I explain in the section on meditation. This, among other remedies, can release energy from forgotten events in the past that have locked us into patterns.

To break the pattern of emotional indulgence, one needs to apply many techniques, but especially, a genuine effort has to be made.

Empowering and Degenerative Emotions

Not all emotional states are to be resisted. Take one example: grief. When we lose a close friend it is natural to feel grief. Even the most advanced beings will shiver with the keenness of grief. The correct response is to enter fully into the emotion of loss. Feel the nuances, recall the significant moments, and speak openly any unresolved or pent-up sentiments. The memory of such a friendship should remain sharp and clear. The pain carried as fresh and cutting. This is all appropriate.

What is not appropriate is when we replay the emotions over and over. Dwelling on them in the solar-plexus until, instead of it being a fresh cut to the heart which we carry with poise and maturity, it becomes chronic, swollen and septic. Feel the pain, feel it fully, remember it, but know how to leave it. For healing, these emotions have to be 'forgotten', to sink into the subconscious where they can transform away from our interfering sight.

This broken-record quality of replaying an anguish over and over in a characteristic way, is one of the marks of degenerative emotion. It is not possible to fully explain this – you will need to examine it first in others, then in yourself, until you can recognise the difference between degenerative and empowering emotion. Then cut yourself free from the former.

It is clearer to describe the antidote. The first step is to make the effort to remain calm and adaptable in the face of situations which are not going according to expectations. When plans and desires are cut across, or interfered with in unsatisfactory ways, catch yourself after the initial disappointment (which is only natural). Before the rollercoaster of emotions build beyond control, step in and say, "OK, I will find a way to accommodate this unpleasant situation." Then change your attitude. Adopt the view that not only is this disruption accommodate-able, but in fact it will be a superior tactic to what you originally had in mind. This means exploiting the situation and turning a disadvantage into a boon: 'turning your hat around'.

I am speaking here of a type of control and release. Control yourself. Step in as the master of your inner house, take leadership and shift focus. Release the world to follow *its* plan, instead of yours. Then re-engage again as a partner in a new pattern. The world is saying this is a better idea. Accept, and roll with it. Always seek where new opportunity is revealing itself.

The next step, learn how to break from a task or activity that is not working out. Pull back when you are becoming drained by an unresolvable set of circumstances. I'm not suggesting you become weak through lack of determination. Break the insane obsession that is going nowhere by switching attention for awhile, then return to the difficulty when fresher. Or give it up completely in those cases where you realise persevering is idiocy.

A variation on this in the inter-personal sphere: when you find yourself trying to explain something to a person who is just not getting it. This can become infuriating when what you are explaining is so plain and obvious in your mind, but the other person refuses to 'get it'. Don't allow the frustration to build into antagonism. Stop! Realise that there has to be a reason they are not getting your view-point, and you can't see it. Don't keep repeating yourself again and again. Stop and know there is a blockage that is very relevant. This has to be resolved before further attempts at communicating your view-point. Catch yourself. Pull out of the emotional escalation. Control, then release the tension.

In its wider sense, you could call this a form of inner discipline of the mind. The final step in this process is to engage in meditative practice of a silent mind. I discuss that further in the section on meditation.

What underlies the whole complex of this type of emotion, is a mysterious similarity across humankind of a unique type of self-absorption. It is not in any way intentional or deliberate on the part of all of us who pride ourselves on our individuality and self-direction – nothing could be further from the truth. It is marked by ignorance and willlessness. This kind of consuming emotion is a malaise of our species, and when combined with cruelty and obsessive sexual fantasy, is nothing less than a vicious and ruthless enslavement of humanity.

What can we do? Only one thing: free ourselves. What is required is a specific kind of effort – that of actively freeing ourselves from automated sleep. When the unique emotion of this kind of effort is 'given off', it is food for all those who are also engaged in the *work*. As distinct from the other emotions I have been discussing, this does not debilitate the one making the effort – rather it strengthens and frees.

One more thing about this collective mind – its manipulation. Small and great events have a strange way of triggering the network of anxiety. There is a malicious force that consciously keeps the collective anxiety-nerve in a series of spasms. All practitioners of this Path need to not only free themselves from the domination of this human condition, but also clairvoyantly see the manipulative force behind its constant stimulation.

Love

This particular emotion requires special attention. In previous periods of humanity, and no doubt in the future, it will not present itself as requiring special attention.

The overwhelming emotional attraction that we currently call love, also infatuation, is one specific type of love. Infatuation is an inferior reference to it. It is deeply consuming, and I find it hard to imagine one could progress far without having experienced it. It is a projection onto another of a deep personal connection with a particular aspect of the original prototype of our species. This prototype is a being which we must meet at some point on the journey to our centre. It vivifies the heart in a profound way and must at all cost be respected, as must those upon whom our projection falls.

It must also, come unstuck. But never allow this emotion to fall from the expansive pressure in the chest, to the dark pain of the solar-plexus with its corresponding emotion: hate or resentment. Always honour and respect this event of love, its place of occurrence, and its associated people. And never expect any one person to carry all this for you – don't let your love become a burden for another. This experience is an important test.

Of course there are other types of love, which grow slowly in the heart, or come upon us in ways totally unfamiliar, without the activation of desire. These are more profound, and it is they that we all have to reach. This type of love lasts beyond the grave and flows to us from before birth, but that is another subject for another time, and anyway, is better discovered for oneself.

Chapter 12

Influences

Influences I

We exist in a world of influences. Do not subscribe to the hubris that you are the master of your fate. You are not the master of anything. So it is, that those who call themselves master, are fools. The world in which we live is filled with unseen forces. These forces are for the most part, autonomous beings with their own awareness.

A landscape of history is associated with these beings. Multiple struggles exist between these forces of which human kind is completely ignorant. I am no expert on this landscape, but I have seen enough to sketch some important features.

There are some beings who do not want the proper evolution of humanity's consciousness. There are others who strive for their own vision of humanity's method and end – possibly often a beneficial vision, though not necessarily the 'official' version. There are also certain forces intimately involved with the direction of human evolution, who belong of our own kind, and of our predecessors, whose methods would surprise you. A lot of what happens to the world of human kind can be seen from a very different viewpoint: what may appear evil from a limited perspective, will be seen to be good from a meta-perspective.

One of the first points to realise about influence is the concept of *trajectory*. Think of the trajectory of an arrow shot into the air: first it shoots up, curves off, then descends. This is how the impulses, from the guiding forces of humanity, take shape in the world. Everything falls at the end, reverting to its opposite tendency. So do not judge the heavy material finale as the only evidence.

Take Communism, for example. I'd start with Jesus Christ, later I'd identify the writings of Charles Dickens and the work of Robert Owen, then Karl Marx, who in my opinion added in the major corruptions. But in essence, there was a recognition of the lives and rights of the vast mass of ordinary people. Compassion on a material plane. This impulse led to Democracy and the Socialist world, which all those in the developed nations now live in – it is the basis of our lives and perspective, no matter which politics you follow, or which party governs.

Communism is one trajectory-falling tentacle of this original impulse. In many ways it reverted to causing the opposite effect of its intention – instead of lifting up the common strata of society, it in some obvious ways retarded them. But that is not a criticism of the original impulse. It is a criticism of the means, and an example of how all impulses circle back upon themselves. This is a law of manifestation, and should always be remembered when attempting our own influence.

We accept that every person's life, no matter their social position, is of intrinsic value, but this has not always been the case. An impulse: to pull the focus of value down from the privileged few to the many, bringing with it a new attitude of dignity. Beginning with Christ's 'love one another' and the promise that each little person could become God; then embroiling itself in gross materialism and descending into brutality and greed, which persists un-deflated even today. Nonetheless, this impulse has transformed the individual's view-point of humanity from *outside*.

Children are born into this 'mind' through *no inner struggle of their own*. They are the recipients of an attitude of shared self-worth. It has taken thousands of years and the sufferings of millions of people and animals, to evolve to the currently accepted view of the world and our place in it – a transformation from the *inside* for society as a whole.

I mention animals because, at the time of writing, the continued extension of this impulse is now beginning to encompass birds and animals. It is only incipient, yet across the world, changes in laws are including animals in their protection from unnecessary suffering. Although this has been done in past civilisations, it is now coming from the common-mind up, instead of from enlightened lawmakers down. We are yet to see this further extended to plants, but who knows…

A blatant example of the pervasiveness of this impulse is the spontaneous common anguish at the death of single solders. Gone are the days of hundreds of thousands of solders dying daily, with hardly an eyebrow raised. This is why it is essential today for politicians to label an enemy as an amorphous blob – undistinguished and inhuman. A vast change has come about in humanity, which has elevated the value of each individual.

But we need to see into the spirit of an influence to assess its value. Don't be distracted by the inevitable ugly manifestations. One current example of this original impulse is the 'cult of the individual'. With its venality and self-satisfaction it is an ugly posture of greed, and denial of the inter-relational influence upon us of all living beings. Yet its original intent was quite the opposite.

The same could be said of the 1960s and 70s, of the drugs and sexual revolution. Despite the prodigious efforts of conservatives across the globe, our world has changed forever.

Let's observe the difference between the contraception pill, and the basic acceptance of a child and mother – no matter what social status, how often is the word 'illegitimate' used today? The contraception pill came to humanity without effort, whereas the stigma of unmarried mothers and their children has been a tortuous path, and is still a struggle in the mind of society. One was without effort, the other with.

Let me ask you to ponder: from which forces came the contraception pill, or the atom bomb? Both examples of technological change having dramatic consequences upon our perceptions, expectations and behaviour which came from *outside*, not from the slow evolution of internal shifts in human consciousness. Think about this carefully. A powerful change inserted into our species' consciousness with no effort on our behalf. What forces brought this, and for what purpose?

This distinction between *outside* and *inside* is critical to understanding influence. Transformations from *inside*, through long struggle, suffering and realisation, have tremendous potency and sustain. Those which arrive from *outside* are brittle and unreliable.

It is so easy to become discouraged at the path of humanity, when only the outer manifestation is considered. The outer is always degrading – that is the rule. The seed, the sprout, the tree, the fruit, the decay … the seed. To see the true movement of humanity you must look deep: see the seed.

Some people have, from ancient times, been releasing from the school of our species – they have graduated. They move on to the next school. Let's call it the advanced school. Some of these, as post-graduate study, choose the Arc of Humanity. Even now you may perceive their influence; it's not that difficult to observe.

Influences II

This brings us to the Short and the Long Paths. Let's get one thing clear, the strategy of this book is committed to the Short Path – graduation within *this* life. Thus it is most important to eschew the path of the Hero. We need life, not nobility or grand gesture, to complete our task. In a 'real' world, this task of the Short Path is understood, recognised and allowed for. Alas, our current world is unreal, so we must dissemble.

But the Long Path is valid, and much effort is spent to guide its course – which is not guaranteed by any means. The fate of humanity is currently very brittle.

The Buddha's leading disciple said to him one day "Half of the road to enlightenment is in the companions we choose." "Wrong!" said the Buddha, "it is all of the road".

We are unavoidably influenced by the social world we inhabit. The Long Path utilizes this truth. It is a question of magnetism – people are attracted to changes in social attitudes. Those on the Short Path also use this, but they are not swept by the group mind. They consciously and carefully choose the influences they require, and always retain their core centre, their purpose.

A point has been made here previously about the benefits of groups in the development process. (I really should call this the un-development process, but that's another story.) This is important. We must utilise the powerful effects of group energy. But always remember, the achievements attained through group processes are never as strong as those attained alone.

The problem is of course, that alone we go in circles. It takes others to pin us against the wall. If you feel that because you are on the Short Path you can avoid the group, you are a fool. As with teachers, those on the Short Path seek every beneficial influence – the difference is they retain within themselves the function of Influence Broker. They choose, and not one influence, but many.

Now we come to ideals. I have seen many comments on the ideals of our times. To give a few: the ideals of motherhood, the ideals of relationships, of telling the truth, honesty, love, compassion, dignity, wealth, world sanity, peace and war.

Notice one thing: these all have to do with other people. Our relationship with society. This is all connected with the Long Path. It has nothing whatsoever to do with the Short Path.

The Long Path is designed purely to prepare individual people to jump to the Short Path. At some point, everyone who wishes to graduate must take the small lonely path. Truth is always you, alone, in that awesome vastness. There is no escape. Aloneness is the most treasured joy of those who finally awaken to the seriousness of their path.

But there is also profound value in the Long Path. Minds far greater than ours are feeding seeds into the common mind. Don't forget there is still a post-graduate course, and best absorb the knowledge being cultivated in the world, prior to your ejection.

Before I discuss the Long Path's role for those on the Short Path, let's first cover an important point. Everyone on the Short Path cultivates the rules and guidelines of this Path. But a serious problem arises when, in the kitchen, with a glass of wine in hand, someone asks you for advice, and you realise that your concepts have no foundation in the other person's life. Your Short Path arguments and methods are useless to someone who is just wanting to know how to handle their relationship with their new partner's children.

Alas, I must inform you, that you need to learn and understand at least the basic concepts of the Long Path. Your advice to a mother of four with parent problems to go into the desert alone with a can of sardines, is not going to get any applause, or even a polite ear.

We must study the Long Path, at least to be of some usefulness to the world in which we ply our trade.

The Long Path becomes relevant to us when we take up the lessons of the *task*. Where we manifest the efforts of our inner life in the outer world. We so easily fool ourselves, that it becomes essential to act in the world. Not just for the purpose of actualising and revising the inner strategy. It is also for knowing who we really are – not just who we believe ourselves to be. 'It is by their acts you shall know them'; it is by observing the effect of your influence upon the world around you that you discover who you really are, who you are 'becoming'.

We on the Short Path, lend our energy to those who are seeding and guiding the Long Path, as our offering, and as our required tasks. But, always, this is only the second stage of our *task* exercises. The first stage must always be utterly meaningless activities – such is our self-importance, acting for the sake of acting is the primary lesson. Only once this has been sealed into our being, do we risk helping our advanced brothers and sisters. Else we would be a nuisance and a burden to them.

The critical difference between the Long and the Short Paths, is that the Short Path requires *self-generation*. The Long Path creates an influential environment which lifts the person due to exposure and absorption. This has been the role of organised religions. Whether they were useful in achieving this goal is another question.

There is also a serious question as to whether you, as a unique human being, can really benefit from the Long Path – after all, its goal is to lift the human species to a higher plane, long after you are dead and gone! In my opinion, we only have the Short Path – anything else is the domain of beings far beyond our comprehension.

Self-generated means that we must generate from within ourselves, the moods, knowledge and freedom. We do not rely on others, or other things – like alcohol or power plants – to shift our assemblage point. We must shift it by our own intention. Of course we utilise every available influence, but only as a temporary assistance to break the trance, to cut through the constant inner singing of our personal National Anthem. Eventually this must be achieved through will.

From the viewpoint of the Short Path, the human world is almost completely bullshit. Humanity is self-absorbed in its own reflection – its prospects do not look good. From the viewpoint of the Long Path there is an enormous amount of richness and value in our social world. Such is the dilemma of our position. You must distinguish who you are dealing with, but also see for yourself, as the I Ching says: what food you need to fill your own mouth.

Unfortunately the influences of the Long Path are not useful for the Short Path, because the Long Path utilises identification to achieve its goal. Identification is death on the Short Path. We belong to no nation, no religion, no profession, no family, no gender. These are influences we partake of, like chocolate and ice-cream. Enjoy the offerings that come our way, but really, these are alien people we move amongst, be it your fellow countrymen, your parents, your religious friends, your children, your partner. All those who are not committed to the single task of life are ghosts, and they shall blow away sooner or later. We must be able to love and let go ... like the mushroom that lives but for a day.

Some people will find this offensive. It is. But I didn't make it that way. It is the rule of the bird. And it applies to every living creature, on or off the Path.

Chapter 13

The Parallel Lines

The image of the Parallel Lines is an excellent trope to assist understanding the journey of the spirit. There are two facets of this trope. I don't intend to address the primary facet, except to draw attention to it: primarily, it is a direct representation of the Journey of Silence. Make no mistake, the fog is here. It is now. In front of our eyes – in our mind. It is the world we recognise about us at this moment, and as we enter mental silence, we face and enter the fog. Crossing the Parallel Lines is crossing through the fog – from one reality, through a buffer zone, to another reality.

So as I leave aside this facet, know that it is the primary statement. A statement of immediacy. Only personally can we validate this. The real task is not out in front of acclaiming crowds, but quiet and unglamorous. We quietly move away to a solitary small place, and there we concentrate. Freeze the matrix, silence the mind.

The Parallel Lines is also an effective trope of a life journey, and this is the journey that I have directed all my efforts towards since joining this Path. It sums up my actions, as I have personally travelled this journey, and so I have attempted to help others who are struggling along its road. I have not always been successful, I admit, but then that's how it goes.

The journey is from the self we find ourselves to be, when we begin. It is towards the self that we really are, which is far from whom we at first perceive ourselves to be. The self on one side, to that on the other, of the Parallel Lines. What I will outline here is only a general landscape, individual variations are of course the nature of this game. Yet it is surprising how common these stages and their sequence are for travellers who have spoken of their journey, or those that I have observed.

At first, the world is sealed. It is concrete. We may be a nervous or insecure type, but that is just our temperament, and says nothing about the cohesion of the world we live in. Most people live their entire lives without the slightest idea, let alone desire, to know of the existence of our parallel self. The journey to cross is heralded by some event, different for everyone. It is a message sent from our true being. For me it was a book on Siddhartha, given to me by my sister. Something awoke in me at that point, like a soft breeze from a foreign land.

I presume this would happen to many people, but they would lack something inside with which to answer the call – something unconscious. An indefinable force inside us, that pushes us to seek more scents of that peculiar foreignness.

The second major event is the first time that the first line is pierced. A momentous event, for really, after this we are never the same again. How does it happen? Usually a drastic assault. A close encounter with death, a drug experience, a severe sickness. The beam is broken. The world is never solid again. This is also a common experience. But without a conscious intention to pursue the opening, or the tools to make sense of it, most patch themselves back together again as best they can, and attempt to rejoin the common madness.

This second event is mostly out of our control, without much conscious grasp. It is a physical crack in the energetic shell.

The third major event is quite different. This one is also another crack in the wall, but this time something astounding happens for the first time. We experience a 'gathering together' of hitherto disparate and fragmented aspects of our being. I call this our first *enlightenment*. We understand! We recognise our path. Not only is this another piercing of the wall, but our consciousness grasps the significance of it for our situation as a living being. Our life's purpose. We are still novices on the journey, but a true shift has happened. It needs so much more to fill out the possibility, but I see this as a recognition of something deep inside, stirring for the first time.

From here on dreams become important, and no longer to be taken as the conditioning of world-bound struggles. This also marks the beginning of the conscious employment of all the techniques and associations that become the tool box of the traveller on this Path. All these ideas, exercises, and their resultant experiences, form the process of bolstering our being for the pressures of the road. Lining the tunnel through the fog. More importantly, preparing us to withstand the severe conditions we will find on the other side of the fog.

We learn to break down our endless self-talk, with its attendant attitudes and prejudices. We enter a relationship with death. We learn to grapple with our egos. We learn to handle the first strings of power.

All the things that are the basic substance of almost every school of learning in this game. Little do we realise that as time goes by, the consequences of all this attention and rearranging of our life situations, has gradually led us through the fog. One day we awaken to the horror that this was not a game. We look back and see that the people and the world left behind are gone forever. We are alone in a phantom world. This is so strange and hard to describe. It is the same world as everyone about us shares, with a few extra bits, but for them it is real, and for us it is phantom. It is as if we have slipped behind some membrane and observe what others observe, but in a dreamlike way.

Then comes the fourth major event. A shattering breakdown. Could be accompanied by serious illness, and usually takes many years to overcome. It is the final consequence of our dabbling with death. At this point we lose the desire to live. If we do not actually die, we are rent apart from the desires and ambitions of not just our fellow humans, but of even our old self. We no longer care what we do – everything is equal. We should be dead, but we are alive, and frankly nothing matters anymore.

At this point, many travellers have trouble even getting out of bed. And then they take up any job – it no longer matters what. Something meaningless is fine. This is where the efforts made earlier on the Path come to our aid. Going forth through momentum alone, desire now being absent. We continue many of our previous practices simply out of habit, and a recognition that they are the best way to live – no other reason.

Thus we have fully broken through the first parallel line. We wander about on the other side in a kind of exposed dream. After a little time we realise that we have to do something to fill in time until our 'second death' – the death of the body. That might be years, decades off. Most travellers, here, take up a completely new career. But the feeling of detachment never again leaves them – it is no longer a groovy idea, it is a *fact of bone*. So the next part of the journey begins – the path between the parallel lines.

The road through no-man's-land

From here on it becomes increasingly difficult to describe in words the twists and turns of the road. In fact little is generally said of what to expect. So I would like to touch on a few things that I believe could have been better covered in the literature surrounding this part of the journey.

The picture is one of a slow fading out of the old self, and the gradual dawning of the new. This takes many years. Don't think because of the dramatic events of the first barrier's destruction, that all becomes immediately revealed. The old identity is dead, despite its lingering influence, but unfortunately the new does not rush to the rescue. We have during this period a delicate balance. The burden of difference from our fellow humans can become unbearable.

Often do we long to return to being normal. Loneliness and sadness have sources deep within the universe. The winds hereabouts carry us to unbelievable heights and comparable lows. Don't shield yourself from the life of feeling, but know how to protect yourself from dangerous extremes. How to find and sustain equilibrium.

Severance from spontaneous companionship with the populace of our old world is without respite. Two things prevents us from this respite. Firstly, when we attempt to identify again with our old world, it becomes obvious that we can't stand it. All the colour and excitement of that posture, its activities and attitudes, on closer inspection are revealed in their true hollowness and meaninglessness.

Secondly, even when we push back our disgust and muck in with the crowd, we discover it doesn't work. We just can't pull it off. And what's worse, others notice this. An uncomfortable anxiety arises in people around us, due to something that has shifted in our core. Progressing further, it becomes possible to mask this effect for extended periods, but this trick is not usually available to the novice. Disassociation stamps all our interactions.

The other side of this is a sudden increase in sensitivity and seriousness of living. A two edged sword. Capable of extending our senses into everything around us, feeling intimately into people, animals, plants, objects, clouds, creeks, hills, winds and nonmaterial entities – spirits at large, and dead people. Intense experiences of both joy, but also pain. We see potential and damage. A far larger world opens and when we *see* our fellow humans, they appear cramped into their own self-limited containers of mind.

But we are human, and we must live and participate in the common struggle. Time goes on, and our journey takes us into the world of humanity, with strange consequences.

Relationships

Those relationships which existed prior to penetration of the first identity barrier are usually over by now. We instinctively realise that ordinary relationships no longer work. We may experiment with some, but our seeing quickly reveals the hidden agendas that people bring with them: to draw us down into their unresolvable, emotional landscape. Unresolvable, because they don't want to resolve them, they want our support *in* them. They want our energy. No, the only relationships that will now work are with others who are on the same road. These also have the emotional games, but there is always a more powerful thread that comes to our assistance again and again.

Friends

If for some reason, a few old friends are retained, a struggle usually ensues where they strive to pull us back to the old self they knew. This is a curious pantomime, not without its humour. It never works, and they either accept the new situation or drop away. But new friends can be found, who are sympathetic to our Path. They help somewhat to alleviate that longing for human companionship temporarily, but really they are no substitute for finding our own spirit family.

Family.

Our biological family can't be jettisoned so easily, especially if you are female. And as we grow older, there are responsibilities to ageing parents, children, brothers or sisters. Unfortunately, they have our number, and exert immense pressure to adopt their world view. This becomes more a mere nuisance than the previous emotional battleground. Still, never underestimate their subversive influence through persistent pressure.

Our spirit family, however, I hold to be very important to seek out. It is not that, in theory, the journey can't be done alone, but in practice the energetic support and experiences from linking up are so advantageous, that to ignore this is pure folly. Also, there is a mysterious connection here, between our spirit family and our true self. We have been conditioned to believe in the absoluteness of our individuality – there are some drastic rearrangements in the fundamental concept of self coming our way.

Work.

This has not properly been discussed anywhere, as far as I know. Once we have dabbled in the 'do anything' phase of no-man's-land, we recognise that there is a natural shift toward activities that speak more of our true self. This is the development of what I call the spirit-vehicle. It can be confused with our true self. Part of the journey through the second barrier is the experience of the *expression* of what I'll call our 'second self'. Our second self is closer to our true self, but the path to our true self is never so easily satisfied.

I said the *expression*. Our second self seeks *expression*, and we cast about for an appropriate form to give it a compatible vehicle. It will choose its own vehicle, don't you worry about that, but still we must do what we can. We never know what specific preparation will prove to be the critical one, so we follow both the path of heart and the path of intelligence, in constant preparation for the 'second coming'.

We may come up with a number of possible vehicles. These are skills we hone, and can become extremely proficient in, to the point of calling them acts of power. But we also need to make a living, and thus learn skills that we can trade in the market place. Our deeper self has still not arrived so we don't have the luxury of its vast connections.

There is the danger here that we identify with our career to such an extent, that we lose the way again, and fall into a new version of our original world. It is imperative that we sustain the practices that helped us through the first wall. Most important is the group of practices which mitigate against the draining of power. Impeccability, non-resentment and recapitulation. Thus we continue to quietly store more power through all our tasks.

The task.

Quite often, as we draw closer to the second wall, we are set a special task. We are lucky if this becomes obvious. I call this the *edifice test*. My own experience with, I speak of later.

We walk along a street and choose which *edifices* to enter – mostly on the basis of reason, or other people's influence. But one day we are directed by the voice of our true self to enter a large *edifice*, and we extricate ourselves from its caverns and corridors not just through our own skill. Finally, reaching a point where we are forced to rely on the sole guidance of our true self. A scary but critical test of the reality of our relationship to this mysterious force. This is our task, to carry us through the wall, the second of the Parallel Lines.

It is usually a huge task, which requires the exhaustion of all resources, and may or may not result in success – that doesn't seem to matter. What matters is the ability to gather up our full force, and place it on the altar. What is the altar? By that time, we know what the altar is, and that brings me to a key to the second wall.

The second self is the child of the true self. It is its creation, whereas the first self is the creation of parents, school, culture. It is so hard, at first, to know just what we are looking for when seeking our true self. The second wall is pierced via a validation of the relationship with our true self. It is impossible to fully word this. It is like a vast whale rising up to us. It knows what to do! You can trust it, but first it must come to you – and for that to happen, you must attract it through a lifetime of discipline and heart.

Part III

Personal

*Far off
in a lonely land
he danced his dance
    no one ever saw it
    no one ever knew
    the unbelievable glory
    the laughter and the pain
    the fire and the love –
        alone
        and proud
        he danced!
watched only
by his death.*

*When at last he finished
he turned
and went his way.*

Chapter 14

The Journey

This story from my life, I have written for one primary purpose. I want to detail a journey based on a view of the world which is not current in the dominant cultures of the globe. This journey has an intent. That intent is to engage directly with the major mysteries and facts of life, not just in an intellectual way, but as a whole body experience and knowledge. This journey is to be seen as a symbol of life, of an intent which should lie at the base of any intelligent person's path through this world.

The fact is that we die. The mystery is death. Why we are here and why we die. To live life in uncovering the answers to this mystery is the only purpose worthy of our birthright. That current cultures place almost no emphasis on this purpose, or dismiss it with some superficial attitudes with which we are supposed to feel satisfied, is a sign of the degeneration of these cultures. There can only be one stance to this life condition we find ourselves in – full dedication to a complete-being investigation. Any other purpose to life is plain stupidity, or worse – cowardice.

Due to the nature of this journey, there is a lot of symbolic significance associated with certain events. Personal symbolism is a dangerous mind game. It is a form of madness, but also gives meaning to life. Where the line lies between madness and truth is not easy to discern. I have seen too many people lose their way in the forest of symbolism. Caution with assigning meaning to otherwise arbitrary events is essential. To keep one eye on the *facts* evolving in front of the body, and the *facts* evolving in the inner landscape of meaning, without either disembowelling the other, is a skill and wisdom all too often in scant supply. I do not want to, in any way, encourage this madness in those who cannot control their minds, yet without assigning significance to events as signposts and soul-mirrors, we are left with a barren spirit and pointless life. I can only warn. Do not allow the mind to spin out of control with gratuitous ghosts feeding off self-obsession, and destroying the inner refuge.

Introduction.

I was introduced to the primary material about the age of twenty-three, and worked hard on every possible aspect available for the next four years. It is interesting how dedicated I was during that time. I was able to substantiate the validity of the work; passed through the initial enlightenments, which put me squarely on the Path for the rest of my life. I still had not established a connection with Death, nor with the spirit of the universe (that was to come only after many years). But the connection with Death, my own death, I knew was the next task to complete.

I saw the appointment up ahead, and knew I had to work my way towards it step by step. I mapped out the course … after all, how does one map out the course to one's own death? I knew it was a case of evoking it. I also knew, without a shadow of doubt, that I could go no further in the pursuit of true knowledge about who I am and why I am here in life, on this earth, until this threshold was passed. I also knew the risk. I may die.

What am I saying? Of course I knew I would have to die. But we always hold to the hope that our death would be of the inner world, not the physical body. And yet, it is the physical body we hold up to death. And Death may very well take it. So be it, there was no choice … only one road, and through the Portal of Death it went. Thus the Journey began.

Before leaving, I had a potent dream. I was outside a building, and from this building came a reeking of horror, as some terrible slaughter had happened there. I made my way in, around the back, and the terrifying fear and horror intensified as I stood at the back door, and looked in at something my mind refused to recall.

The Preparations.

How to find my way to Death? How to evoke my own death?

I reckoned that I had to begin where I was. I lived in a fictional world – I accepted that. I knew that I existed in a composite of elements delivered to me since birth, that compromised my reality. I accepted this was false – I intuitively knew that I could touch nothing. All I could touch was a facsimile of reality. But that was a start! There was no other place to begin. So I worked the facsimile into the fantasy of Death, banking on the possibility that Death would see me, through the fantasy, and deign to allow an audience.

I began by working up an emotional concept of my own death. Reading books and poems of death. Seeking out any death-reference that seemed to touch me. Writing songs and poems of death. Watching films that had a strong reference to death. Everything I could think of, everything I could find that could evoke some feeling of what it meant that my life would end.

Looking back after many years, I came to realise at that stage I was struggling with the *first death*. The death of the persona. The *second death* is the death of the body, which could happen at any time.

After working hard on all practices and on the evocation of death, it was time to set out. I carefully rounded up my affairs. There was no reason to write a will, but did write sufficient to act as a farewell. I sold up all my things, except for those which no buyer wanted – those I kept, and put away. That was only my acoustic and electric guitars. Someone almost bought them, but declined at the last moment. My silver flute, I took with me – seemed appropriate somehow.

I resigned from my job. On the last day of my job we went to the bar at the university I was working at as an auditor, and got a bit drunk with the boss – why not? I've never been a purist. I never told a living soul what my purpose was at this time – this was a journey for me, my life and my death. There was no other person who needed to know. This was my journey. But it was also the journey of those whom I would never see again, and I wanted to respect that relationship, in their terms (my boss liked drinking beer).

While looking out the window on that last day at work, a little tipsy, who should I see on the grass outside the building? My previous yoga teacher, with his pupils. What a wonderful coincidence – the man who in some way also represented the life I was bidding for, represented in his own aspiration and in his yoga path. I took off down the steps and out onto the grass where they sat, in full view of the people who knew me as their auditor, from out their windows (who knows, maybe no one was looking). Alas, my yoga teacher was not the man I wished he would be. That was to be a recurring experience for the remainder of my life. At a crucial moment, those who should see, see not.

He had his head in some scheme of his own; that was fine. Sitting with them, paid my respects to their symbology. After all, it was my life I was paying respect to.

I also paid respect to my parents. They would never understand what I was doing. I had realised that long ago, and unlike many others, I had no desire to drag them into my world. So without direct words, I said my goodbyes – even if I should return, there was no guarantee they would be alive to see me again. Said goodbye to special friends – the house, the trees, the suburb I had known so thoroughly as a child, and any people with whom I had had a connection.

Packed my bags and dad drove me to the airport. He didn't know the purpose of my trip this time, but unbeknownst to me, he was also facing his own death. We were very similar in this matter – both saw death as a personal, private business. We didn't say much on the way to the airport. I mentioned again the time I let him down, the time I changed, though I don't think he really cared. We both knew something was different about this trip.

Said goodbye to dad, boarded the plane, and I was on my last journey. First stop Kuala Lumpa in Malaysia.

Malaysia.

Arriving in the early morning, there was no need to stay in Kuala Lumpa. It was some years since I had been here, and it was a fast changing city, but I still had a rough idea of where the road north entered the centre of the city. Catching the bus into the city I walked to the start of the road north. It was quite weird to be standing there in the centre of a strange city, on a large busy road, hitchhiking. Having hitchhiked a lot in Malaysia, I found the wealthy Chinese in their Mercedes to be good company, so I hoped for some success again. I was not to be disappointed.

With luck on my side I arrived in Ipoh before night fall, and made my way to the Youth Hostel. Ipoh has one of the best night food markets in Asia, so I was well fed that night. There is a special technique for deciding what stall to eat from: pay less attention to the food, and more to the cook. A cook who is alive, friendly and on the ball – trust his food. Works most of the time.

Next day I travelled all the way to George Town, Penang. Things had changed here also. The centre of traveller activity in the old days was on the west coast of the island. That had almost disappeared by now, so I stayed in George Town itself, in those wonderful Chinese hotels just down the road from the opium den, with the men playing Mahjong in the hall outside my room. I had a small room downstairs, which had good acoustics. Here I had some vivid astral travelling dreams – returned to my home city and friends.

That wonderful sound of the muezzin's call to prayer wafted into my small cave of a room. Sitting quietly alone I would practise this singing style along with that haunting sound.

Not wishing to stay long in Penang this time, I flew to Medan in Sumatra. This was a pattern of mine. Get out of Australia and rest up in Lake Toba before heading north to Thailand, and then the big leap – into India, the real stuff. South East Asia is a holiday camp – a great place to begin *the process*. *The process* is a name I give to how in Australia I acquire a layer of false identity. A facade, created by the Australia culture, which in this respect is the same for all western cultures. It causes people to become lost in self-perception games and an infinite number of petty attitudes. These attitudes seep deeper into us the longer we stay in the culture, until we become clones, out of touch with our real self.

This is a hard concept or perception to explain to anyone who hasn't had their facade removed. I have always found travelling in Asia caused this layer to eventually fall off like cakes of plaster-of-Paris. But, ultimately, it is India that strips me back to the bone, so I can live.

Lake Toba, Sumatra.

Staying in Medan a few days I had some very strong experiences, which I had best not speak of here. *The process* was beginning. Then the bone-jarring, tortuous trip by mini-bus to Lake Toba. Lake Toba is one of the natural beauties of the world: an island, in a lake, on a mountain. I have stayed here a few times over the years. The first was in the early days, when there was only one house where travellers stayed. That place has been bypassed and the man and his family have also been bypassed, impoverished – it is sad to see places where so much once happened, become sidelined. No one knows about it anymore.

On another trip here about three years earlier I had stayed at a great place on the water's edge, where Julie, a gorgeous and sparky local girl who spoke good English, had caught my eye. She was young as was I, and I was very attracted to her. We liked each other but she was a 'good' girl, and as I later realised, quite intelligent. Nothing happened between us except a 'connection'. These connections often happen while travelling.

I enquired if she was still around. Yes they said, she now owned a tourist lodge around the island, not far away, and she was soon to get married. One day I walked around with little on my mind except my walking exercise. This was a practice of concentration I had been building where I walk barefoot.

There is a special skill to walking barefoot. The danger of injuring your feet is acute, so the only remedy is to watch every place each foot will be put down. This requires looking ahead with one part of the mind, scanning the 'path of footing' – about four steps at a glance – while also looking specifically at the precise next foot placing. One can get very good at this, to the extent that one gains a relaxed attention, and yet still be able to enjoy the surroundings. This is the way humanity walked for thousands of years. With the advent of strong shoes, we now hardly ever look where our feet fall, and instead we spend our time in internal dialogue.

The peak of this exercise here at Toba, was one day while returning from a long walk, moving steadily on the path around the lake, an old local man came to the path, turning onto it exactly at my point. He also was shoeless, but of course he was an old master at barefoot walking. Still, I am proud to say, I held my own – it's all about the attentive casualness, the vibe one can sustain. No problem for him, but I was a newbie. We walked side by side for some time, and eventually he turned off – he gave me a quiet smile. I took it as an honour.

I walked into Julie's lodge kitchen, and inquired of her whereabouts, fully expecting she would never have remembered me, one among thousands of tourists that came through. I sat with a tea, and waited, aimlessly taking in the environmental feelings of the room. This is my main pastime when travelling – absorption of life's landscape.

Then she walked in. My body went into a convulsion I have never experienced before. She was not a pretty woman, never really had been, but she had a quality about her. Totally unexpectedly, my entire nervous system was in chaos and agitation, though I held it together from the outside.

I was in complete confusion – not a familiar mood, I can assure you. There was a line of etheric fire that went between us. I recall a greeting – she said she remembered me. My confusion was due to this: this woman was three years older now, and mature. Maturity has always been a fiercely attractive feature for me, but there was more. We had a connection way beyond the normal-unusual. I knew in an instant we were 'old companions'. I couldn't handle it. Here I was on the final pathway to my death, and she was about to get married. I also saw in an instant she was going to marry a good man – she wasn't stupid enough to make a mistake there – but not one she loved. It was part of her culture, which she had partially escaped from due to her association with tourists, but not to the extent she wanted to live outside of it. I saw all this in her face and felt it in my bones.

I sat there looking at my cup. What could I do? I was still too inexperienced in the Path to be able to stand above this. I saw what my life would become if I were to close the gap, even if that would be possible. It wasn't a path I could switch to. I had to leave her behind. I stood up and left, in a state of utter nervous agitation that I could barely hold together. Now I could well have been making all this up in my own mind – she could have been thinking of the tomatoes she was going to put in the evening's dinner. But I don't think so, and all my knowledge gained since tells me that was not the case.

Was I a coward? Yes, I think I was. But what choice did I have? I had set my intent to walk to the door of life, and that could not be changed. But what about her? I let her down, I have no doubt, and one day we will meet again. I hope then I will be able to repair the damage.

I borrowed a guitar from the owners of the lodge I was staying at and played some great music, sitting watching the lake. One night, a strange experience happened. There was one of those boorish Australian tourists staying with us. This is a special type of person – an 'ocker', a real Australian dag. They come to Indonesia to drink and get cheap sex. Mostly they go to Bali, but occasionally are found further afield. They often have a coarse semi-violent air about them, that is reminiscent of Australian pub front-bars.

This man was raving on about all the hippy fools who come to Bali and get stoned, deriding them on and on, and boring everyone. Then a strange thing happened. As the daylight went, the air became colder and colder – an unnatural coldness. I saw this man was possessed by a malicious spirit; not one of your really evil types, just a typical, gross bad spirit. At a high point, I had a blinding insight. Everything this man was saying was about himself. Sure, he used alcohol not marijuana, but nonetheless it was a perfect self-description (I have since come to realise this is a very common thing). So I told him. I lifted my head from the guitar, and said my first words all night. "You're talking about yourself."

Boy! Did that shatter the air! Well I thought, I had to do something, as the situation was growing unbearable. He hit the roof, and denied it profusely, but the tide turned then, and his influence over the situation died away. It was a lesson on people and spirits I have never forgotten.

I came upon a sorcerer in the market place. Indonesia, especially Sumatra, is full of sorcerers. Walking along a back path I came across him selling items laid out before him, to a small crowd. One look at him and I realised this was no novice! He emanated power, and it was not a power that I felt friendly or even wise – just he knew his business, and I had no intention of getting caught in it. I turned and walked off as quickly and as casually as possible. This has always been an overriding principle for me on the Path. Never get involved with any practitioners who are in any way dodgy. Magic is a land full of nefarious beings that are to be bypassed without a backward glance, or any indication that one has seen them. It is simply too dangerous, and there are always those who are more powerful than oneself. More than that, as one builds power oneself, one becomes identified on the magician's radar. Power feeds off power – never forget it!

While at Lake Toba I had a forceful vision in the middle of a dream. It was just of a man's face, but it left me with a pressing question. I felt, incorrectly as it turned out, that this was the dream double of a man I had met along the way, and had been too self-absorbed not to notice that he was 'special'. This bothered me considerably, and I admit the possibility still bothers me today, that I could encounter a person whom I mistook for an ordinary being, but who was, in fact, a significant person, either in their own right or in relation to me.

This is always an issue when meeting people, visiting places or looking at things. Everything carries a *load*. On the surface it may look just another object, like all the other objects that surround us. But it is not: it carries a power. That power may be in itself, and of itself, or it may be because it has a special significance to us personally and for our journey. This is also the case with omens and signs. It is imperative that anyone on the Path learn to *see* this type of *load* – it is an astral *load*.

I was deeply troubled that I had missed something. Someone I had been acquainted with was, for me especially, a personage of power, and I had not seen it. I resolved to always look two, three or four times at every person that I meet, to ascertain if behind their casual façade they were indeed a being with power. That I had missed this caused considerable anguish in me – it must never happen again.

As it turned out, this man was still ahead on my road. Had I been more experienced on the Path I would have recognised that was the case.

I spent two or three glorious weeks at Lake Toba (troubled by the Julie thing) and after living on rice, fish, and fruit, I reckoned I was ready for the next phase of the Journey. So with an aching heart, I left this paradise and made my way back to George Town. Where I met a young German man.

George Town, Penang.

Back in George Town, I acquired a beautiful room high in another Chinese hotel. This was an old style room, with wooden windows that opened out across the town. Friends met there in the evening, drinking Chinese tea while watching the evening come on, and heard the clatter and boom of city life, a constant accompaniment in all Asian cities. But, for the discerning ear, there was an extra set of sounds that occasionally became identified out of the chaos.

At any time of day, I could distinguish a set of sounds that seemed vaguely musical. I was left with this conundrum: was it a case of the cacophony spontaneously manifesting as music? Or was it indeed music? But if it was music, why did it happen in short bursts at any possible time of day or night? This became the mystery of the room, and I would draw attention to it when we were meeting and talking prior to the night's excursions.

One night, we set off in a new direction (which I love to do – just off down a different lane, who knows what one will find?) and while walking through the maze of people, vehicles, and alleyways, we came across the music. It was indeed musicians, and it was a Chinese funeral. We were later told that these Taoist funerals would go for days, and the musicians or priests would spontaneously start up some of that weird music at any time of day or night. The mystery solved, somehow I was a little disappointed.

Here in George Town I met Hans, a big young affable German hippy. He gravitated to me, so I began to introduce him to the world, and some of the mysteries and complexities that underlie our superficial skimming of that world. We developed a fond friendship, until he met up with his tempter – a young New Zealand man. He was one of those stupid gung-ho types who thought the world was their playground, including heroin. I have never touched heroin, and I have consistently warned people away from it. Opium users I can tolerate, as it somehow does not rot the soul, though it is still powerfully addictive. Anything that is physically addictive has always held an abhorrence for me all my life. Perhaps because I know I am an addictive personality in some ways, so I instinctively reject the slightest chance of getting caught in that trap. But heroin carries another more sinister vibe. Suffice to say, it is bad news, and I told Hans, no! He didn't listen.

They were only experimenting with smoking heroin. Don't know the difference and don't want to know. Anyway this did not surface to my awareness until Bangkok, so I had plenty of time to establish a good connection with Hans. When we left George Town, we all travelled together in a taxi across the border into Thailand, and then to Ko Samui – a paradise island on the east coast of Thailand.

Ko Samui, Thailand.

These islands have been serially discovered and ruined by the flood of tourists to Thailand. At the time I arrived at Ko Samui it was still fairly pristine, though not for the purists, who had already moved on to the next undiscovered island. But I liked a little bit of westerner-friendly facilities. I was still in enjoyment mode – India was up ahead. I had every justification in relaxing and pleasuring myself, and events subsequently proved that only too true.

I set up in a grass hut right on the beach. In George Town I had bought a bamboo flute. One of those with a hole at the top over which a small piece of rice paper was licked and stuck on, in a special way to produce a vibration that enhanced the flute's sound. It was a skill to get this just right, and it added a touch of something like a 'reed' sound. I had also acquired a set of fine sand papers, and was able to polish the flute to a beautiful finish. I continued to rub it with my hands and oil to get the final finish. This took a long time, and I worked at it with the diligence and attitude of a spiritual practice, until the flute acquired a power of its own. It looked like it was made of ivory.

I almost never played it until the end of my stay at Ko Samui – I had a great love of playing small bamboo flutes. One night near the end of my time there I sat on the beach in the moonlight and played for a long time – a memorable evening.

Heaven on earth. Sleeping in the hut, lying on the beach and swimming in the crystal clear sea water. Separated from Hans for the most part during this period, as my personal preparations had begun. I initiated an intensive series of 'not-doing' exercises. Every not-doing I could think of – there was little here to stop me. Of course I never disclosed the reasons for my odd behaviour as I was also trying to encounter the not-doing of being thought of as crazy. This I believe was very difficult for Hans, as he had known me as an intelligent and sane person, even a teacher. So to see me doing crazy things, and to hear other people's disdain, caused him some anguish and confusion. I couldn't help this, for I was on an unchangeable track, and all I could do was follow and intensify that journey to its utmost. This was in the end, a journey I walked alone.

One particular not-doing I utilised was to answer a question with a completely irrelevant set of words. I recall even resorting to the word 'bananas' to one serious question, and I'm sure everyone thought I was. A few special events occurred here which I should relate.

There was a dog on the water line, with a bad wound on the side of its head. One of those dingo-ancestor dog breeds, very common on the Malaysia peninsular. The wound was out of reach of its tongue, so it became infected and slowly began to eat into the brain. I saw it each day, limply trying for hours and hours to scratch at the wound with one of its paws. I seemed to be one of the few who noticed it. This brought on one of those recurring experiences in Asia, of animals, people or situations which one could do nothing to resolve. Either it was out of the realm of possible help by a passing traveller due one's limited resources, or the situation was beyond one's understanding. There are always conditions surrounding these horrific scenes, and a proper response requires knowledge of those conditions. This is too difficult to detail, as every situation is different.

I have always been impressed with those people who cease their own momentum, and take up the cause of some horrendous situation. I have done this myself where I can see a direct and effective action. But I am only one person travelling through a strange land, and spreading out from my position are thousands of horrific situations in which animals or people are caught with no remedy or escape. In the end, I am the same. Especially this journey of mine – I felt an instinctive rapport with this poor dog.

We cannot save everyone. At some point in life we have to stop and realize that we are caught in the same trap. By whatever means, none of us are going to escape death, and the process is never pleasant. At some point we have to stop and recognise this bond we have with all living-dying beings on this planet, in the universe. We are all on an irreversible slope into the beak of death. The most compassionate thing we can do is to acknowledge our common fate – to extend our heart to every being whose time has come, and say, "Yes, I am you. And it is alright."

A westerner working in one of the food places along the beach procured a rifle from somewhere, and shot the dog – the locals would have done nothing. I am reminded of a comment by T. E. Lawrence, that when a camel or person is dying in the desert, the Bedouin will never kill it to quicken its end, shortening its pain, as the British will do. They claim that every living being deserves all of its allotted time to make its peace with God in its own way, and at its own pace. I don't know the answer to this. I understand and yet I don't. What I do know is that Asia, especially, throws up situations to the sensitive traveller that are inherently unresolvable. The only dignified response is to hold those unresolvables in our hands, and not dismiss the agony with a superficial answer, just to avoid the pain of the realisation that some of the most important things in life have no solution. Don't run from that realisation. Stand there and let it sweep through your being. Bear it as a being that will die, and not as a coward who fears and hides from Death.

I also fell in love here. Not the type of love I could say was involved with Julie in Sumatra; that was something between beings. This was a love within beings. This woman I never spoke to, or even properly met, though I know she was aware of me. She was an almost perfect representation of my anima. This is a phenomena I have become aware of throughout my life. My anima has a physical form, and when I meet anyone who has similar features, I cannot but help be intensely attracted. I know exactly what those physical features are. I first encountered this when I was a young teenager, and it has been repeated numerous times throughout my life. This woman at the beach, not only had these features, but was also a very mature character – that was obvious.

Looking back, I would have to say nothing on this journey occurred by accident. I see my encounter with this woman, in the mature form I perceived, as an omen that my anima was with me on the journey. I have always known that women who bear these features do so as a complete accident of physical birth. They do not necessarily have any inner connection with me, though that has never been an easy realisation to sustain in their presence. Our anima and animus are to be respected in their form, without forgetting there exists within the other person an individual who is not our anima or animus, and who does not want to live their life playing out that fantasy for another.

The last event I want to describe from Ko Samui was a fore-runner of the purpose of this journey. At the end of the beach there was a high rock outcrop, climbable to the top. I occasionally went there to do pujas. One afternoon I had a revelation there, when I first spontaneously and un-selfconsciously began talking to a bush, as *being to being*. This was a very emotional breakthrough – one I had known of, but not until then fully experienced. So this rock had become a special place of power for me.

Another late afternoon, there was a big storm approaching the island. Knowing this was the time I had been waiting for, I packed up all my belongings, to leave everything tidy and complete, and left them in the grass hut. I made my way to the rock, and began my last puja. I suspected this would not be my death, but it was a metonym of that event, and who knows, it very well might be my last – one cannot tell when that moment will come.

I presented myself to the storm, with lightening striking about me, on water and land. Being exposed on a high rock in an electrical storm was extremely dangerous. This was a crucial gesture, to say, "If you want to take me, here I am." Knowing this type of gesture was a necessary part of beckoning my own death, I was ready. If this was to be it, I would go facing forward. This was the moment I laid down the last card, and stated my intention for the whole journey, and if it was to end here, so be it.

It didn't end there, but such elation and freedom flowed from this gesture that I knew I was ready. Still I wanted to delay the final leap into India some time yet. After this event, my time at Ko Samui was over, so I headed north to Bangkok.

Bangkok.

I stayed at the old Malaysian Hotel, a seedy place which was then the centre for tourists in Bangkok, but soon moved around the corner to a nicer, less pretentious hotel. It was in the Malaysian Hotel that I met Hans and his New Zealand friend, smoking heroin. What to do? At this time in my journey I was conscious that one of the primary problems with people in the world, is that they do not know how to actually leave a debilitating situation. I had seen this in many workplaces – people who wanted to get out, but couldn't do the final act of walking out. This was my assessment at the time; not wholly inaccurate, though now I take a broader and more understanding view – that the act of leaving is extremely simple. It just requires precedence and practise. People throw up endless reasons why they can't leave. All bullshit. Once the decision is made, the feet walk. To see another do it, is one of the most powerful impressions for following.

This was in my mind, while sitting in the room with Hans and his friend when they lit up a smoke of heroin. I had done the ground work with Hans. He knew in his soul I did not approve, even if his mind was uncertain. My response was also strongly physical. My body acted: it stood up, and walked out. I have always been uncertain whether my action was self-righteous and arrogant. Was it effective? I expect I'll never know.

It was in Bangkok that I met the man whose face appeared in front of me in the vision I had back at Lake Toba. He was an unusual Malaysian man, one of those charismatic and inherently potent people, who spoke excellent English. He had hitched up with a young German girl I had also met before, and whom I liked very much. This man was one of the children of God, but he didn't know it. I was not at that point in life where I could have assisted him in this aspect of himself, though I could clearly see it. Unfortunately, he was preoccupied with selfish and mundane events. He was using this young girl to get to Europe, and as part of his plan they were carrying a quantity of drugs to help with his finances in Germany. Intuitively, picking up on this without being told, as usual, I put my foot in it, much to his displeasure. Again, as so often on this journey, what could I do?

I'll tell you what I did, and I accept, as with every other similar situation, I may well have been wrong and could very likely behave differently today. Not wanting to burden their minds and fate with my admonitions and concern, I said goodbye to them, wished them well. Closed off that book of my heart's journey, left them behind, turned the corner, and set sail for the next adventure. I took the bus to Chiang Mai.

Chiang Mai.

Chiang Mai was a sleepy town in the 1970s. Haven't been back since, but I'm told that it has changed considerably. Some wonderful experiences there, but to keep on track with my story, all I wish to say is that those experiences only further solidified my purpose and validated my journey.

I stayed in a hotel run by a young homosexual Thai man, who explained the difficulties he had in a society that did not condone his type of sexuality. I borrowed a guitar, and in my room played some of the best music of my life. Some of the locals would gather outside, downstairs, to listen. Around the same time each afternoon I would light incense, watching it drift past me out the window while I played. The languid, sensuous enfolding stream of incense smoke drifting across in front of me and out the window, became the persistent leitmotif of my aesthetic vision.

I relate one interesting small snippet, which for me acted as a remembered omen. It occurred on the way to a music venue to which I had not been before, accompanied by a friend. We had bought some ice-blocks on sticks along the way. Unbeknown to my friend I had been again focused on my underlying purpose, while still participating outwardly in the current situation. This had become a continuous practice, a second sense for me on this journey. I was always engaged in two worlds at the same time. One, the current world of people and places; the other, my deeper driving journey to death. While conscious of these two overlapping worlds, my friend asked if we were going the right way.

"Yes" I said confidently.

"How do you know?" he asked.

"Because I have a used ice-block stick in my hand, and we are just passing a rubbish bin." I replied, and so it was – we soon arrived at the venue.

To appreciate this you need to know that that was perhaps the only rubbish bin I passed or saw in my entire journey through Asia on this trip. They were almost completely unknown in Asia at that time. For reasons described, I was conscious that this was more than a coincidence, and more than an issue of finding the venue.

They were pleasant times in a lazy peaceful town that Chiang Mai was back then. Next, I headed for the Golden Triangle.

Karen tribe

I made my way to a small village of the Karen tribe, at the top end of Thailand, the Golden Triangle. This village had become a travellers lodge. On arrival, there was a little party going on that night at the restaurant, the only one in the village, where a number of travellers had congregated. Not being enough room for us at the restaurant-lodge to sleep, the owner walked me and another man down the road to the chief's hut, where we could stay. Interestingly, he brought his motor bike along, which he walked beside him, engine running and lights on. At the time I found this a bit odd, but later realised this was dangerous bandit country. He was making a show to warn away any lurkers, plus being ready if we had to make a quick getaway. Travellers were terribly naive back then, though if anything that has only increased these days.

The chief's hut was basic and pleasant. I was very attracted to the simplicity of these people's lives, in some respects. One night as dusk fell, we all sat on the veranda with a single oil flame burning. No conversation, either between the other traveller and me, or between the chief and his wife. We just sat and watched the night. I feel a longing for that simplicity in my bones, and would like to return there once my mad dash through the world has exhausted.

With some companions we climbed the mountain and visited a tribal village high in the hills, right on the edge of Burma. There I tasted the best rice I have ever eaten – plain rice, so fluffy and flavoursome in its natural state. In the evening we tried the local opium custom – lying on our sides, someone brought around the pipe. This was the first and only time I smoked opium. A very sensuous and visual experience, drifting on the edge of dream in an ocean of colour. I have never been attracted to smoking opium again, not just because of the addictive dangers which I have always studiously avoided, but because such experiences are common for me as an astral adventurer – there is no need to chemically induce them.

During the night there were whispers and noises, something happening outside, but we slept safely. We returned down the mountain the next day to hear that a group like ours was robbed at gun point only hours before.

I took a boat to Chiang Rai, stayed with a tough looking man with "Face Danger" tattooed on his arm, and his beautiful saucy daughter. Then returned to Bangkok, via Chiang Mai.

On the return bus trip another interesting experience occurred. Out the window I was watching the creek and rocks off to the side of the road. At one point I thought I saw the shadow of a possibility that a man was there on one of the rocks mid-creek. I was sure this was just a play of lights. But it occurred to me right then that we had a power to manifest what we wish to see, at least on the margins of our world. So I said to myself, there *is* a man there – with a strong degree of scepticism that this would not work. Like a switch in the mind, I chose the world that had the man, and there he was! I was left with a distinct sense of the fluidity and self-fulfilling propensity of our existence. I pondered the implication of this upon my own journey, my own intent to manifest my own death. Like a switch: one way – or the other? Was it that simple?

Bangkok again.

Bangkok was different this time. Avoiding the main tourist area I stayed at a lesser known hotel in a different part of the city. This was a sacred time for me. I was about to dive head first into India. I had been there numerous times before, so I knew what I was in for. And I knew why I was going this time. An almost unbearable anguish invaded my being, as I waited for my departure. I had the habit of staying in dormitory rooms, as I had little money, so I became acquainted with other travellers and their own journeys. This led to interesting insights into my fellow humans, and what they see as their purpose or lack thereof, in life.

My booking was a one way flight (all my flights on this trip were one way) on Friday the 13th. At the airport, to my surprise, they told me my flight was cancelled. Possibly due to the superstitious nature of Asians, though no one would tell me exactly why the flight had been cancelled. They had rescheduled me on the next flight a few days later, but alas my visa also expired on the 13th, forcing me to over-stay my visa. This led to a rather curious experience with a Thai immigration official, trying to explain that it was not my fault. After arguing and demanding to scrutinise his regulations, it slowly dawned that this was one of those situations where we from Western countries grow up under the illusion of conditional justice. An inbuilt sense of 'fault' and 'rights'. It was not my 'fault' so I assumed it was within my 'rights' to expect the Thai immigration to waive any penalty for overstaying my visa.

That was not the world I was now living in. This was a salient lesson to me, and has remained with me ever since. Our justice is conditional upon blame and fault. Theirs was not. They had a rule, and if you broke it you had only two options – pay the fine, or pay a slightly lesser amount as a bribe. I railed against this, but eventually I came around to realise that not all cultures cared for the individual's part in anything. There were rules and penalties – concepts of personal fault were not an issue. In many cultures when a rule was broken, a price had to be paid. Who paid was irrelevant. This was not a matter of punishment of the person, but punishment for the breaking of a rule. Traditional Aboriginal culture of Australia is similar to this, where it is all about restoring natural balance, rather than about individual culpability. I have since come to see some intelligence in these differing approaches to justice.

Nonetheless, in my situation it was much more a case of 'couldn't care less', just pay up, one way or another. He was bored, and the rights of some dirty tourist were completely irrelevant to him. I paid the fine – to pay the bribe seemed to be rewarding him for his stubbornness. But I relate this because it stuck in my mind as a last obstacle to surmount before I was allowed to begin the real purpose of my journey. Somehow there was a symbolic gesture in that obstacle, and its timing was crucial on my journey, so I recount it for mythical purposes as it was woven into the karma of my last dance.

The pleasant South-East Asian holiday was over. It was time to step up to the main task. I was ready, I knew where I was going, though not the actual places, and I knew why I was going there. I boarded the plane for India.

India: Delhi

Arrived very late at night, taxied to my favourite hotel in Paharganj, the Vishal. These were the days before this area spawned so many hotels, and only a few were the traveller's favourites. The Vishal was a central meeting place for travellers back then. I took a room on the very top floor, and went to bed exhausted, but excited.

Next morning I looked out the window to the street below, and there sat a man cross-legged, meditating – right on the early morning pavement – India! Oh how it made my body and heart want to shout for joy! I was back. This country for me has always been a deep calling, ever since the day I first crossed into India from Pakistan, after travelling overland from London as a young man. As soon as I crossed the border, I knew I had come home.

On this journey, as on my previous trips to India, I navigated in the mode of *power*. This means never determining beforehand where I would be going. I allowed *power* to tell me where it wanted me to go. Watching for any sign that could be an indication of the direction to take. There is a reason for this. I am not interested in finding palaces, temples or whatever. What I am seeking are experiences that will transform me. Those experiences could happen anywhere, so there is absolutely no point in planning anything. The other advantage of this type of travel is that one can never be disappointed – if some direction is blocked, one simply goes another way. So I can relax and allow the flow of the journey to take over, allow the flow of the Gods to dictate where they shall meet me.

A significant pantomime played out one night. There is a concentration technique I use where a lighted stick of incense is placed flat on a table. The idea is to return to it, moving it out over the edge of the table every few minutes, else it would extinguish when burned to the table's edge. The catch is, how far out do you push the stick over the edge? The tendency is to push the incense stick out a fair way, as then you don't have to keep coming back to it so often. Thus less chance you'll forget. In fact it works the other way, where by pushing it over the edge a small distance you have to return sooner. It is precisely that which enables you to remember – the longer between returning your attention to the incense stick, the more likely you will forget it.

So I was playing this as I read a book and practised my flute. Due to the significance of the situation, having just arrived in India possibly for my last journey, the occasion took on symbolic meaning for me. This transferred to the game. The incense stick became 'my life' – that was always part of the game, in order to instil a bit of emotion into the play. But now I understood this with new meaning, a new seriousness of intent. So for the honour of the event I lit a second stick and placed it alongside the first – the two beings of my life: the physical-bodied me and the dream-bodied me. I think I also was hoping to elongate my existence a bit.

The first stick eventually reached the end of the incense section of the stick, as I sat pouring over the scene – it was too serious now to do anything but sit and watch them burn. But to my utter amazement, the wood-only part at the end kept burning, on the table itself! That had never happened to me before. And then so with the second stick also. To my jaw-dropping disbelief, as I prepared myself for the final extinguishment of the first stick, from below the table on my left, a little beetle crawled onto the table top and walked across the still burning first stick, then across and over the second stick. It did a u-turn and crossed back over both again and off over the edge of the table, back on the left side. Then the sticks burned out.

By this time in my experience with India, I had developed a relationship with the Gods – not the big name deities, but the Beings themselves who roam the land, by whatever name. I knew when they came by, when they pushed me beyond my limits, and when they ushered me into their confidence, which only happened after a lot of painful transformations on my part. This time they said, "Kashmir". So I boarded a bus to Jammu.

A very long journey, but two important things happened. One was the experience of the Indian road; the other was the state I was able to acquire before we arrived in Jammu.

The Indian road trick. I have to describe this – where a person slips like a dream through the chaos of traffic. Relaxed and alive, drifting among the rickshaws, trucks, bull-pulled wagons, snarling buses, bikes and people. I have seen a woman casually cross a busy multi-crossroad. As if sleepwalking, she moved gracefully across the very centre of the chaotic traffic to the other side of the road – a perfectly normal occurrence.

From my front row seat of the bus I watched the road ahead, from early morning till well into the night. I saw the old roads of India, and the new, with the occasional sadhu drifting listlessly and indifferently towards us on the road, like a mirage. The roads then were still casual and narrow, with a comfortable mix of traffic and people.

Ever since I have had a longing for the Indian road, just to walk, relaxed and alert, through the kaleidoscope of road-side life. An important lesson for our walk through life.

But unfortunately, on this journey I was tortured the whole way. A protruding piece of iron sticking into my ribs, that I was unable to avoid. Hour after hour this pain persisted in my side, until my body went numb, my mind went numb, and I sat in complete inner silence as the bus jostled and roared on through the afternoon light and into the night. The whole experience was a blessing. I held to this for the rest of the journey – an omen of the underlying purpose. It was always going to be a task of releasing through inner freedom. I had to turn my inner realm around, to where the physical drama was checked, sublimated.

Jammu was a grubby highway town. I stayed the night in one of those dives you find in such places, then caught the bus in the dawn to Srinagar. These were all local buses – no windows. We climbed up through the passes. On the top of one pass we stopped for lunch at the most delightful food house, overlooking the valleys far below. Finally with the dying light, we entered Srinagar through rows of autumn trees. It was a paradise on earth.

Kashmir: Srinagar

I stayed in an old area of the canals, used by some travellers before Dal Lake swamped everything with its murky-watered glitter. It was a houseboat, beautiful and well-furnished, in a lock close to a road. I would sit and look out the window at the kingfishers on the tie ropes. The calmness, aloneness and quietness had a healing effect, and prepared me again from the inside out. This meditative recluse centred me for the journey through India that lay ahead. After a week of rest, I left for Windrush, Pahalgam.

Pahalgam

Pahalgam is a small mountain town – crisp air, smell of pine wood. Following along a little road beside the brook, you came out at Windrush, a large guest house, where the magical journey really begins. Pahalgam is the place where all the sadhus come for the pilgrimage to the Shiva ice-lingam up in the high valleys. There was a trek on, which happened once each year, when the full moon shone fully on the ice pillar in a cave. Two days, with no warm clothing? I decided to make my base at Windrush – there would be hard adventures enough for me ahead.

In the hills above Windrush there was a small wood on a plateau edge, overlooking the valley and the town. To this day that image has remained deeply and symbolically embedded in my imagination. In the mornings at Windrush I would sit out on the lawn in front of the guest house, alongside the ice-cold, snow-sourced stream. Which was flowing so fast it became a real test of courage and strength for those few who crossed it on foot. I practised yoga on the lawn, and gazed at the stream – it was a sanctuary for holy men and women. I idly wondered how a world would be in which one lived in this state of constant pleasure, like the old rajas and princes. In retrospect, I see this was not an idle wonder.

I had a small room separate from the house, back behind, upstream, with a window that looked directly onto the stream. Studying the I Ching and gazed into the water … timeless caravanserai. I never found a more beautiful place in all of India. One night I heard the most wonderful singing of monks. This was a choir with beautiful high and deep bass voices, like a Russian choir. It went on and on. I knew it was not a physical choir, but it was so wonderful and so strong I really was thrown, and transported. I had thought to ask the locals in the morning if a monastery existed nearby, but inside I knew I was hearing astrally. Possibly sponsored by the rushing stream outside, though this was the only time while there that I heard this singing. I allowed myself to absorb its beauty, knowing I was blessed to hear such beautiful music, from wherever it was coming.

The main house dormitory was a large room, at the front of which was an alcove, and one could lie there and listen to the ever present sound of the stream rush ... I realised why it was called Windrush. Windrush is a magical name in those parts of India, so it had dual citizenship in my mind.

I met here a thoughtful German man, who was studying the story of Christ's journey to Kashmir. He wanted to write a book on it, and had visited some remote monastery where documents on this were recorded. When he got to the monastery, he was told the abbot was not there. In fact he hadn't been there for some time – he was dead actually, and they weren't sure when he would return, but he had the keys to the room where the documents were stored. I spoke with my German friend about death. I think we had a meeting.

There were some interesting characters at Windrush. One day, with intense awareness, I was washing my breakfast bowls in the stream out on the front lawn, where we all placed ourselves for our morning rituals – some doing yoga, some eating or meditating, some smoking hashish. As I stood up and turned around, a group of people faced me and broke into song. I was taken aback! Why were these people singing to me? Like I was some kind of guru? It was quite embarrassing, especially because I knew I was deep in acute awareness and on a definitive journey – how had my cover been blown? It was like a Bollywood movie! But then the world rearranged and I saw it was just a situational coincidence – they only happened to strike up just behind me, with no interest in me whatsoever. But I wondered, was it a coincidence? In India, coincidences don't exist.

Another day, I realised I had been too introverted and unsocial in this amazing place with so many interesting travellers. After finishing my fruit, honey and yoghurt breakfast as usual, and washing up in the ice-water stream in the morning sun on the front lawn, I saw a self-styled young guru sitting close with his admiring woman friend. What the heck! I'll break my pattern and go speak with him, before he might approach me: this is a rule of conduct in the world of these faux-gurus. He who makes the first move is lower, he who responds, higher. What did I care? I already sussed he was an ego strutter, but that did not mean he wasn't an interesting man, so I went up and said hello.

Immediately I knew it was a mistake. A slight, telling, smug smile crossed his lips, with a subtle gesture to his devotee girlfriend, as if to say, "See, another student approaches me." In a flash I said to myself, never again – it just doesn't work. You have to play their game if you want to have a decent exchange with such people. Turned out he was from Australia, and had even graduated from Military Officer school. I didn't reveal that I had also – competition was too far from my agenda. He was now an 'enlightened' man, travelling India and knew all about everything. I thought to myself, I hope India is kind to him, and I left them. But then, I'm sure he is still on the Path, and if so I bet he is far less arrogant these days. The Path sorts out such people in no uncertain terms.

I returned to Srinagar, and who should I meet in the market, in the midst of the rushing, flowing street? Hans. Like a lost child from out of a time warp. He'd had some important experiences on a lake in Nepal. I was pleased for him, though there were still clouds in my joy.

Gulmarg

I found my way to Gulmarg, for reasons I can't recall. The bus full of those Kashmir Jewish types – quite distinctive features, beautiful women. I climbed a high hill to a small guest house on the very edge of a cliff that ran away forever over the Kashmir Valley. Towering snow-capped mountains looked on from afar.

This place had a lawn in front, on which one could sit and quietly drink tea while watching over the cliff, and the dreamscape land beyond. Kashmir was proving to be a world of great beauty. An experience here caught me from the side. I had a mouth organ, which was my main instrument at that time. A small boy who lived at the house was watching me play. He was one of those wide-eyed kids that have an attraction to music. One day he asked me to give him my mouth organ. Well, no, I was enjoying it and had only just mastered it for my purposes. And I would never get another on this journey. So I kindly shook my head. A few weeks later I lost it into the canal waters of Srinagar. I felt a proper arsehole.

I adopted a meditational posture at this lodge. I would sit on the lawn in front, just a few meters from the edge of the cliff, beyond which stretched away the great valley of Kashmir. Sitting there half the day, in silence, watching … watching everything. One day I received a gift. I had been observing the birds. This was a particular pleasure of mine – not just the birds, but every non-human creature I observed closely and absorbed their 'mind'.

I had been watching the small birds, as they flitted and danced close to the bushes at the cliff edge. Then I watched the larger birds, as they had a different dance; they weren't so flighty, and also moved slightly higher. One of these was the crow – I particularly liked the crows. For some time now I had developed a close association with crows. Moving up the size category, the birds became less frequent and also their flight paths changed. They preferred the tops of trees that grew along the cliff edge, especially the pine trees. Then the eagles, which flew higher, dancing with the updrafts, executing beautiful hovering manoeuvres with the wind.

A thought occurred to me – I looked high into the sky with the idea that there could be a bird which flew far above all the others, way up in the clouds. To my utter amazement, a profoundly moving experience occurred. I saw a bird, a tiny speck, way up in the sky. It was moving in a straight flight line from behind and left of me. I watched it with wonder as it flew in a dedicated silent and graceful line straight out over the mountain range we were on, straight out high above and over, across the Kashmir Valley. It was a small insignificant yet stupendous sight. I kept my eyes glued as it glided into that vast panorama, so far above the tussle and squabble of life that fought its daily battle below. This was a magnificent symbol of spiritual beauty, played out in a spectacular landscape – the valley spread out below, the snowy peaks looking on in the distance from all around, and this one tiny speck, with absolute dedicated intent. I watched till it disappeared into the distant skyline. Never deviating from its singular trajectory. I so wanted to be that being!

I stopped that exercise right there. But there were many others. I recall one night watching a peeled area of the wall in my room. This was a rendered wall, which had begun to peel away in layers, creating around its edge a myriad of textures in which I saw an endless sequence of images, especially people's faces. My eyes went around and around in manifestations of images. I can't recall another time in my life where this phenomenon was so powerful. Finally I had to break away, as there was no end to the sequence.

Srinagar again

I left Gulmarg at last – had to tear myself away. Back in Srinagar, I moved to a place outside of town: Nagin Lake. This was a peaceful, clean lake with only one or two houseboats. Here I settled in to enjoy the gifts on offer. Swimming in the middle of the lake, playing my flute out on the lake in the night. Learning to use a shikara – the small wooden canoes they all use in this area, where you squat at the front and paddle on each side. Also playing a guitar they had there, with two strings missing. I became good at this guitar as the missing strings were the two outside ones. I made up songs on the four strings, and sat out front of the houseboat looking across the lake at the mountains, playing music.

A strange occurrence happened here. In this tranquil area there was little to disturb the atmosphere. However, after a few days I noticed that the houseboat owner, who lived on the next houseboat, had a small physical defect – his big toe on one foot was curled under. At first this was a minor observation, but after about a week at the place, it began to become a symbol for a strange disturbance that existed here. This was a subtle underlying feeling that only became apparent after about a week, and by the time I left, I was really glad to be leaving. This man's toe had become a manifestation of some psychological problem that quietly lurked behind the scene. It was never a serious issue, but just kept nagging beneath the surface.

One day another traveller and I paddled our shikara all the way into Srinagar town, via the backwater lanes. On the way, an interesting little cameo event occurred. We were paddling toward a bridge underpass, when we saw one of those congestion situations build quickly: too many boats converging on the narrow underpass. In this situation, it was natural to stall, and wait till the others who were claiming the first right of access, had passed. That is still my preferred approach, but in this instance I got a sudden urge to challenge them, and called to my friend "Let's go for it!". We paddled furiously into the melee, demanding passage by our very energy. We succeeded, much to our mutual surprise, and it stands till now as an example of how one can create a passage in life by sheer energy and audacity.

That all went well, but on the way back we took a wrong turn. We knew the general direction, but our waterway became more and more blocked with hyacinth, until, in the night, we realised we were lost. Not a pleasant feeling. Deciding to stop, we stepped off the boat on to the shore to sit awhile. There was no one around to ask direction, but while we sat there a change came upon us from nowhere, a new sense of confidence. We got back into the boat and paddled on, to discover that the hyacinth slowly grew less and less, till miraculously we found our way out and home.

That experience was another that has remained with me as an example of the principle, that when in a tight spot where all seems lost, stop for a moment, and stand outside the scene. Somehow that allows fresh energy to enter the problem. It is not a fix in every situation, but is a standard tool in our kit. The difficulty is in being able to break from the problem, from its consuming hold on us, to find a solution. The solution often comes precisely by breaking the focus, and looking elsewhere, recalling we are larger than whatever the problem is.

One night, I heard a woman coughing – all night long. The next morning a boat pulled up and someone came, possibly a healer. I did not know if it was a doctor or some other type of healer. Looking out the window, I caught a glimpse of the boat pulling away, and saw the face of an extraordinary woman sitting in the boat. To this day I still don't know if the woman I saw was the patient or the healer, but her face was striking. It was so powerful. A power that can only come through suffering. I was to know this myself, later in my journey.

Another day I took the guitar and paddled my shikara off along the lake, stopping at a pleasant green bank, under a tree. I sat and played, and a few locals stopped and settled beside me to listen. Indians love music. After I had played for awhile, I looked at my companions. Then I noticed something about them with a start of surprise – they were lepers! I had stopped at a leper colony! Without freaking, I calmly packed up and said goodbye, back into my boat and paddled off – I knew you can't so easily catch this disease, but nonetheless, it did unsettle me a little.

I felt refreshed and ready for action, but what to do? I don't know where I got the idea, but it came somehow that I should go across the Himalayas to Ladakh. The season was closing in, but there was still some time, as long as the snows didn't come early and block the passes. If that were to occur while I was half way, then I don't know what would happen as these mountains close down for the entire winter with no way in or out. With carefree abandon and audacity, as in the earlier related bridge underpass event, I decided to risk it. I caught a bus to Sonamarg.

Sonamarg

Sonamarg was a frontier town, a mere strip of buildings along the road to Leh, with the mountains literally running down behind the buildings. The last town before the famous Zoji La pass. Quite a pretty landscape, around a dingy village. The men would sit around with clay pots of charcoal fire underneath their blanket shawls. I also bought a blanket, as it looked like I would need one ... it wasn't going to be enough.

Then in the morning, I and a few others walked to the boom gates at the base of the pass road. Only one way traffic could navigate the pass, so batches of vehicles took turns. We hired a ride on a goods truck. This was the daring way to go: to sit in a cramped bus for two days on the rough and dangerous road that crosses the Himalayas was definitely not for me.

On top of the truck, above the driver's cabin, there is a small open enclosure, where we sat with luxurious views. We could also jump down under the tarp behind when police came by, to avoid the driver getting hit with an on-the-spot payout for carrying foreigners. That was the theory, as he explained to us, but unfortunately for him we were usually too slow – I think he eventually lost all the money we paid him for the trip.

On the way up Zoji La pass, we climbed above the vegetation, the lammergeiers hovering above us on the upwinds, the road wet and slippery – there had already been an early snow fall. Every male passenger on any vehicle had to get out and help push, or at least walk beside the struggling vehicles. We reached the top, where devoid of all vegetation, the high plateau stretched away before us.

This was one of the most spectacular experiences I have ever had. The road winds its way through the multi-coloured mountains. I was amazed to see such colour changes in the hills – purples, reds, yellows. We sat atop the truck, with a panoramic view of the majestic Himalayas. By night we finally made it to Kargil, an ancient town on the old silk road. Not much there, and we slept in a dive the drivers use.

Woken before dawn, we crept out onto the dark cold street, where the truck drivers had fires lit beneath their engines to warm them up – a little disconcerting to see fires under a truck ... under the petrol tank!? Off we went again into the spectacular barren landscape, with its dramatic sheer drops, its winding up and down mountain zigzags. Along the way we stopped at small truck stops for tea or lunch.

One chai-stop stuck in my memory, as I could see myself retiring to such a place. At the bottom of a long winding, downhill road, beside a mountain stream – the Buddhist chortens with prayer stones laid along the walls between them – across the stream, was a simple but good conditioned home with an orchid along the stream edge. This was a kind of place after my heart, where I could picture myself living out my final years, in meditation and fruit tendering.

The second night we stopped in a tiny village at the bottom of one such valley, and I realised my bedding preparations (nil, except for that woollen blanket-shawl) were not going to come anywhere near keeping me warm. It was a desperation moment. I had to find something to put over me or I'd freeze to death. I walked back among the huts and without any local language I said and gestured 'blanket'. No, was the answer, but I simply couldn't afford to give up, so I just kept pestering until finally, thank God! someone gave me a heavy woollen blanket.

Late on the third day, we crossed the final, highest pass, and came down into the valley of Leh.

Leh

A wonderful place. I shall restrict myself to the important events, but the cobbled streets, old women in their top-hats and fur-skin back-warmers, young women wearing turquoise head-hoods served us food in the big kitchen, with huge pots lining the walls – a place to remember. This was still early days for foreigners in Leh, so it presented much as an unspoilt Ladakhi town.

In the evening I walked up the ridge line above the town, to a small sitting place that overlooked the valley. I meditated there while watching the sunset against a spectacular skyline, then walked back along the quiet lanes into town. I was constantly amazed on these walks how the backs of my hands looked almost black. It was not the darkness coming on, and although I had a tan from sitting on the roof of the truck for three days, this was more than that – I never did understand what happened to my skin after those sunset poojas.

Some important events are so small, that often it is a real skill to grab them and recognise their significance. I was on my journey to death – not just accepting it could happen, but actively intending to meet my death. This made for a very different journey than that of a tourist. Events become symbolic, wistful. There is a constant farewell going on. Two people in small café, at a magical twist in the road, as the lane comes down around the old Palace wall, the start of town. Talking with me, as I watched a cow grazing the rubbish just outside the café, at the peak of the turn in the road. I said, "There is a lot happening here in India, all the time – so much… like, look at this cow here." And they both froze in midair. The conversation fell like a trapdoor. What happened? I don't know, but the world stopped for all of us there in that moment.

Another time, I was in a dingy side-street café, when the sound of deep rumbling penetrated through the walls. I had never heard that sound before. It stopped, then around the corner came a mischievous young man with a slight grin on his face. I later heard this sound again when a monk was healing someone in the compound where I stayed – penetrating through the walls, it went on for a long time. I eventually saw a shrunken monk tiptoeing away.

This was the apex of my journey, a high point in the landscape. I was fit, light, and daring. So I figured, after one teetering brinkmanship experience, it was time to visit the *old ones*. I waited till after dark, late. I prepared everything in my pack once again, as in Thailand. I may not return. Over the back wall, past a couple of foreigners chatting in the night light. Said "Hi", over I went and through a small maze of buildings which I had staked out earlier, to the road heading north, up the valley behind the town.

Soon, I was outside the town-edge dwellings, and into the wilderness scene that is this whole region. Leh had previously been a prosperous farming valley, till the war with China came. Walking up the valley, I employed a few accelerators – various not-doings to pump up the urjong. Stopping randomly, turning in small circles, walking backward – the usual tools in such circumstances.

I came across a road, and at the same time saw a truck's headlights coming down the road … in just sufficient distance, that if I kept going I would be a moving object in a moon-lit desert hillside. This was a military area, things were still touchy with the Chinese. Not a good place to be picked up as a suspicious person walking alone on a barren hillside after midnight. Definitely not a good look, I thought to myself.

Plan change. Back to the edge of the road – right there on the bank above the road, in full obvious view of the oncoming truck. I squatted, shawl around me, as silent as time. The truck came around the bend with its full front lights, and I went still. The truck drove straight on by.

Astounded, I thought, let's go further. I walked high up the valley wall, and meditated for an hour or two. The night was spectacular.

Filled to the brim, I walked back down the hill, till I met my death again and purchased my final ticket. Coming through the silent sleeping town. My feet echoing slightly in the dark on the cobbled stone road. I came around the corner, face to face with a line of dogs – all walking abreast, filling the laneway. There were maybe eight dogs across. They stopped dead, while I gird my loins and held my stride. I grasped in an instant this was going to be a bluff-down scene. Let me explain something – dogs in India are rarely tied up. They sleep through the day, and roam in packs at night, doing real doggy stuff, when they are in their own game without the complexities of humans. It's a different world. A dog's world.

I walked straight toward their line, as they stood still and stared at me. Someone had to give, there was no room for me to pass. Unfortunately, or fortunately, the dog directly in front of me was the leader. Somehow in the moment, that was plainly obvious. I headed straight for him. I didn't rush, I kept my measured stride as I tried to pull off being a bigger dog. At the very last moment, as I neared the line, a smaller dog next to the boss, yelped, and backed out – I passed through the gap, next to the boss dog, from whom I heard a deep growl.

I walked free, the boss dog kept his face, it was win-win, except for the little dog who broke, yet I think it was just his place in the pecking order of the gang. Unfortunately, that marked my fate. It was an encounter, as I look back, with my death, who was also taking a look at me. I gained a fatal hubris from this encounter – I felt too good about it. Something was bound to happen.

I left Leh on a local bus to Lamayuru Monastery where I hoped to stay the night. This is a bizarre place on a dirt cliff, a village below and Tibetan Monastery above, with the most dramatic Himalayan landscape all around. Yes, I could stay in the dormitory – thank God! The only other traveller there was a German man, who was sensibly prepared. I wasn't. I still had no adequate warm gear, especially for the night. This was where I began to experience the cold getting into my bones, which intensified before I left the mountains.

I had to do something for the night, or I was going to freeze to death! I did become a little anxious here, which happens often in India. But then had a brainwave! The dirty old thread-bare carpet on the floor! Quickly I got to it and rolled it up in a tube, put it on the bed and crawled in with every bit of clothing I could find. If I just lay still I could create a smidgen of warmth. The night passed, just tolerable.

I had a beautiful sojourn in this Monastery, which has remained with me ever since. Although it seemed remote from me, nonetheless it touched me in that way which some places do instinctively, as if I had lived there before.

Next morning the German and I hit the highway, hitchhiking across the Himalayas. They were Salad Days indeed! Ending in the back of a truck for both of us unfortunately – we missed most of the scenery. It was very cold, and I only had my thin woollen blanket. But in the extremes of this travelling I had a delightful interlude. I stayed in Kargil, but this time for a day or so. There was a hotel there, and also a girl whom I fell in love with, and she with me. It was an absolutely delightful experience, walking together along the creek. She was with a man, so we just waved from afar and felt the wind.

Off again with a bunch of Tibetans, in the back of a truck. We crossed Zoji La pass – there had already been a snow fall so a little concern from all, as once the road is closed there's no escape. I heard they don't appreciate idiotic foreigners eating their food resources, which has to last all winter. We crossed, and came down into The Valley – Kashmir. I didn't stay, moved on, knowing my time in the mountains was over and the serious work had to begin. I made my way to Delhi again.

Delhi and Agra

Back in my favourite Delhi hotel, Vishal. I was travelling lean now, just a bench was fine for me. But I concealed upon my baggage a precious item: a silver flute. I could rarely play this flute, although I was by now accomplished on it. Due to the risk of it being stolen, I kept it for special moments. And one was the peak. Long been a symbol of 'fluting' since my youth, when I first heard it done by Paul Horn: the Taj Mahal.

I was silently ecstatic at the thought – this was when it was still allowed to play music in the Taj. I booked the train for Agra and waking early the next day, set out for New Delhi train station. Heading down Paharganj in the early morning, I felt like god, with a spring in my shoe. I walked too close to a large male dog, who bit me.

Right. There you go. It happened.

In Agra I saw a doctor, who asked me, "What did the dog look like?" Strong, I said. Very confident and strong. "Well," he said "Don't worry, if it was healthy you have nothing to worry about." He also explained that of course there is a latency of effect, during which the dog may feel its old self, but is already infected. Rabies.

He put it this way. If you want to have the treatment, it is a very big needle that has to pierce the wall of your stomach. I was impressed with his description, as the needle had to be repeated for seven or more days. He said the treatment can feel worse than the illness, except of course, it isn't. So I had to make a decision: strong dog = healthy dog = most likely not got rabies but can't be absolutely sure, vs. a very painful treatment to catch the slim risk. I took his advice, and just carried on. Knowing this was significant, but the absolute risk was low – I wasn't being foolish, just paranoid about the consequences of being wrong.

I stayed at a dormitory hotel, just up from the front gates of the Taj. In this dorm was also a certain woman. I awoke from a night's sleep to see her sitting in the bunk across from me, topless. She just sat there bare-breasted, with a soft listless look. She was no naïve youngster – she was in her late twenties, and a competent traveller. Just that that never happens in India – you never see a woman's breast, unless by accident bathing at some Ghat.

This type of behaviour was being rumoured by the new middle class – they didn't care what we foreigners did in rooms, but on the beach, or in a public place, it was simply not-on as far as they were concerned. Hindu code was very strict. But we travellers could basically do what we liked, as long as we didn't outrage the locals. So there was no big deal at waking up looking at a pair of beautiful breasts. Still, I did take notice of this woman, as in some odd way I liked her, though intuitively I felt she was walking too close to the edge.

The Taj. I timed it, arrived after dark, few people were there. The guard smiled when he saw I had a flute. I sat at the back of the inner circle of this stupendous building. It is truly a mighty shrine to sound. The slightest noise would echo almost infinitely, with a specially unique and attractive treble – sound ricocheted through crystals into the finest long tale. Into this I played my flute for about an hour.

It was perhaps the most fabulous experience I have been given in this life. Two young Sikhs came in and sat near. When my little concert was over, I was dumbstruck. The two Sikhs came and thanked me. I walked home in this turmoil of such a profound musical experience, coupled with the possibility of dying of rabies in India. I felt good, had a good grip, and was able to balance the recognition that this was the meeting, this was death – with the realisation of the fabulous carnival unfolding all around me. That part wasn't too hard.

But I was walking on eggshells. Something happened in Jaipur. I was travelling to the camel festival in Pushkar. That was to be the final staging ground. In Jaipur I went to the wrong restaurant. To know a healthy place to eat in those days, was to see how many customers they had. Mostly travellers eat at low level food shops, and they are fun places, full of energy. Occasionally, we weaken, and desire something a little more delightful in the way of Indian cuisine. And such places do exist. Usually though, one is somewhat apprehensive. The fact of not being well frequented by the masses – are they still OK? And the answer is mostly NO! But what can you do? You have to give it a go.

At a table in just such a place the other foreigner at a table said, in the course of our conversation, the old furphy, "You don't drink the local water, you'll get sick; you drink the local water, you don't get sick!" Like a fool I said, "Yeah." and drank the water. I was not to know then, but this act niggled me until much later when I belatedly saw the significance.

I was in this city for a few days, and loved to walk down the road between the Old City and the park. A beautiful park. One day, I saw a crazy man running through the street crowd. He was crazy alright, just like I had been reading can happen to people infected with rabies. On the way home that evening, I felt a little strange, as if my consciousness slipped a little. That was odd … oh well, let's keep moving on. I journeyed by bus to Pushkar.

Pushkar

The trap was not yet closed, but I knew what was happening. This was it: I was lining up to meet death and it was thus I surveyed Pushkar. I loved the bus ride, seeing the old men in their turbans and moustaches, sitting on the side of the road smoking chillums. Somehow I got from the bus station to a place that was called an ashram. God knows why. But I was taken upstairs and shown a space on the floor I could have, in the dormitory. He pointed to a small hand sticking out from the wall, above this space. "The hand of God." he said. And I thought, that'll come in handy. I had much cause to look at that hand over the next few weeks.

I was becoming aware of some of the symptoms of rabies. The real possibility that I would die in Pushkar of rabies was not lost on me, I can assure you. This was a very intense experience. Firstly, there is some kind of madness, then a fear of water (that part really had me in a twist), and last there's mouth frothing and death. How many days? I wasn't sure. I still hoped it unlikely, but I also knew this was no ordinary situation – I have come on this journey for a purpose, and now it was happening.

Pushkar was about to hold its famous yearly Camel Festival. I stayed through the festival and after, in the shadow behind the festival. My bed consisted of a segment of a dog's-leg room – the doggy side of that leg – where there were just two of us. A piece of mud-pack floor, on the second level, with a flat roof on top from where you could see the lake, the peacocks, and the monkeys. I had a cotton ground-cover. There was a door on my right, just past my feet, and a window opposite, looking over the town. With God's hand above me, it was a perfect location for the unfurling drama.

Around the corner of the dorm, a row of people. Unusual people. One man was making chillums, and beautiful ones at that, which he sold for his livelihood. He was a genuine person. Another man was most interesting. He meditated. All day. He would lie down and sleep for awhile, or eat, then get back to the wall, and meditate, with no regard to night or day. I found that dedication admirable.

There were some serious people travelling India then, and still are, though harder to find in the throng. They were such a self-composed bunch of people. I felt like they all belonged to that tribe of India-living foreigners, and so in some way all knew each other. I didn't know anyone, and felt outside, though perhaps we all feel that way. But it mattered little to me, as I had my own agenda on fire.

Before the crowds invaded, I explored and came to know the town. It was centred on a long street, which ran around the sacred lake – a manifestation of Vishnu. That's queer, I thought, with me being a Shaivite. Along this road, at an intersection in the centre of town, was a chai shop, which was the prime chai shop of the town, for though it was basic, it had the position. It was here one day that I met the madman.

I was leaving the chai shop, to go home, when right outside the shop, some young men were taunting a mentally-ill man. He was the village madman, though more on the quiet side than some village madmen I have seen. He was 'simple', and the taunters were from out-of-town

– Indian visitors to the lake and festival. It was a disturbing moment, not just for the poor man at the centre, but for everyone watching. Someone should have stopped them, but in India that doesn't always happen. This event later became very significant. This was my introduction to the village madman. That made at least two of us.

There was a wonderful family-run restaurant at the other end of town, operated by the older brother with the younger ones helping, or sleeping on the floor. Every morning I walked to this restaurant for tea and curd, to which I added bananas purchased at a little fruit stall along the main drag. I would meditate in the morning, then go for breakfast, return to meditate and yoga. When primed, I'd head out for the day's adventure.

Pushkar is nestled around a lake, between two hills on top of which are temples, one on each peak. Around the lake on the other side, there was a group of foreigners living as sadhus in basic public areas along the road. Further round, directly across from my patch, was the Burning Ghat, with a number of Indian sadhus around their central fire. They also played music there – amplified music, which I think only appeared for the festival. The common musical technique among the locals of Rajasthan is a harmonium, voice and percussion, sometimes with clackers and dancer.

One day I saw the woman of she-with-the-naked-breasts in the Agra morning story. She was walking through the main centre behind an arrogant man from the white sadhus camp. I felt sorry for her, but I reflected I knew nothing of her life. Still, I felt concern.

I climbed to both hill temples outside the town. One was easier – a very pleasant summit with a stone courtyard around the shrine. From this temple there was an excellent view across Pushkar. I just sat there gazing to the town and desert all around. A sadhu was striding purposefully around the shrine, saying a mantra – quite a few times. The other temple was at the top of a gigantic set of stone-laid stairs. There were seats along the way, to rest, and one needed them! At the top I saw a foreign woman in a sari, who was living at the temple. That's a bit odd, I thought. She might be interesting, but I never saw her again. I think there were two of them there, doing god knows what.

The people began pouring in, plus the camels, the show-people, and the noise, which grew to deafening proportions at the height of the festival – 24 hours a day! I couldn't believe that level of sound, all meshed in together, could go at it all night long. But they do that in India.

Leading up to the big day, the intensity steadily grew. I especially enjoyed the evening – the time Indians like the best, when they all come out to walk the streets. I would plan my day, so that I was ready by that time. Then off I would go exploring. One memorable night I heard from my room the sound of a man's singing. What caused me to pluck his bit from the massive cacophony was that he was playing the microphone amplifier for feedback, just like Jimi Hendrix. I was very impressed, and set off through the maze to find him.

What I found was a phantasmagorical scene. At the end of a wide long double road, leading up to a hill on which was perched some temple structure, was a rough platform point. The musicians were on this point, and the people below mulled and danced across the streets. There was the singer – a handsome rugged looking farmer playing the harmonium, and singing into the microphone with a mischievous yet competent grin. Around the circle were a drummer and a priest-looking man who was a bit of a fool. But what really took my eye was a foreign woman, playing flute. She was positively white, and beautiful in a plain, calm sort of way. I was so taken by her and the singer, that I made my way to a ledge just near, and went into meditation.

Unfortunately this sublime experience was ruined by the priest, who kept calling out to me to come and drum. I had no desire to act – I just wanted to hear. Eventually I had to get down and back into the crowd, just to get away from his proximity. But it was too late as that disturbance caused the session to end and it never repeated – the singer walked off. I felt that woman's presence was my anima, come to see and play music at the end of my journey. She was ethereal. I never saw her again.

Another night, I stepped into a small temple. Quickly and quietly I slipped inside and stood still beside the entrance. I watched. Among other things, I saw to my left a couple of naked sadhus. One was a striking young man, with a fierce yet contained posture. He at least looked like he knew what he was doing. I slipped away, as I had come. The gypsy women would walk the streets till late at night, singing and laughing in large tight groups. I walked along the camel grounds, where the gypsies camped and traded their camels. The men were pictures of dignity – just like their camels – with their moustache, turban and noble mien.

The big day came, and the streets were packed solid. I couldn't get out of my ashram. There was a large stone at the front, on which I would usually stand surveying the street before launching myself on my daily adventures. This day I could get to the stone, but no further.

So I turned off a back way and came down into the town via little byways that wove through the town, till I connived to get into the lane next to the main street.

As I walked along – everyone tightly compressed together – I was 'scooped' from behind to the sound of laughter, and delivered effortlessly to the side by …? I couldn't conceive of what was happening, till it walked mildly past me. An old bull with large horns – 'twas them that went under my bum for the transport across the lane, so he could cruise through. Everyone behind enjoying it, those up front oblivious. And so was the bull oblivious – he did it with calm nonchalance. I couldn't get through to the centre of town, the press of people was extreme. There simply was no room to move, except I could squeeze out.

The day was mania in a degree I could never have believed possible. I was gobsmacked at the volume of sound and activity that persisted for-seemingly-ever. But I was beginning to feel strange. I was getting a head condition. A dull ache, and a dizziness. I thought if it wasn't for the fact that this was not a healthy condition, I could quite enjoy it. It was also a terror. I was sick. I didn't recognise the symptoms. I was becoming more generally ill – feeble.

I considered leaving the ashram and heading to the other side of the lake, past the white sadhus, not wishing to offend the world with my last event. I didn't get the luxury of time. Next morning I came out of the night with a serious illness. I couldn't move from my bed. This was it. There was only one action I could perform – moving the sickness away with my hand. Beneath the little hand of God, I moved my hand, pushing away the spirit which was killing me. I had no other option, there was nothing else I could do, except think. "Shit! I've got rabies!!!"

"Oh well, here we go." I was ready for death. This was a good place to die, I was content. I had cleaned up and smoothed off every pocket of my life, and now I was ready to die – for the adventure of it! Nonetheless, I wasn't going to let this thing get me without some form of fight, and the only action left to me was the hand. Let me tell you, I put a lot of shakti into that hand movement.

In the middle of the day, lying there with my hand turning above me, I saw someone at the door, looking in – then look at me. It was the madman.

I don't know why, but for some reason, I felt immensely honoured. I can't explain, but somehow his appearance represented some acceptance. We looked at each other, then he went away. He had never been in the ashram before or after. I ploughed onward. It was a long day and longer night, what can I say? It was a nightmare of terror and determination.

The other side.

Next day, I was still alive, and slightly better. At one point, I realised that I may not have rabies. My symptoms were very much like amoebic dysentery. I had been reading! (The water in Jaipur restaurant! The bastard I was stupid enough to let fool me into drinking local water.) Some hope, to get a handle on this bizarre experience.

I found myself alive, when the whole day before, it was obvious I was in for a very nasty death. After a few days, I was feeling better, which I later saw was attributable to the fact I hadn't eaten for days – further evidence for dysentery. I arranged to move from the dormitory to a room, down in the courtyard.

I saw a doctor, who was actually a 'failed-two-year-training' doctor – we were lucky to have him. He confirmed it was amoebic dysentery, then proceeded to give a vitamin shot in the arse with me wondering if his needle was clean – see, I was thinking again in survival mode. He gave me two pills, which he said were the exact opposite of what I knew they actually were for. And I knew one of them had been condemned in western countries for causing eye problems.

He didn't give me exactly what would kill the bug, and which incredibly, I had on me – he threw me when he said no, that won't help. He was wrong! That, in fact, was the precise anti-bacterial drug which I was later given in Australia, and ironically I had it but didn't use it. It didn't really matter, the disease calmed down as I knew what inflamed it. It just would have been quicker.

I was very week and feeble, but I had been through the most extreme experience of my life. I had a deep compressed core, underneath, like a hard board. Like the woman's face in Kashmir after the night of coughing, there was this profound power. Walking down the street in the early morning on my way to breakfast, I was nearing the centre of town, when a small boy raced around the corner, and stopped dead at the sight of me. My eyes 'landed' on him like a solid plank of hardwood. I can't explain better, but for some reason our eyes locked, and something from me transferred to him. Some degree of intensity, which caused him to spin on his heal and race back around the corner. Just a moment in life where something intense jumps out at you, and you act like in dream. I walked on to breakfast. I did feel a bit sorry for him, but then, perhaps one day he will know what that look meant.

Coming home from breakfast one morning, by coincidence I found myself walking side by side down the road with another man. It was one of those unexpected cases of alignment, and it was compounded as we both walked at the same quiet pace down the road like some kind of 'High Noon'. It was a bit embarrassing, yet somehow right – we just walked on.

He was an interesting man, who I had seen occasionally from before the festival – there was a group of us 'old-timers' who saw each other from time to time but never talked. He lived in a small upstairs apartment near the centre of town, and was a serious yet calm personality. Sort of person I could befriend – a bit like me. Strange how we walked side by side as in a dream, along the centre of the almost empty main road of town – as if he was my double. I never saw him again.

One evening I went down to another food place, which I had seldom visited. It was a hangout for groovy young people. I don't know why I had never frequented this place before, it was perfectly pleasant. This night they were very busy. I was like a walking ghost. As I walked in, the place was full, and I stood at the door quietly gazing across the seats to find one that was empty. I finally saw one, so I headed for it, and sat down. It was at a large table, with people talking and eating. I just saw the seat and took it, in a very ordinary framework of events. I composed myself for what I knew would be a long wait for food.

I gazed down the table, a man who was leaning forward, sat back, and to my amazement this surreal scene transformed in front of all of us. I realised in a dream-like shock that I was sitting at the head of the table, of a tribe of freaks I had little to do with. Like finding yourself in your grown-up children's party. They were OK. But for a moment, there was a pause in the conversation, as I sat at the table head of a strange tribe. Maybe they weren't so strange a tribe …

The moment passed, the night transpired, a crowd came and went, but I felt an extraordinary intense appreciation of being alive, and a humility for a journey that had taken me to such majestic sights. At that table, an uncanny moment was shared in a split second. Every dog has his day, and my being had been shattered. I was split wide open. A walking live-wire on a flimsy lead.

Slowly I gained an improvement in my physical body, which enabled me to walk better. But my psyche was broken. My will went into coma. It took another five years before I felt back to somewhere near my normal confidence and strength. Nothing would be normal again, at least normal in the terms of my old self. That self died.

I was a child again. Yet my mind was strong. I knew where I was, how I got there, where I was going, and how far I had travelled. I had succeeded in cracking my shell, and what a tough shell it turned out to be. That was the victory. Now I had to survive.

I recovered enough, that one day when I walked to and stood on the large stone at the front of the ashram, I realised, "I can leave." I saw it all in an instant. I saw that I could be anywhere, it really didn't matter – it would still be this incredible and mysterious world in which I stayed alight like a flame, till puff! Except that I saw I could create my future.

On that stone, I knew the deed had been done, the lever had switched. A new world, a new life was now beginning. I had the tools to build this new ship, anywhere. Everywhere was just a coloured wall – an Indian temple, a tree, a laneway, a person – a kaleidoscope. I had a new task. My preference was to live in India, but I knew I had to return to Australia. THE task, was complete. I had travelled the path to my death, I had gone all the way, and looked into the eyes of Kali. I was free.

The Return.

There were two farewells. One night taking my flute up to the rooftop, I played a final concert for India. That was a treasured experience. Then one day I heard music from the other side of the lake – perhaps it was the amplified sadhus at the Burning Ghat. This was sublime and hauntingly relaxed Indian singing to harmonium and drums. His voice just stole my heart. It was the most beautiful sentiment I had ever heard. I didn't go over to find him. I stayed there and accepted it as a passing gift, that has remained embedded in my life. I expect I'll hear it again on my next death.

The owner of the ashram and his family women-folk said that I should bath in the lake before I left. They were very adamant, so I went. I am not usually a swimmer in Indian rivers, tanks or lakes. They are filthy. Okay, maybe their total belief bestowed the power to not get sick, but I kept on the side of prudence in bathing situations. And yet they were so insistent that I saw their correctness.

I went to the water's edge, where they bathe, and walked in up to my ankles (should be safe enough, my mental guardian said). It was a healing moment. I talked with the lake, and the town, and the experience which wove me into this place on earth. I likely would never see this 'place-of-my-death' again. I grabbed my bag, and left.

Back to the Vishal hotel, Delhi. Then I flew to Kathmandu. This was a flight deal, stop-over in Kathmandu. And who should I see? The woman I fell in love with in Kargil, in the Himalayas. She and her husband. She was pleased to see me – we really liked each other – but I was too fragile to play my part as I would have wished. It was truly beautiful we met again, at the conclusion to each of our journeys.

I was barely functioning – I just kept to myself, and walked the streets. Anyway, I got sick again – a case of giardia, a nasty form of parasite. Not pleasant as a send-off, but I was used to boiled eggs and rice. In Bangkok I ate too much of this meal, and had to do diaphragm-breathing exercises all night to avoid serious cramps. I got over it, and who should I meet?

Hans, the young German I travelled with in Malaysia, and last saw in the early days of Kashmir. With his friends still – they were also in China Town where I had decided to stay this time. All of us there had little stomach for the popular hotel area. He and his friends had a Thai woman prostitute staying with them. She was a beautiful looking woman with a mature, serious face, and a quiet accepting look. She had come from the country – some family story, and she was left with no choice. I liked her, she was a sensible human, which is not common. But what could I do?

I was again in no position to do anything, but keep on my own feet. I said goodbye to Hans and the others, gave the girl a knowing exchange, and left. Hans was a bit upset, but what else was possible? I submerged into chance again.

A man in the hotel, a foreigner, talked with me in my room one evening. He finally stopped, and said, in a purposeful voice, "The way I see it," he said, "everyone is trapped in their own world. Doesn't matter what level of society, what country or gender, what grows around us through life becomes a prison from which we can't break free."

He continued, "It is the same for every person, animal or whatever. We all become sealed into our world like a shell. The primary task must be to break that shell. That's what it's all about. It's simple, and it's the same for everyone, rich or poor."

I grinned at him and said, "Yes."

Afterword

Subsequent to this journey, after my return, I had a dream.

I was caught in a fast flowing river, cascading down through the mountains. It broadened out but remained a strong current which swept me, in the middle of the river, towards two towering outcrops of rock looming ahead. The water rushed towards these great rocks, swelling up as it flowed between them, through a huge natural gateway.

The significance of this was beyond me then, yet I knew it was a critical passageway through which everything in the river must pass. I also passed through.

On the other side of the gateway, I was caught in a small, tight back-loop current which swept me around and underneath the right-hand rock pillar. Beneath that great rock there was a deep, quiet little pool where I found myself holding onto a rocky ledge, catching my breath. Two other people were there with me.

Then from deep in the water beneath me, under the great rock pillar, I saw a horrifying ghoulish creature come forth. It hooked one of my companions by the feet and dragged him down into the depths. It returned and took the other person. I waited for it to come and take me, but it never returned.

I struggled out of the pool and climbed up the steep embankment. This took me higher and higher, till I was looking down on the whole rock gateway scene. I scrambled on and on, and after a very long time made my way upstream through the mountains, back the way I had flowed in the river. It seemed to take many years.

At last I entered the rushing current again. But this time I somehow knew what to do.

As I was swept along the cascading river, I worked strenuously yet calmly with the idiosyncrasies of the current, to manoeuvre myself towards the left bank of the river. I accomplished this by a specific movement of dropping down to the bottom of the riverbed, and then pushing myself up and to the left. In this way I slowly managed to approach the left bank, sufficiently to be pulled into a small side current which veered off the main river, just a little before the mighty rock gateway. It flowed into a tributary that carried me over a slight edge and down the left side of the valley.

The small stream meandered tranquilly through glades and forests, and eventually I pulled myself out and onto a soft grassy creekbank. The atmosphere was ancient and beautiful – a quiet forest opening beside the tranquil stream. There I sat and absorbed the restful ambience of nature in its pure original state. I had the intuition that an old tribe of natives lived nearby, and I was eager to meet them.

I will leave the reader to ponder the significance of this dream. Needless to say, its symbology is in itself ancient, and has given me much solace over the years.

Chapter 15

The Threshold

Self-sufficiency of *view*

One of the most essential aspects of the Path is self-sufficiency of *view*. What you are engaged in, are practicing, your direction and purpose: what constitutes your '*view* of the world' and your place in that *view*. All this is no one's business but yours, and yours alone. Self-sufficiency of *view*, means you feel no need or desire to explain or talk about your *view* to anyone. In fact it is recommended you keep completely silent unless someone of serious intent demonstrates they are ripe to communicate.

There is no real rule not to speak of your *view*, though it is recommended against. What is essential is that you have no need or desire to speak of it. You are sufficient unto your path, and what others think or feel about that is of no consequence to your inner process, your inner road. You will have to take what others think into account in considering external actions, but not internal actions.

There is a rule to not speak of your specific practices. It is imperative to be extremely circumspect about speaking of the techniques you are currently practicing – that is a very different matter. But to speak of your inner posture and understanding of the world, these matters are solely your concern alone. Speak to your circle of spirit if necessary, and to your guides or teachers, but everyone else around you – it is simply not their business to know, and they would not understand. Just leave them alone. Keep this foremost in your mind while reading the following story.

Their right or readiness to understand is not the point. It is self-sufficiency of centre that has to be acquired. This is essential to absorb into our deepest core. The world flows by on its inevitable winds of chance, but we who follow this Path have no business being vulnerable to the world's caprice in anyway whatsoever.

Thus my threshold experience which I am about to relate, is a story that has never been told to anyone. It was my personal achievement, for which I paid with enormous effort, and was sufficient unto itself. This point is important to understand, as we live in a world which values communication and community, values the exchange and disputation of attitudes. This world is of no concern to those who seek companionship with the being that lies at the core of our inner and outer universe.

I was at a crossroads on my path. I had passed the initial phases, had acquired all the knowledge I needed, and only had to apply this in practice for a suitable period of years. I retired to an out-of-the-way place, and set about a steady and intensive period of practice of all the techniques I had learned. Once these years had completed I was ready to face the next phase: application of my prepared inner being in the obstacle course of the world. This required a task.

Due to my excessive practices, I had pushed my body to a serious point of ill-health. I had only just succeeded in bringing it back to some semblance of capacity, after about two years of dedicated struggle. Due to my retreat, I had run almost completely out of financial and material resources.

In this state, I saw that I had to set myself a task that would push me to my limit (again), in order to reclaim my physical life. So I was in a position of conscious readiness when the call came.

It came one day as I was walking the road between my house and my nearest friend's place – about 8 km through the empty countryside. I recall the exact moment precisely. My car was no longer registered, so walking and bicycling had become my mode of transport. Like a message stick handed down from heaven, the idea plus the method dawned on me with complete clarity. I knew exactly what lay ahead.

I was not aware of the extent to what that task would demand, but I was aware of the task itself, and the fact that Spirit had *indicated* it to me. This last point is important.

We walk through life much like a person on a footpath, with a series of buildings on either side – large, small, grand, mysterious, dangerous, safe, boring, simple, happy – every type of experience presents its front door to us. We usually have to choose, or not choose, to enter these 'buildings'. I call them *edifices*, and I have written already of this metaphor.

When confronting the threshold, it is absolutely necessary to choose an *edifice* to enter, not by our own preferences and desires, but by the *indication* of Spirit. It is only the continuing memory that Spirit *indicated* entry, which informs and sustains us through the passageways of the *edifice*, and eventually accompanies us out the other end.

What I saw on that country road was the idea of setting up a restaurant. There were a group of us with time available to operate it, and another group with some assets to assist securing a loan to start-up the business. I knew a particular woman whom I felt would be good at running the restaurant, although things did not turn out that way. That was fine, as I had no fixed expectations about how the main idea would manifest.

I had enough experience in life by this time to realise that most people are unreliable, and so I would be able to count on very few of the approximately twenty people who were willing to join. In fact, life had shown me, never enter into anything unless you are willing to carry and bring to completion the whole affair alone. But a restaurant was not an easy operation to run single-handed, and I was very lucky to find one or two people who were willing to apply themselves beyond their limits. One person in particular proved to be of sterling character, and as such I was able to share with her a great deal of the shakti I was accumulating from the whole venture.

From start to finish, it was a farce. I only wish someone had detailed the whole journey – no one would have believed it! We could have produced a great comedy television serial from the daily material that flowed past our incredulous eyes.

First there were the meetings. Most of the people at the centre of the group were also engaged in what you could call new-age spiritual interests and gatherings. I was exploring these at the time as I was involved in trying to understand my fellow humans, especially those who showed some interest in spiritual matters. It was impossible to convey to people that the true path of spirit is far from new-age dallyings with which they preoccupy and consoled themselves.

Many of the people in this group had a karmic connection, and as such this restaurant endeavour was a perfect opportunity for me to share some hint of what the real work of spirit entailed. Being unable to explain this directly, due to their lack of preparation for such concepts, I sought to confront their energy bodies with the *work* in its raw state. I had only to hope that somewhere on their future road through life, they would progress sufficiently to be able to retrieve from this experience, data which would be of valuable service to them and their ultimate destination.

The meetings were hilarious. Everyone came together highly enthused with the prospect of being involved in a popular, community restaurant. Looking around the group, I would roll my inner eyes with anticipation of how most of these people would all fall to the side as soon as the going got tough or confusing. It came to pass exactly so, and to my great delight, there were some surprising exceptions, which only went to reinforce in me the knowledge that one can never tell who will prove to have spines of courage and stamina, and who were made of paper.

Something of immense significance happened at these initial meetings. There were different factions, even then. And it grew side-slappingly bizarre how these factions eventually saturated people's minds. One faction, I will refer to as the Grey and Windy faction. We nicknamed them such because they displayed throughout this venture certain characteristics: Grey was always exercising his grey matter, and was generally colourless and boring. He believed himself to be above everyone else, and seemed to spend most of his life thinking up things of almost complete irrelevance for everyone else to do! To the rest of the members, who were inherently vibrant personalities, this man was close to being one of the living dead.

Windy was an interesting character, but almost completely without substance, who blew one way one day and the other the next. She was way out of her depth, and clung to Grey like a priest clings to his crucifix. A pity she didn't cling to someone of more substance, as she may have salvaged some of her inherent potential to become real. Alas that was not to be.

The Grey and Windy faction I identified immediately as trouble. At first I had hopes for Windy, and tried to fire up her courage to stand strong and take a risk – to throw herself into the business fully. She didn't have the mettle. We sailed a different course.

When I first took proper stock of Grey, my heart leapt for joy – here was trouble, and in cahoots with Windy, I was in for a fun ride. These people were going to make life very difficult for everyone, which in the end came down to me. For a person in my position on the Path, I couldn't have asked for anything more precious. Little did I know what heights of ecstasy were in store.

One meeting, our troublesome couple Grey and Windy (they were just entering a relationship then) brought along the most wonderful person I had ever encountered. In our day and age, when tyrants are few and far between, when you are not allowed to abuse and murder people at the drop of a hat, it is very difficult to find real arseholes. So when Grey and Windy brought into the room a man called Boofhead, my inner joy barometer went through the ceiling. I simply could not believe my luck!

Here was perhaps the worst bully one could ever imagine in civilised society. And he had fallen into my lap! What a gift, what a treasure! I raised my eyes to the Lord, and praised His holy name, that He had vouchsafed to me such an opportunity. I felt the shakti rising up my spine sitting there in the room that first day – could barely contain myself. Driving a friend home that night, who expressed anxiety about this person's presence in the venture – what could I say? No one would ever understand. I just bit my lip and said, "Oh, he may turn out okay."

Okay? He was fabulous! A nastier piece of work you could never hope to find. This man was going to reap for me an avalanche of power from this venture – way beyond my wildest hopes. I had no one to share this realisation with, but as I have said, that was not my concern.

At one meeting the group made a classic mistake. I tried to warn them against it, but to no avail – they were swayed by a moment of idiocy. One member of the group had a flash of stupidity. He was a tad prone to such flashes, which he then throws slabs of emotion behind. Otherwise he is a genuine seeker of truth, at least within his own parameters. Seeking within our own parameters is a basic flaw on the Path. It makes for a worthy person, but that is insufficient. We have to seek outside our own parameters, and for that we require forces that will break those parameters, consistently.

Otherwise we continue to rotate in our own predefined ruts, forever thinking we are making progress when all we are doing is going in circles. I should add that this man, Trent, does break out of his parameters, but what I am referring to here is a question of degrees. Unless we are willing to engage consistently in actions and thoughts we resist, dislike, avoid, disagree with, then we will never store sufficient *alien* energy to make progress on the Path.

So Trent somehow got it into his head that we didn't need much time to settle in to the new operations of running a restaurant, before we had our opening night. What a disaster that spark of idiocy turned out to be. I suspect that mistake actually caused the eventual collapse of the business, but only by symbolic precedence – there was much more pragmatic material that brought the business to its knees. The main one being the immaturity of the people themselves.

We had the luck of the gods in setting up the business: finding the right restaurant, getting cheap finance, creating the décor, renovating it to our style and mood, and drawing on huge quantities of willing enthusiasm which all set us off to a good start. There was a real feeling of goodwill all round in those early days. The spirits were with us, and supported the spread of our popularity. The restaurant put forth a beautiful energy into the town. In full, the life of the business went for a year and a half, and for the first nine months it was a wonderful place to share and learn. In the minds of many members, the last nine months overshadowed and cast a grim pall upon the memory of the venture, but that was not true. For at least half of its life, this little restaurant was a glowing spark of beauty and nourishment for all who participated – staff and customers.

To understand my personal inner adventure, there is a feature which is essential to practise again and again on this road. Commitment. Complete and utter commitment. Complete to the point that absolutely nothing of our own is withheld. This is not a moral concept. This is an energetic practice.

The difference between those who have aligned themselves with Spirit, and the average person, is seen energetically around the feet. The average person has *roots* going down into the ground. Like a plant, or more like a mushroom actually. But it is the nature of these *roots* which bind people to the earth: they are unable to move. If you watch children, you rarely see such *roots*, although some children develop them soon. In the main, they do not appear to become tenacious until mid-twenties, but it is really only in under five-year-olds that we see good clear space beneath the feet.

Those who have succeeded in making this Path an actuality in their life, have a different energetic configuration. They literally dance like flames above the ground – and they can move with lightening speed, on the slightest innuendo. How is this possible?

Because they practise commitment constantly in their life. Not commitment to morals, other people, or social and political concepts. Commitment to Spirit's demands. To do this they have to be capable of lifting their entire energetic presence completely off the ground, in an instant.

If you have lingering desires, tasks undone, feelings of regret or unfinished business like guilt and shame, obligations that tie you, or simply the inability to give up components of your life, then you have *roots*. It is those *roots* which bind us down, and make us poor servants of Spirit.

Whenever we get a chance, we practise the ability to push aside every aspect of our lives. To 'give ourselves completely' to a task. This is practised in many ways, and I have touched on quite a few in earlier chapters. This restaurant venture offered me a superb opportunity to practise it again.

I worked at the restaurant from about 8am to midnight. Six days and nights a week, often not getting home till after 1am. All I did at home was sleep and wash my clothes. On Sunday I did the books, as I was also the accountant of the business. For 18 months my life was on hold, pushed to the side, and I lived completely from within the framework of running a cooperative restaurant.

I was not the only one. Julie also did the same. At one point she asked me if she should throw herself into this venture, as she could see how much it would consume her life. She wasn't sure she was up to it. I told her to grab it with both hands, because I knew this was an opportunity that comes rarely in our lives, for a number of reasons. It was not just a consuming task – there are plenty of those, and I love them also. No, this was more, this task was unique. I only wish I could have convinced a few more people to partake of this feast, but unfortunately most of them thought their own little plans were more important. It is rare to find people who can see the Gift of Spirit when it is offered.

The opening night

Our Opening Night came. We had the place looking beautiful. Tony had done some excellent woodwork, Grey and Windy had pitched in usefully and rustled up a great swag of people, as well as decorated out the walls with art works. The place was packed, and we hadn't a clue what we were doing. But we staggered bravely on! The only member of our group who actually was a professional cook, was nowhere to be seen. The music and conversation kept the atmosphere alive and bubbling – it was in the kitchen that we were panicking.

I was battling at the stove, preparing meals as fast as I could go, but that wasn't anywhere near fast enough – we were getting a long way behind. In the panic and chaos I recall one moment in which the whole scene lost all meaning – I stood staring blankly at a row of orders, without a clue what to do next. One of those moments you just want to crawl off to bed. Julie however was on the ball, and leaned forward, pointed to one order and said, "Do that one!" and I did, and we were off again into the endless train of madness, meals after meals. Complete novices.

I recall that evening with fondness, but actually, customer-wise it was a disaster. Some people waited hours for their meal. I don't think we ever really recovered our reputation after that night. What we should have done was to leave the Opening Night for a month or two, instead of a week or two. I suppose some of the blame was mine and I should have put my foot down when the idiotic idea was floated. Never mind, I told myself, we're off and running, and what happens, happens. It was a fabulous place, so much was learnt and experienced.

Running the restaurant

The evenings were a party every night. The mood was friendly and the people, both workers and customers were always interesting. During the day, we'd start work at early morning, and just as everyone else was taking a lunch break, we went into overdrive. Finally stopping about 4pm, when we could get an hour's sleep or rest, before it all began again for the night shift.

What a motley crew we were. I couldn't imagine a weirder bunch of people. The other main helper we had, in the actual hard work of running the restaurant, was Mark. He was the only person with whom I shared some of my *view*. He had sufficient background understanding for me to be able to explain a few things about how best to use the situation to gain shakti. He did try, although I felt it was a big leap for him.

In the end, it came down to who was willing to do the work. This was such a long journey – so much happened in every day, that I can't possibly go into details. One thing stood out: work, work, work. We would have meetings that were bordering on the unbelievable – insane comedies. Grey would turn up with long agendas of miserable little tedious demands, in complete oblivion to the overriding issue: we who did the daily work were fast becoming utterly exhausted.

The work fell to three of us, and without that trio, the whole place would have folded very quickly. Everyone else delighted in waltzing in to play restaurants for an evening, a Saturday morning, or to help out with a little cooking here and there: as a kind of quaint pastime.

Don't misunderstand me, we were grateful for every bit of assistance that came our way, but it became obvious that an inverse relationship developed between those who worked and those who caused trouble by indulging in factions and intrigues.

We had one man, Tony, who fulfilled an important role – he mixed around with everyone and was able to smooth out or lubricate the machinery, such that many problems could be diffused before they blew up. I called him *flux*. Unfortunately he left for an overseas trip after some months, and no one else was able to take his place. I did seriously consider I should take on that role myself, but in reality, I didn't have the spare time nor energy to do it. I let it drop, knowing well the consequences.

It was obvious that if members would come in and work regularly, side by side, they would develop a completely different view than if they only took a passing interest. Some members preferred to work away from everyone else, and thus set up little side-scenes. This was okay as far as offering diversity for our customers, but did nothing to heal the gradually growing insanity that eventually overtook the whole venture.

This was a wonderful experience for me on so many levels. I thoroughly enjoyed myself from start to finish, even when I was exhausted and without answers. I have the ability to enjoy myself even while experiencing frustration and pain – I split into two people, one who does the grinding activity, and another who watches from above knowing what it really means.

One of these experiences was to gain an intimate insight into how complete insanity lies just below our daily mind. I watched as people fell into pits of pure madness. Since then, I have developed a keen awareness of the derangement that pervades people's minds and lives, but at that time I was unaccustomed to this phenomenon, at least to that degree.

I was placed in the position of manager, although in tune with our new-age credentials, they called me 'facilitator', which was supposed to mean that I did nothing of my own decision but simply implemented the requests of other members. Well that was largely what I did, so I guess the name was appropriate. If I really had been the manager, I would have run the place completely differently. As it was, I spent most of my managerial effort trying to balance and accommodate a barrage of conflicting requests from everyone.

I didn't mind this role, though it did mean that people would constantly come to me agitating with their anger and frustration, requiring that I act in their interest. But as soon as I did, and others disagreed, I was left to defend the decision, while my agitators disappeared without trace. Human nature – I didn't mind. It was all good fun really. Nonetheless it reinforced my view that most people are spineless and not to be counted on in a tight spot. Still, that is no reason not to like them.

After constant and vociferous agitation and request from many members, I rescheduled Grey and Windy away from their plumb Friday night spot. I felt this was not really fair to them, as they had built up their own clientele for that evening. However the agitators also had a good argument, and in the end, the balance went against Grey and Windy, for which they never forgave me. Such is the role of facilitator. They moved to Saturday night and reset themselves up in that spot, and then wouldn't you believe it, the people who so vehemently wanted Friday night eventually flagged and decided they didn't want it after all! I offered it back to Grey and Windy. Such a mess, but that is how cooperatives work.

No one is in charge, so it becomes a free-for-all to demand whatever fancy takes your mind. Yet I was prepared. I knew from the outset, this venture was not about business success. It was about interactive learning between people. That was its ultimate group purpose, aside from my personal purpose. The purpose and intent of the whole venture was for a group of like-minded people to come together and learn about human nature – how difficult it is to work together and how basically stupid and petty most humans are. How nonetheless, it is still possible to unite and act as single body despite the differences.

And we did that, thanks to the wonderful inclusion of Boofhead. But I digress ... I will come to that magical moment later.

The fracturing

The in-fighting and antagonisms, the misunderstandings and pettiness, eventually conspired to undermine the reputation of the restaurant. But a critical moment was required to pull it down completely. That moment came due to the final exhaustion of the working trio: Julie, Mark and myself. We simply could not continue. There was unbelievable pressure from all the mal-contents, the shifting factions, all the no-hopers who preferred to criticise workers instead of come in to work themselves. We pleaded with them to cease their machinations and just lend a hand, but no, that was beneath them. They preferred to spend their time belittling and intriguing. So we just kept working – there was nothing else to do if the business was to sustain.

The restaurant was still a vibrant place, despite the best efforts of the member-saboteurs, due to the excellent and loyal customer relations we three had built up personally, when we were confronted with two facts. First was our inability to go on without respite – we were physically and emotionally exhausted. Second was a proposition by the Grey and Windy faction, who by now had brought in Boofhead, to put in one of their own rope-ins from God-knows-where as manager and to run the restaurant themselves.

As this was a substantial proposal, and we were completely stuffed, we had no option. But we were not fooled. We could see as clear as day, it was not going to work, and the person they had drawn in to run the restaurant, while nice enough, was not up to the demands, and would not get support. We had to let them try, and so reluctantly handed it over, and thankfully spent the first two or three days straight away from the shop.

Of course, it didn't work. We even came in over the ensuing month to help out, as we could see the business collapsing before our eyes, yet there was nothing we could do. Their stand-in soon left, as she was not entirely stupid and saw what a bunch of arseholes the people were who had drawn her in. Plus she also realised that all the horrible stories about us were false. Then, they brought in another tough woman, who destroyed what was still remaining of the business's reputation. In the end we were forced to take it back on, even if only to find some way out of the mess, as quickly and cheaply as possible.

We had handed over an internally damaged yet still thriving business to these self-righteous and bombastic buffoons, who reduced it to a shell, and then handed it back to us. Actually we took it back – there was still a membership who could validate decisions, and this decision was so obvious there was no other option.

During this time it became clear that we had to sell the business. Get out in any way possible that could be as financially painless as we could manage. Boofhead tried his hand at selling, and succeeded in stuffing it up. It always amazes me how such people care nothing for the facts, and rely on aggression and intimidation to try and get their way.

When the three of us regained control of the operations, we also got back the books – the accounts. In them was a note from a local accountant. It became apparent the Grey and Windy faction had been so worked up that I must have been stealing money from the business, they sent the books off to a professional accountant to scrutinise. Rumours had been circulating that I was stealing money in some way, which I didn't take seriously – the idea simply wasn't in my consciousness. And anyway, what money? For God's sake, we were all being paid a pittance for working six days and nights a week. There was no money.

Julie and I used to actually work the Fruit and Vegetable shops each morning to snavel the bargains, just to scrimp a few dollars here and there. We did everything we could to keep costs down and promote the restaurant.

So what did the accountant find? No sign of any fraud - the books were all in order. So her little note said. I had to laugh, thinking of her going over those endless papers. As an accountant myself, I did the whole thing on paper, and it balanced to the very cent! I spent countless hours poring over those figures, and it tickled me pink to know that someone else had seen the effort I had gone to. When I brought the books to our business Tax Accountant, he took one look at the two large boxes of papers, and was amazed at the trouble I had taken with them. I think he took my final Profit and Loss and Balance Sheet without question – not that I minded. Although I would have loved to see someone else follow my trail through the numbers.

Doing the books was just another task I accepted with glee – I left no stone unturned in this experience, to milk the maximum power from applying myself to the absolute limit of diligence and delight.

I had two roles in this venture, this group. As a psychic channeller who came to our group said to me at the beginning: I had to wear two hats. One was the physical leadership and the other was the spiritual leadership. An almost impossible mix. The spiritual side had to be interpreted as the role in uniting the soul of the group, as the unique spiritual aims I pursued were too remote for the others.

The physical leadership was easy, because I had much experience in that field, plus I had some excellent assistance – always a critical factor in this area. The spiritual leadership was far more difficult, as the members refused to engage in the 'mill' of the work. That was the crucible in which learning could manifest, and when so many kept their distance I was unable to reach out to them effectively. My energy was too closely embedded in the restaurant activity itself. We had to meet there to gain any benefit. Those who did, I could help, and assist in major transformations. Shakti was high, and we who did pitch in had fantastic times!

The soul of the group

There was one critical spiritual task that I could assist with – the soul of the group. This group, at least the bulk of them, were intimately connected, and as such I was able to bring together two threads: the bully-hunting task I had loaded on myself, and the evolutionary path of the group. By strengthening the empowerment of the group, it was possible to affect each member of the group.

In my delightful encounters with Boofhead, I had been successful in demonstrating his incompetence and his incompatibility with the soul of the group. This had the wonderful dual outcome of delivering the coup-de-grace to all three of the idiots who had been causing such trouble, plus uniting the group into a position in which they were able to strike a decisive blow, as a unit, as a team, to the people who had been annoying them throughout the whole venture.

It really was a magnificent moment. With careful diligence I had been successful in manoeuvring Boofhead into a position of obvious vulnerability. Yet he was still a strong contender, and to empower the group to deliver the killing blow was the outcome of a strategy active since the first meeting.

My method was to not overtly intrigue or connive against him. I held to my own integrity and sustained a position that would not allow him to land a blow on me. It was primarily a strategy of defence, not attack, in which I avoided offering him any opportunity to figuratively corner or strike me. As a target I made myself invisible. This was significant in the final battle, as had I exposed myself in any way – gone on the offensive – I would not have been able to round up the team for the last task. My influence would have been compromised.

Thus I allowed his own brutal nature to reveal itself again and again. Despite his innate ability to push through all the resistance from other members, due to his aggressiveness and their timidity, he nonetheless, accumulated a huge store of antagonism in their minds. Plus a similar store of karmic debt in the realm of the energetic scales of natural balance. Surprising how long it took for the group to respond, but the timing was as it had to be, as I watched carefully and played my cards astutely.

The first intimation that the coup-de-grace was afoot, was the reappearance of one of our members, Maryke. She is one of those people who likes to belong to things, but wanders in and out as the mood fits her. It is just her nature, and generally no one minds. Everyone else was either too timid, or insufficiently influential in the group. I could not launch the attack myself, because I intuitively acknowledged that would compromise my ability to bring about the final blow with the minimum of rebound.

Maryke was perfect for the task of galvanising the group – she had no baggage, as she had been absent much of the time, plus she had a naturally assertive and indignant spirit. She was not one to tolerate injustice and was prepared to say so. I realised her significant role in this game, when on the first day she returned and came into the kitchen, the conversation turned to the outrageous behaviour of Boofhead, Grey and Windy. In an instant I saw that she could play the necessary catalyst role, for the potency of group cohesion.

I applied myself to the task with care and sensitivity, and was able to encourage her to channel and sustain her energy in firing up the whole group. Ultimately, they were so inflamed with outraged, long-pent frustration that they called a Special General Meeting, to decide the membership status of Boofhead once and for all. They were all highly stirred up.

It was almost too much to bear for me. I could see the opportunity ripening before my eyes, while I scurried around like a sheep-dog, clearing away all the little obstructions – so that the energy was not distracted from the primary objective. Not overplaying my hand, nor revealing my intent, yet I could not allow the impetus to wane. A matter of balance.

The meeting began, and we were amazed to see that Boofhead turned coward at the final moment. As did Grey – they sent in poor Windy alone to fight for them! Imagine that, these two big male bullies sending in their female lap-dog to defend their egos at the final moment. Can you think of a more cowardly manifestation of the characters they had been all through this venture?

Everyone else turned up: the core group of supportive members, who in this final act, overcame their own petty squabbles and factions and joined together to put matters right at last. The meeting was emotional and fiery. Give Windy her due, she battled hard. I was most impressed that she put up such a quality defence for so long. I didn't realise she had it in her, and I salute her. Pity she opted for the wrong side, she could have been a useful trooper.

But the group's assault was not enough. Even Maryke's participation was not going to finalise it – she was not sufficiently involved to be useful when the stories began coming out. She was a piece of the puzzle in that she rounded up the members to act, but that was all. The meeting reached a stalemate, when everyone had had their say, argued with Windy, yet she had held out. Consensus was not able to resolve the matter. A decision and a vote had to be taken, but strangely at the last moment, everyone lost their nerve.

I had been mostly watching during the meeting, and saying very little – a few quick points now and then, a clarification here and there. I saw the momentum stall, and knew if the moment wasn't grasped, we would lose the day, and everyone would back away. Unity would be lost due to the exhaustion of emotion. I had one of those rare magical moments in life, where the room went quiet in a pregnant pause, and I knew my piece in the puzzle was at hand. With one of those secret inner delights, at the acknowledgement of the incredible situation, its intensity, I said the words: "No resolution by consensus is possible, so let's vote."

Windy looked at me horrified that I had turned against her also. She had secretly always hoped I would be supportive of her – God knows why, after all they had done: attacking me over such a long time. But she still had a subconscious bond to me, so she felt it like a final betrayal.

I wasn't betraying anything. I knew precisely what I was doing, and I did it! We took the vote. Boofhead was expelled from membership of the Cooperative. Relief swept the members, except for Windy, who practically broke down right there and then from the stress. She cleared out as fast as she could go. But the moment was euphoric for all the others. In one blow, Boofhead, Grey and Windy had been nailed to the wall. And the group had done it! The spirit of the group had finally shone through, and they all basked in exultation.

In my personal tasks of bully-hunting and healing the soul of the group, I had succeeded. However, that was only the peak of the mountain. We still had to walk the downhill road to the exit gates – a long and difficult path lay ahead of us.

That night, after the meeting, a few of us felt, firstly, sorry for Windy, and secondly, that we needed to deliver the decision of the meeting to

Boofhead himself. So we drove around trying to find them. We even ended up at some house that we felt sure they were inside, but no one answered the door. Sensing we were pushing this a bit far, after some discussion, we decided to leave it go – the meeting's decision was sufficient. Boofhead would hear alright, and he would not care for formalities – he'd never cared for them up till then.

The Threshold

The restaurant limped on after that for another four or five months. The usual working trio held it together, with the usual cameo inputs from a couple of others who had the little spots they enjoyed. What followed was the agony of two things: dissolving the Cooperative, and selling the business. That process soon turned into a nightmare.

Now comes the *threshold* moment itself. I need to explain what I mean by this term.

In traversing this Path, we are confronted by something both extraordinary and mysterious. We soon come to acknowledge that *there is something there*. I avoid the word God, because that word already has loaded into it, such a train of baggage that it can no longer be utilised to name something ultimately unknown. 'God' is too known, despite what people say. Cultures have been crapping on about God for aeons, so that by now, its mental and emotional baggage has rendered it impotent.

In this book I have used the word Spirit, but that is a vague term, which is why I like it. What are we really talking about? That is the question, and it is a question that cannot be left to faith, or whatever other euphemism you want to use for ignorance. We who are serious about prosecuting *spiritual development the hard way*, are commanded by our inner integrity to know for absolute certainty that this *something* actually exists.

We will never understand it completely, but we have to validate absolutely its existence for ourselves. We cannot accept another's word for it. Therein lies perhaps the greatest struggle for those on the Path: the validation of the existence of an intelligent and dynamic force alive in the universe, alive in our lives. To accomplish this we also have to establish a reciprocal dialogue with this force.

We have heard from those more advanced along the Path, that this thing exists. And we have an inner longing that reaches, searches, desires to believe in it. Mostly this is all conjecture. What we ask for are three things:

1. To know that Spirit exists.
2. To know that It has our developmental interest at heart.
3. To have a meaningful exchange with It.

We begin by speculating Spirit's existence based on the words of others we respect. But we have no personal validation, and as such, if we are true to ourselves, we can't just adopt such a belief. We seek to know for sure. Then we begin to test out our hope, our desire. Mostly we find it falls by way of chance: maybe – maybe not.

As time passes and we apply many of the practices of the Path, we notice that there is a strange relationship between our inner development and our sightings of Spirit. The tests we conduct start to offer more than a fifty-fifty chance. As we progress, we realise that success in our testing is correlated with our ability to align with what Spirit wants. Meaning we discern that Spirit uses a *language*.

We are still unsure, but by accurately reading the signs and omens – a very difficult thing to do, we are so prone to fantasy – some reciprocal manifestations are noticed. Eventually there comes a point when we have extraordinary experiences. By 'testing' I mean that we observe with an unbiased eye. We see that indeed something is tentatively interacting with us, but we retain a deep-seated doubt, because there are so many times when it fails.

At last, we finally gain utility in the *language* of Spirit. Not that it doesn't catch us with new twists, but we become comfortable with knowing what Spirit is requesting of us. It is secreted in the warp and weft of daily events, odd synchronicities and the behaviour of animals, birds, machines: every possible thing imaginable. It has a tag, a stamp, a subtext message that is unmistakable.

At this point we are ready. We are no longer in doubt as to the existence of Spirit and its developmental designs in general, but we retain doubt in our personal connection. Unfortunately, that undermines the whole structure. No matter what, we just can't put to rest this nagging doubt, or rather an acute awareness that real knowledge is lacking.

Then comes the *Edifice Test*. Spirit invites us to step into an *edifice* of events – a channel, a corridor of sequences – and we are drawn further and further towards a final cornering, from which we know that our own resources are fundamentally insufficient. There is no way out. Basically, we are stuffed. We are left in no doubt that the survival exit lies not in our hands – unless we throw the line to Spirit, and trust implicitly without knowing, in utter confusion. Unless we give up, and walk blindly following the mysterious traces of Spirit, then there is no way out. That is the *threshold*, and that is what happened to me in the period subsequent to the cooperative's meeting of unification.

The unification completely collapsed after the big meeting. It did not fracture, it just decayed – there was no purpose to sustain it. Business had decreased to the point where the three stalwarts, Julie, Mark and I, were more than sufficient to maintain the primary running of the restaurant.

It was a very pleasant phase, except for the fact that we couldn't find a way out. The dissolution of the Cooperative was proving complex and tedious. But worse, no one wanted to buy the business. The stress began to tell on me, and I started having panic attacks during the night – I could see no escape. All was dark and the only response was to get up each morning and carry on.

We couldn't walk away from the business, as we still owed the bank a lot of money, which none of us either had or wanted to lose. The only way out was to keep working till we found a buyer – but what if we couldn't? And how long could we sustain the effort to maintain the business as a viable enterprise?

It was during this time that my faith in the signs that had led me on this track, was tested to the limit. I knew perfectly well what was at stake: this was going to be my *threshold* experience, from the very beginning. It was simply the timing. I had done all the preliminary work, I had retired from the world to embed the concepts, the practices, and the knowledge into my being. After digesting everything it was time I re-entered the world under a new personal spirit. But first I had to pass the *edifice test*. To prove I had learnt my lessons. I knew where I was, why I had come this way, and what I was engaged in. But that was not much help – in fact it made the whole thing worse.

If this *edifice test* failed, it meant the failure of my whole journey – my whole purpose and intent, to say nothing of years wasted in error, while I could have been making money like all the rest of my fellow humans. During this dark night of the soul I used to look upon the books I had absorbed, and consider I had been tricked. Perhaps they were all bullshit? All the Taoist, Sufi, Hindu, Buddhist, Mayan, Aboriginal, mystical texts from every possible source that I had studied and applied – all bullshit. They had tricked me! Who were these people who wrote this stuff? Why should I have trusted them?

I knew I had no choice, and the stakes were frighteningly enormous for me personally. I could not go back, I could not step off sideways. I had to strap myself in, and *choose* to believe I was on track. I had dreams of walking in the ocean where my feet lost contact with the sand – all I could do was tread water in the direction of intuition, till my feet touched sand again. I had dreams of losing my way in the bush, and having to rely on one observation: the gentle upward slope of the ground. So long as I could continue to walk uphill, I could keep moving in the absence of any path.

Outwardly I let no one know of this inner struggle. That wouldn't help the situation, and anyway they would not understand. This was my *threshold*, and only I could pass through.

We kept an advertisement in the paper for months, and had some close chances. We nearly sold a few times, but they fell through. I was becoming very annoyed at the bureaucratic pettiness of the Government departments who were responsible for the dissolution of the Cooperative. I told them, "Everyone's gone; let's just call it quits – there's no money, only debt. We all just want to go home and forget it." But no, that was no good. It had to be done by the book. (We became experts in 'the book' over the life of this Cooperative, and more so as people's hearts grew caustic.)

I was pissed off at one Government man in particular. Later I heard that it was only through his personal efforts that we succeeded in bypassing the normal processes, and had our dissolution sent straight to the Government Minister, who signed off on it. Something that only happened in exceptional circumstances. Without my knowing it, Spirit was moving to clear away the obstacles, and I had been pissed off at the very man who was Spirit's instrument. I felt a bit silly after that.

At last we attracted the attention of a genuine buyer, and carefully prepared everything – I prepared the books and the documents of valuation etc, while the others, especially Julie, did the human stuff to smooth our relationship through to the finalisation of the sale. We weren't going to get through the last door without considerable skill and effort.

We walked out on the last day of the year, a triumph, and celebrated our freedom with a picnic at the creek under the singing casuarinas. It was bliss. For about two years we had not been able to simply lie about and enjoy a drop of wine with a real sense of release and relaxation. We were out. My commitment to Spirit had been driven so deep into my bones that I was left in no doubt as to Its relationship with me personally. Spirit remained true to our covenant, and led me safely in the maze of the *edifice*. I was through the *threshold*.

In the end we paid out the original loan, except for the sum of $250 each, which to my admiration of all the primary members who signed the loan guarantee, almost everyone paid. Even those who had very little money. Except, of course, Grey and Windy. Yes, to the end they proved themselves worthless as human beings. And they were the only ones who actually could afford to pay without noticing it. On principle they refused, and eventually the bank gave up pursuing them for it. On principle of being egotistic arseholes. We didn't care one jolt, but I knew, and I still see, their debt is accumulating interest in the books of karma to this day. There is no escape from the debt of our word, nor our pride.

Boofhead lived to bully people again and again – he is still at it, but our paths only cross in the street these days. I still give him a nod and a smile – what a wonderful benefactor he was to my graduation.

Part IV

Peaks

Slowly the day fades
children's voices
a lone bird whistling.

Nowhere to go
scarlet clouds
a level stretch of ground
To rest on.

Peace is so precious
always waiting
royal blue
    behind the fire in the clouds
how can I have been so blind?

Chapter 16

Shakti

Shakti is what it is all about. All the work and subterfuges. The deadly secret that accompanies knowledge, is that it is useless without shakti. Shakti is personal vibrancy – life enhancing energy that bubbles on subtle levels. We were born with a tidal wave of shakti. But over the years, we are taught to dissipate this power, until we walk the streets empty. And death calls.

The secret knowledge is simple: harness this energy – shakti. First it speaks on how to stop the sliding away, the out-pouring of shakti with no return. Then it speaks of how to enhance natural shakti. Those are the two sides. Stem the outward tide from our life, and save what little we have left. Then discover highly insightful ways of building the fire of shakti.

Shakti is luck. Shakti is power. Shakti is possibility. Without possibility, all the knowledge in the world will mean zilch. Shakti is feminine – she gives birth.

Everything I have said and done since my own first awakening, has been a strategy to grow shakti. That is not the essence. The essence is always absolute silence – it can be no other way. Time and again the message from all the great schools, is inner silence. But we have to act. And a shrewd assessment of that fact, shows two significant points:

1. If we give up worry, concern, then focus like a shark on the technicality of our daily world – uninterrupted with thoughts of the personal. If we give up anguish which burns our lights out. If we completely detach from ruminating incessantly: the real mortal sin – endless obsession with an anguishing emotion, over and over. That's the clue that the great evil Nigel is at our door every day, sucking at our vitals. The sin that robs us of our immortality.

2. Then a most mysterious thing begins to happen. That mysterious thing – that's shakti.

Put simply, shakti opens unbelievable possibilities in our life, so why wouldn't we turn to its study with dedication? Surely anything else is stupid. Perhaps we only realise that once we have experienced shakti. Up till then we have to take it on faith. And if we choose the wrong faith we end with shit all over us.

So we are left with two questions:

1. What can I *not* do: to stop shakti dissipating from me?
2. And what can I *do:* to attract, replace, replenish, vibrate, glow this strange substance? Called grace, or 'friendship of the gods'? A lighthouse that can be seen for miles in the subtle worlds? The answer is: *taste.*

Almost everything in this book is about the first question, because that is the way it works. If you acquire knowledge of the second question without the first, you are doomed. The first question is about building will, character and power. Ultimately that means death. Death is what consumes our shakti. Once we befriend death, meaning giving up all claim, facing the open door – once we die, we have the licence to build with impunity.

What drains shakti is clinging. Clinging to life is the deepest claw of all. When we let go of that, as does a person who is dying, then we have the possibility of being allowed a stupendous friendship – which could disappear at any minute.

The story that towers above all others is the bird. The bird arrives in front of us once in our life, and if we let it go, it never returns. There are those who run for the bird! They dive beneath the wings, clinging with love to the bird. The only clinging that brings freedom.

The technique

Although this whole book is about the first question, "What can I not do: to stop shakti dissipating from me?" I will outline the argument of both questions here.

1. Stemming the loss.

The usual case we find is emotional cud-chewing, especially of hurts, but sometimes of ambition. The world teaches us to worry – there are so many good reasons. And more, it chastises you if you do not share this state of concern. That is the world mind, to which we voluntarily give over vast qualities of natural, magical glean. To what…? Think about that for a change, where does it go?

Life becomes flat and boring and we indulge in crankiness, which pumps even more juice out of our inspirational pool. Quarrelling and petty thinking dissipate our heritage. Then we compound it by becoming unreliable, as reliability requires inner strength. Soon we are a sitting duck for death, who dutifully comes.

The way to stop this outward tide of life force is to examine your outgoings. Where you spend energy. To say 'stop obsessive anguish' does not relieve us from sensitivity. How to tune into the world that surrounds you, and yet detach yourself from it all? That is the best question.

The answer is, do both at the same time: tune in and detach. That's the stance of an enquirer into life. Feels intently, knows what is going to happen, likes to engage and play one's part. In fact, devotes complete dedication to a worldly task. Enjoying it beyond measure. Suffering up to one's limit. And yet behind it all, knowing that ultimately nothing matters. Ultimate disconnection from the world mind and its secret denizens.

One can only balance between tuning in and detachment when one has found a fight worthy of one's spirit. And given it up. One can only give everything up in the face of death. Once we pass through that doorway, we are free. Then we can truly detach, because true detachment can't be practised. It only comes as a consequence of death. A deep cutting of the bondage ropes that can't be faked.

People who have passed this way before, noticed a pertinent point: that you need shakti to gain shakti. So what can an aspirant do, who cannot see? The answer: add quality into one's life. To seek quality over convenience. Simple as that. Practise quality, seek quality. But most of all, practise. Practise doing everything to the best of your ability. Seeing your life before you, and instead of criticising or complaining about it, pick small tasks and do them well.

The reason is simple – even doing one small task with intentional quality, begins to turn the mighty wheel. But more, it reaps a reward, a nourishment to the spirit, a dose of shakti. The more we repeat, become a person who can complete tasks, a reliable person, a person who is known for quality work, the more we drink in shakti. A boost to our shakti can help us to do it again, to apply the theory as previously stated. Knowledge and shakti together – that is what we aim for.

I can't even begin to state how imperative it is to adopt the practice of doing everything to the highest quality. This is what distinguishes all people – those who can be relied upon to consistently produce the highest quality work in every task, no matter how small and insignificant, always stand out from the crowd. Too often we make the mistake of thinking we will do important things well, and it doesn't matter about the rest. That we will look after a house we own, but not one we rent. That 'good enough' is fine for menial tasks. Wrong, wrong, wrong! Remember – this is your life, and where you are, what you are doing IS your life. We have one choice, to live every moment to its highest value, or slide into the lazy masses whose lives are meaningless. It all begins with one small action – in a split second we take one road or the other.

Every light that glows inside us – be it action, thought or feeling – expends shakti. Some expenditure returns greater shakti, some just loses it forever. Expending shakti to climb a mountain renews shakti, as long as we don't dissipate it by giving-up, complaining, or wasting the journey on petty thoughts and words. Watch intently every time we expend shakti. Remove everything unnecessary from our lives, and re-work the remaining, such that it builds power rather than loses it. It takes many years and much wisdom to know how to accomplish that.

Position, possession and sex. That's what consumes our shakti. Say what you want, that's the truth. And it's not really these, but our attitude to them, which triggers the suckers to latch onto us. Our obsession and neuroticism. These are the objects of repetitive and futile preoccupation. Thought followed by action, followed by outcomes and reflection: that is the proper use of time. Not gnawing on your leg stumps like a dog with a bone. Truly we rip into ourselves viciously, flagellating our backs with guilt and envy. Decisive mind-focus, and mind-silence, that is the method. Instead, we get this soap opera of continuous mental drivel, that loops endlessly around and around.

Words are also devastating. Unfortunately, for some people words are a release valve for emotion. They spray words about like sewerage, as it is a way to react to emotional intensity. Empty words, words with no deliberation, gratuitous words without commitment. They carry away our shakti in barrow-loads. Loose with words, is a suck-out.

Still, mind is the worst – self-abusing, self-accusing, self-deluding: this mood where we pour over our hurts. Then the surface-thinking, superficial-living, television-watching mind where we follow entertainment while telling ourselves we are being positive. Both words and mind leak, because they are distractions from the elephant in the corner – the mystery of our being that is alive, and will die. It's all a deep dislocation of the spinal column of reality – the truth table.

That is the whole trick – once you have a grasp on the reality of your life, your situation, then you can better engage with less relevant issues, as you come to them from outside, not inside. Build inner strength first, then navigate the world's maze.

The most common manifestation of shakti-leakage is resentment. When we stew over the past, or re-run old songs of woe, of 'how we was wronged'. Giving up resentment, or feeling we have been diddled somehow, would be the greatest achievement in stopping the general rot. That's my best rule of thumb, but alas, without all the work combined, knowing about the disintegrating power of resentment will change nothing. Still – give it a go, if nothing else in this whole book.

2. Enhancement.

Although this is not the place to go deeply into this aspect, still a few things should be said. As stemming the loss is concerned with outflow, so enhancement is concerned with inflow. Inflow means feeding. There are three types of food we eat: mouth food, air, and impressions. Impressions are the big issue.

Food in through the mouth, and air, are the basic feeding which keeps the physical fuelled. However, impressions cover a huge range. Essentially we are perceivers, and as such impressions are the stuff of life, the stuff of the world in which we live, which impacts upon our perceptual receptors. We take in sensations, and they change our inner core.

For example, we may eat food via the mouth, but the taste of that food is an impression. The smell of the air is an impression: although the quality of the air is a food for the lungs, the feelings of that quality are impressions. Taste is the essence of impression food, and it is often overlooked when referring to health. We are told about vitamins, minerals, proteins, carbohydrates, and so on, but we are not sufficiently informed of the healing benefit of taste, both variety and quality, and the expansion of capacity to taste. Taste is also about learning and maturing. I speak of taste in its broadest sense.

When young, I liked certain things, but I've moved on. I have learnt to appreciate many things far beyond my childhood preferences. For example I liked certain foods – food I was usually fed, but also those I liked immediately, most of which was not especially healthy. I have explored many cultural foods now, and have learnt to appreciate quality in many areas. This gives immensely greater enjoyment than I ever knew in my youth. I had intensity, but a narrow field of play. People forget this, and I am saddened when I see some cling viciously to their old childhood attitudes to food. By viciously, I mean there is no way you will ever get them to enjoy foods outside their cramped cubby of old tastes. Oh, they may try to change, just to please you, but turn your back and they are back into their old ways like sleeping donkeys. Taste can be acquired! That is the best story in town.

This is the subject of a further work, but for now, know that the key lies in the quality of intensity, coupled with constantly seeking new impressions. It is these two together, that when combined in profound ways, is the skilled approach of enhancing shakti. When you add the intentional – wind from within – you have a potent brew.

Chapter 17

Meditation

This book would not be complete without raising the practice of meditation. In truth, all depends on the successful accumulation of the meditative state.

Meditation is much more than the practice itself. It encompasses the whole shift in world view we seek to actualise on this Path, and it contains the ultimate solution to our condition. I will begin with a short summery of the practice in its most general understanding. There are so many schools of meditation, and they all have techniques of great value. This book does not need to be a substitute for such a vast array of material that is available on the subject. However, there is a need to clarify and reduce much of the obscurity surrounding this topic.

There are four basic stages of meditation: concentration, contemplation, visualisation and meditation.

A. Concentration.

The method used is called Gazing. That is a perfect term because concentration has to be performed with sustained focus, without strain or staring. This is an external focusing practice, and it is done in a relaxed mood with either the eyes or the ears. We gaze at an object in a long and restful pose.

There are many different types of gazing, and each is unique, although exactly the same method is employed. There are differences in application, but the underlying basis is always the same. The types are the objects, and they dictate the effects and the experiences. Anything can serve as an object for gazing, but there are some usual starting points:

Eyes: rocks, leaves, skyline, clouds, fire, flame, smoke, ants, shadows.

Ears: waves, instrumental music, frogs, crickets, rain, traffic, wind.
Skin: breathing, wind-on-skin, stone-on-skin.

The method is to slowly allow the focal point to move across or around the object, gradually exploring the minutest variations. By gradual movement, it is able to avoid fixation and retain concentration.

This is a large subject on its own, and I will not go into the details here. It is very simple to explore oneself. The value is enormous. It has the ability to allow us to suspend inner thoughts by providing an external focus, which assists in maintaining the practice for long periods of time. It is recommended you be cautious with the variations of water gazing – people have died doing this without experience and preparation: ice, streams, pools, steam, mist, fog.

In all these practices, the sitting method is critical. Of course you can practise all these in standing, lying and walking, but the base position is always sitting. The crucial aspect is the spine. For all these practices, the sitting position should ensure your spine is perfectly erect. The Holy Grail of sitting positions is the tight cross-legged yogi position with the legs entwined. This allows for excellent balance, and the best alignment of body-energy.

Not everyone is capable of that position, so there are appropriate alternatives. Sitting cross-legged on a mat, of natural fibre, is a very enjoyable position. There are a number of leg positions you can explore. For long periods, have your back against a wall. If you are able, you should construct your own support post. Go to the trouble of selecting and preparing your own tree trunk/branch and digging it into the ground. This is especially good in setting up for distance gazing, where you can be outside – e.g. skyline and cloud gazing.

Sitting erect without support is a preferred position if you are able, and you should practise it, as it offers numerous advantages. Not just for body alignment, but also for when you are walking in the wilderness, and you are able at any point to adopt the stationary sitting position.

Another excellent position is the low meditation stool. Make your own, as it is not difficult – one cross slab and two end post pieces, are the basics. Build it high enough to place your feet and calves underneath comfortably. It is also possible to sit in this position without a stool if you practise it, but for long periods, the blood tends to become cut off, which is not good. It is a prize position of yoga practitioners.

Having said that the spine should be erect, I will add that for some practices this is not necessary. One position that can be effective is the large chair – large enough to support your head, and be able to sleep in. The reason for this is that there is one good practice, where you begin with gazing, but allow yourself to drift into the half-sleep state. Sitting in a comfortable chair is enough of a discomfort from lying down, yet comfortable enough to drift off, creating the conditions for spending long periods in a half-sleep state where dream practices can be engaged with effectively.

Lying down can also be useful, so long as you are not in the slightest bit sleepy. This is good for body gazing practices, such as watching the flow of energy up and down your body.

Generally, you should have a place dedicated to meditation practices, not used for anything else. A place easy to go to, with a special mat that you only use for meditation. The area of wilderness meditation positions is a whole other field, and very interesting. I would like to speak of this in a subsequent book.

B. Contemplation

Once the power of concentration has been acquired, a form of contemplation can be practised that can penetrate into the mysteries. This form of contemplation is often called 'pondering'. Its place in the types of meditation is controversial, because it involves thinking, and in essence meditation is all about cessation of thinking. Thus, there is a trap in contemplation where we believe ourselves to be engaged in a meditative practice, whereas in fact we are simply postponing silence and indulging in our age-old vice of constant thoughts.

So long as active contemplation focuses on feeling and digging deeper into the contradictions of life, or seeking to penetrate into the hidden meanings of events and words of wisdom, then it can be beneficial. This book has so much material for contemplation, that I feel it unnecessary to go into this further for now. Suffice to know that all the ideas expressed in this book should be pondered in a meditative and contemplative state. The sub-text of knowledge will seep into the lower strata of our being, there to become true creative impulses.

However, I will draw a basic outline of how contemplation operates for those on the Path. There are two aspects:

1. Contemplation of paradox, conflict, the irreconcilable. If we constrain ourselves to ideas which are familiar, which don't create anxiety, situations we understand, things complete – in other

words 'comfortable' – then we remain asleep. Contemplation has to be employed for awakening, and for that we require dissonance.

We must present before scenarios that don't resolve, and strive to resolve them. In all ways possible. This rule is too often forgotten by those on the Path. Its implications are astounding. That we should place ourselves in situations of unbearable anguish, either in a volatile way or in a profoundly deep-resonation way, is one of the absolute commands for those who seek to 'go beyond'.

2. Realisation. This area of contemplation will be discussed in detail in a subsequent book. This is so critical to the entire Path, that it needs a separate and comprehensive treatment. It is, however, an advanced technique when activated consciously, and as such becomes a feature in the life of a Practitioner of the Path.

Both these aspects of contemplation belong to the activities of Practitioners, which is the focus of my next volume on *spiritual development the hard way*.

C. Visualisation

This transfers the quality of focus, acquired in the Gazing exercises, internally. The idea has two components, but the first is the main one. Before I explain it, I'll just say that the second component is to focus on objects in dream. I am leaving that because it has to do with dream work, which is outside the scope of this book.

Seat yourself in a comfortable position again. Calm your mind and body. There are many objects for focusing in visualisation. I will deal with a few. Some people claim they can't visualise at all. That is probably not accurate in many cases, but whatever, don't despair. Try listening meditations instead, as they are a good alternative – it is possible to hear internal music. In fact you can create whole symphonic journeys in aural-imagination.

The classic method is to visualise a composite object. Visualise an Archetypal figure that has many aspects of power and mood, such as the Rosy Cross, Avalokitesvara, Durga, Mt. Everest, or an endless ocean. Always start with something beneficial. But never forget the second half of the classic approach – dismantle the image completely, till it is absolutely erased from your mind. That part is often forgotten.

You don't have to use such highly charged objects. In fact it may be better to use simple, non-emotive objects like stones, trees or apples. One area of visualisation is geometric shapes. Again, always dismantle the image effectively.

There are three specific visualisations I wish to explain in detail: perspective repositioning, journeys and memory visualisations.

Perspective Repositioning

Lie down on the floor. Close your eyes. Imagine looking out from the viewpoint you experienced before closing your eyes – looking up from the floor. The task is to break this default expectation of body-identification. Begin by imagining you are standing above yourself, looking at your prone form. See your clothes, your hands, your head.

Move to the other side of the room. Look at yourself from that angle. Move around – walk around your body looking at it from different angles. Then float to the ceiling and look down on your body from the ceiling – picture your body lying below you on the floor, as you touch the ceiling with your back.

Now float to the door or window – move outside the house and walk down the path. Walk or float away from the house, along the road, looking at the other places around your house.

When you are ready – ensure you save enough energy for the end – come back to the room and see your body again lying there. Enter into your body *gently*, then open your eyes.

This is one example of perspective repositioning, especially from body-identification. There are many variations and extensions of this. Always the idea is to view something from a perspective that is not customary. This can be aided by placing stumps around your house, and standing on them occasionally. It is surprising how pleasant and relaxing it is to stand at an elevated level from your normal bodily position.

Journeys

These are visualisations which construct a journey in an imagined place. They are only limited by your imagination, and it can be useful to construct the elements beforehand so you can include many archetypal aspects. There are so many variations that there is no way to categorise or reproduce them here. However, to demonstrate, here is a simple one that I briefly referred to earlier in the book.

Imagine you are sitting at the end of a grassy clearing in a forest on the edge of the mountain side – you can see out over the whole valley and beyond. You are quite high up, although the mountains continue up, towering snow-clad behind.

You can see down in the valley the road you will be taking. See the forest path winding its way down the mountain to meet the valley road. Not far along this road there is a small village, and a creek. The village is built on both sides of the creek, and the road crosses a simple wooden bridge just before the village outskirts. The road goes on beyond the village and you can see it like a ribbon laid along the widening valley.

Further on, looking past the valley near the horizon, you see the shining lights of a great city beneath a gleaming white mountain .

You stand up, and walk down the forest path. Notice the trees and shrubs, the birds, the patches of grass. It is hard climbing down in some places and you have to go carefully. Make your way gradually along the path, not rushing, taking in features of the wilderness as you pass. Notice when you enter cultivated areas as you near the valley floor.

Walk up to the road then travel along it while watching the creek. Sit beside the creek at an old tree which reaches over the water. Notice the fish and the quality of the stream. Take your time – look up at the clouds and sky, the eagles hovering high above. Move on to the bridge just before the village, and as you cross listen for any sounds – the creek, the birds, noises from the village. Pass into the village and notice the type of houses and shops that you pass.

Continue on in this way, talking to people you meet, drinking tea in the rest-houses, journeying on past the village and over the valley edges to the next valley – on and on till you come close to the large city. Look at its glimmering and shimmering – what a beautiful place! And towering above it is the solitary mountain, covered in snow. The shinning city is nestled beneath the mountain.

Before you enter the city, you have to decide why you have come this way. No one is allowed to enter this city unless they have a purpose in their life. Sit at the side of the road and ponder: what is the purpose in your life?

Memory Visualisations

There are two parts to this, and if not practised correctly, it has the danger of slipping into a memory trap, where like old people, you repeat the same old stories. Old people do this as part of the dying process, and it is beneficial in only a general way. Mostly, it becomes an indulgence, dwelling on a tiny selection of fond recollections. That is not what we are about here.

There are many systems to constructively release the past, but after trying quite a few, from numerous traditions, I will present here what I found to be the most effective technique.

1. *Memory Book:* acquire for yourself a special book of blank pages. Don't show this book to anyone – it is your book of memories which you alone will utilise for cleansing your past. In this book, make lists of all the items you can recall from life. These lists will criss-cross each other, but they must be a thorough matrix of memory patterns. They are lists of people, places, activities and feelings.

2. *Item List:* Here are some examples of category headings to get you going. Write your list of major events or periods to review, under each of these headings:

    - Begin with a list of every class at every educational institution you have ever attended.
    - List all the people you have ever known, broken into groups like family, work, leisure, sport, childhood friends, school friends, teachers, and so on. Naturally these will be the significant people in your life. Less significant people will also be recalled under the other headings.
    - Houses and rooms you have lived in. Include bedrooms, bathrooms, kitchens, toilets, lounge rooms, verandas.
    - Countries, towns and cities you have lived in.
    - Sports and games you have played, sub-classified by the places where you have played them.
    - Relationships, especially sexual experiences, but also arguments and romantic moments.
    - Traumatic events.
    - Exhilarating and ecstatic events.
    - Work places.
    - Travel, including buses, trains, planes, taxis and other similar vehicles.
    - Vehicles you have owned – including push bikes, skate boards, boats, cars and motor bikes.

- Animals – pets and non-pets that you have known.
- Wilderness places you have visited.
- Sunsets and sunrises you can recall.
- Meals you can recall, especially including restaurants.
- Promises you have made.

1. **Structured recall.**
    a. The process is important to understand. Firstly identify where you are up to in your lists, and choose the next item. It is common to feel you should begin with the traumatic or intensely emotional items first, but this is not the case. Try to remove from your understanding of this practice, the idea that you are regressing to remove troublesome energetic events which have a psychological impact on your current life. That may very well be the consequence, but it is not the purpose of this practice.
    b. The purpose is twofold.
        i. First, is to sweep through your entire life, as with a comb, drawing out all the lost memories and releasing the past to its own course instead of secretly clinging through an unexamined attraction. This is done by the realisation of reliving – it is the intensity of this memory reliving that we seek.
        ii. The second is to secure a magical freedom: by offering up to our consciousness, burning in our awareness, the debt of life. This is the process undergone during the death event of every being's life. But we do it now, on purpose and intentionally. We reproduce the death process, where our memories are consumed by the universe. In that consumption, our names are expunged from the records, leaving us free at last to seek what we require, instead of what the forces which sponsored our life require.
    c. You may not understand fully what is involved here, but it only matters that the practice is conducted effectively

- the results will validate. This is one of the secrets of our existence and freedom.
   d. Choosing our item for a session: we sit and focus back on every tiny element of the place or person or event. Recall the colours, the atmosphere, the activities. Move into it slowly and thoroughly, until you begin to feel now the feelings you felt then, at the time you lived those memories. Transport yourself completely back there, and if you are successful, you will really believe yourself to be fully within that memory – because it is always here. In fact, this is a lesson in switching grooves on the time record. It is done through the power of our emotions and feelings.
   e. Dreams: Normally after such a session you will have a strong dream of these memory worlds that continue to run parallel to your current one.

2. **Unstructured recall.**
   a. Once you have first written, and then completed your book of lists, ticking off each one systematically, then you have completed the structured part of the exercise. Now begins the unstructured part. Many people wish to jump straight to the unstructured, while others may find the structured safer. Both are necessary, and should be practised in succession – first the containment then the freedom.
   b. The initial stepping off point: this can be identified from some event that occurred to you during the day, or you can take some illness location in your body. It doesn't matter where you begin. You are following the automatic associations that bubble up spontaneously into your consciousness.
   c. Hidden memories: one image or event conjures another, but we don't wander aimlessly. We wander with awareness and observation. This process allows us to discover hidden memories that our clever patterns and lists could never reveal. These are journeys in memory, dictated by a hidden attraction deep within us. We are usually seeking the thread of intensity in these unstructured exercises.

d. Mundane memories: that name does not restrict excitement and emotion – intensity can often be discovered in the most mundane memories. Allow the memories themselves to pull you to where they are seeking to lead your inner eye. Look around.

e. Dreaming a recall: you will know when you have begun to practise this correctly, when you awaken in the middle of the night, after dreaming a recall of an event in your life which you had totally forgotten. It is the spontaneous bubbling to the surface of intense experiences previously lost to consciousness. It will release huge amounts of energy into your life.

D. Meditation

There are many traditions which teach meditation, and there is a lot of material on the subject, so I will not go into great detail. I do want to set out the core, as so much material is either embedded in cultural ornamentation or approaches from intricate directions. I will try to simplify here what it is we are actually engaged with when we practise meditation.

The whole purpose of meditation is to silence the mind – to still the inner dialogue. Much of the complexity around this subject is because of the inherent difficulty in doing this simple task directly. That is the value of all the different methods, because our mind is a great trickster, and will not relinquish its control easily.

We have two sides to our being: the left and right, the mysterious and the rational, the right and left hemispheres of the brain, the unstructured, spontaneous, and the structured, deliberate, the formless and the formed, the unqualified and the qualified, the uncarved and the carved.

When we are born, as we look out our two eyes and listen with our ears, what we perceive has no order or meaning. It is pure impression. As we grow, we learn that what we perceive has ways of arrangement. And there are some very good reasons for those arrangements.

We learn that some things hurt, and some give pleasure. Some are hard and some are soft, some inside us and some outside us. Over time we are introduced to a deliberate, concerted effort by the world around us to build the most elaborate and abstracted derivatives of arrangement. Most of these have a reason based in our ability to survive and navigate through the world. Some are less practical and involve understandings of who we are, who others are and how we should or should not behave and interact.

All this structure builds on our right side – the left hemisphere of our brain. Our original mind is pure perception which has no qualifications, no arrangements, no order nor form. The unarranged mind remains in the background, and after a short time in life we lose contact with it.

That aspect of us continues nonetheless largely untampered, on our left side of the body and right hemisphere of the brain. It remains active, and connected directly to our senses. But a nano-second after sensual reception of stimuli, we filter the content. We skim the impressions, and in the speed of light have them all nicely slotted into our mental *stencil*.

This *stencil* becomes so consuming and complex that it takes over our whole existence – we will live and die for its constructs.

The rule of the Path is twofold: both sides of our being have to be addressed. The right side has to be purged of dross – unnecessary energy-draining preoccupations, while the left side has to be rediscovered. Meditation is that rediscovery.

Almost everything in this book has addressed the right side of our being – preparing it for the moment of balance. The rule for the right side is also twofold: remove and reorder. Clear away the rubbish (or what we classify as rubbish for our purposes, as nothing is rubbish in itself) and reorder what is left into clear functional lines. The result is a very tight and simplified ship, both in the mind and in life. With the space that has been cleared away, some parts are allocated to our heart – what I have called the Garden – and the rest of it is left completely empty.

It is this empty area that we call meditation.

The method in essence, is simplicity itself. We have it passed down to us from those who have gone before. The first great secret is in our internal thoughts. The second great secret is that silence is cumulative. With these two secrets we set forth, and despite many circuitous routes, we always know we are on a central path the moment when the right side of our being finally cracks, and releases us back to our primal state of perception. The *stencil* is only maintained by our inner thoughts, in which we continue an uninterrupted manifestation of our identity and attitude. Our thoughts constantly rebuild and repair our meaning.

Not that meaning has no value. But it has to step to one side when not needed, so that the magical and enriching purity of unfiltered perception can be retrieved. Our *stencil* is actually draining us of life juice. It is an emanation of death – as soon as the slightest form of order arises, it has to push back the un-ordered, and in doing so, its time is delimited.

At the same time, order also is energising. Both sides of our being offer us different gifts of possibility in the enrichment of our being. Meditation is about tapping the vast wealth that was ours by birthright. No matter who you are, or where you are, this primal perceptual world is always there, waiting behind the fuss, for us to tire and eventually fall back into its arms.

We take these two secrets, internal thoughts and the cumulative nature of silence, and apply them. There are two ways to stop thoughts. One is fast and intense, the other slow and calming. These are the two main meditation practices, no matter what else you feel you are doing.

The intense and fast: in a moment, whether you are walking through your world, or sitting meditating, stop the mind with your will. Like two pincers that reach up to your brain, and simply *switch it off!*

Hold it off! Sustain the suspension for as long as you can. It is much easier if you also simultaneously stop breathing. So many practices you will find utilise this method, and you should avail yourself of as many as you can. Make up your own – find ways to shock your mind into stunned silence.

The slow and the calming: this requires long periods of sitting quietly, in which you gradually calm the body, the heart and mind. The longer the better. A true calm state cannot be achieved in anything less than an hour, and it has to be practised regularly. It can be built up over time, such that it becomes joyous to sit in a state of 'nothing special' for long periods.

People speak of walking meditation, active meditation and even artistic or sport meditations. These are all good practices, but they are not a substitute for sitting meditation. They are more often mindfulness practices – techniques of awareness which I have previously spoken of. They are very important and from them we are able to bring another essential quality into our meditation: self-awareness.

The end result is traditionally referred to through symbolic imagery, of the light being held steady. In the wind and the darkness of the world, of the mind, we hold our flame of awareness steady in its purest state.

The second secret is a promise: every little effort you make is not lost. Silence accumulates until eventually it tips the scales. There are two moments: the major and the minor moments in which the *world stops*. The major moment needs no discussion, for it will come. If not within life then at death. The minor moments are available all the time. Just stop, and look at what is in front of you without attitude or valuation. Look at something as if you had never seen it before in your life, just as a child does. See it as it is, disassociated from functionality, attitude or quality. Look at the colours – not the shapes, just the maze of colours, the shades and hues.

In meditation we apply all kinds of little tools to achieve something which one day you will realise is so simple and direct, flicking the switch in the mind. Silence. That stops the left hemisphere of the brain in its tracks. Leaving the right hemisphere to register the perceptions in their purity. That's all it is. Don't concoct elaborate schemes of importance around it. Just flick the switch.

Holding the light steady
in the dark and the wind

This is an ancient image that has stayed with me for many years and sums up so much of our task on the Path. As a thought, an image, we can take it into consciousness and allow it to vibrate a life of its own.

It has numerous meanings, and I will cover a few here:

In our daily life

Here the light means full functioning, with all our knowledge and capacity available and operating. There are times we move through the world like a multi-armed Hindu God. One hand is awareness, remembering ourselves, and alert. Another hand is the task before us, with which we feel confident and competent. Another hand is our relationships, if not swinging all the time, at least satisfactorily functional – you can't expect relationships to always be on an up. Another hand is financial security, another physical health, and another is pondering the deeper mysteries of life. Another hand has the door closed on all our dark threads, so only the gold threads gleam in our light. We walk like Vishnu, juggling all these balls with skill and joy. Our light shines bright, and why not? Everything is going our way.

Then there other times, when our whole edifice of glory comes crashing down. Pandora's box opens, and out creep the dark threads. We don't give a shit about all this spiritual crap: our body aches, our mind harbours dead rats. Life hurls bummer after bummer at us, and we wish the whole damn mess would just blow away, or at least we would blow away. It's easy to hold the light steady when the weather is calm and balmy. But when the night comes down, and the wind blows a chill through our bones – can we hold the light steady then? Can we warm our own bones, light our own confidence, shine on the path with our own beam? This is not easy. This is where we need to have strong hands, and a strong light.

In meditation

Here the light is our self-awareness, held steady by our will. Silence of the mind, sustained in the darkness of the unknown. In meditation we sit in the absence of self-created images, self-created universe – we sit in the darkness of release. Release from movement, release from emotion, release from thought, release from personality, release from the world – we wait, holding only pure awareness. That is the image of true meditation.

The hands

I especially like the idea of *holding*. We normally hold with our hands. The hands are things of wonder, they create the future, and manifest the past into the present. With hands, we touch the sex of our lover. With hands, we hold the spoon for our old parents, for them to eat when they are too frail to use their own hands. With hands, we smooth the ointment on the wounds of the hurt. With hands, we build houses and vehicles. With hands, we write to friends, and create artistic beauty, expressions of the soul. We hold our hands together in prayer, offering and receiving. With hands, we manifest outwardly the knowledge attained in the past. In that very act of manifesting we learn new knowledge, which builds the world we move into in the future, even after death. The hands also hold our light. This is intimate. Like a candle we hold with one hand and protect from the wind with the other.

The darkness

Nasruddin was asked which was more important, the sun or the moon. "The moon, of course!" he said, "because it shines at night when we need it."

It is easy to see our way when the sun lights up the road. It is easy to know what to do when the world gives us confidence, and people look into our eyes with acceptance and agreement. But there are many times on any road, when darkness falls, and we have to walk blind. When people around reject us, blame, refuse and despise us. When all we see is criticism. Then we have to reach into the heart, and bring forth our own light. To walk in the direction we know to be right only by inner conviction.

Once on the high plateau of Tibet, in the snow and biting wind, Alexandra David-Neel and her companions lost the trail. They had to cross a plain and find the path again through the hills at the other end. There was no sign of where the right track was, and to miss it would most certainly be fatal for them. She knew what to do. She knew she was the only one who had the strength of inner light. She simply said, "Follow me." and off they went into the snow. They found the path when they reached the hills. She, in the absence of a road, laid down the road herself, out of her own will and awareness. That is what we all have to do when we enter the darkness of the Path.

The wind

Emotion. Desires. Cruelty of fate. All these try to blow out our flame. Merciless, and depressing. The world can serve up so much of the rolling force which punches the solar plexus. Again and again, punch after punch. If not the world, then we have the insanity of doing it to ourselves. The wind blows around the house, rattling the doors and windows, forcing the smoke back down the chimney and into the room of safety, where our flame lives. If we haven't built the house strongly, then the flame can be snuffed by a gust. The hands again, build the inner house, the inner room, the sanctuary, in which we host the eternal flame. This is the symbol of our love – our love of everything – love has no object or cause. We love because we love because we love.

Delayed Awakening

The rule is: first we choose the Path, second we Die.

Typically this should take about three years, from the first real launch to the second step.

But why do some people take much longer and even whole lives, to complete this basic second step?

The first step, choosing the Path, would normally mean we begin the exercises. There are plenty of them out there, and for anyone eager, this is an exciting phase. The exercises themselves give the indication we are gaining 'power'. Actually, they lead us away from the second step. Depending on which exercises we practise, in general they are designed to bolster the walls of the well, so we can lower the bucket to fetch the water.

Without this bolstering, the 'bucket lowering' part would not succeed, for many reasons. The walls would collapse before we have the clear water, or after – either way all would be futile.

The 'bucket lowering' is the central core of the practices: meditation. This is the 'awakening' exercise in essence. This exercise leads to silence, inner silence. It is this exercise which invokes Death.

When meditation is combined with the other practices, then we have a wholesome combination, which lowers us to Death in a constructive way.

Death means more than physical death. It means the *death of our false self*. Some call this the ego, but that word is problematic, as it is normally ascribed to our very physical existence – and when that dies, there is no resurrection. That's the end. We don't seek the death of the our physical existence, but we come close to it. We seek the death of the tyrant, and it hangs on to power until the body is so weakened that we face a critical decision: dethrone the tyrant or death final. Death usually involves some physical component. Hopefully, we are not too damaged by this, but it is hard to pass through without a serious physical decrease of one form or another. What we seek is the death of that part of us which is so full-of-ourselves.

Our pride and self-satisfaction. Our secret or not-so-secret belief that we are better than everyone else, even through feeling inferior to everyone else. And more – our total architecture of self – who we identify ourselves to be. All that has to go.

One who has been through this Death has a hollowed-out feeling: inside, you realise, there is nothing. Those who haven't been through this are full in the middle. They have a strong sense-of-self, even when concealed by timidity it is still palpable. They also indulge in criticisms of others, delighting in telling everyone why other people are stuffed-up in some way. The *hollow* ones also will criticise, but you sense with them they are concocting their criticisms, and if you pushed them enough they'd crumble and admit they don't really know. Their criticisms have more to do with a sadness of relationship than desire to express their own inner self.

Here is the paradox: to one who sees, the *hollow* ones have more power and strength in 'self', than the brittle, immortal ones. But that 'self' is a mysterious, nebulous thing they never understand nor grasp. The *hollow* ones could never stand in the centre of the room and demand everyone listen to their opinion. They lack that obvious certitude. They may learn to pretend it, and to put on a show – but look closely, they are *hollow*. Just be careful though, as they could begin to reflect the power of a deeper being through their hollowness.

Death robs us of our rights. Robs us of our convictions, of our demands and desires. Robs us of faux-heaviness, petty seriousness, the longing to be respected and liked, the aching for appreciation. Robs us of immortality – subconsciously we all hold this strange belief that we can never unseat, that we are immortal. That is why close encounters with death always shock us.

So why do some delay between these two steps? Why doesn't the inevitable sequence as expected? What has gone wrong?

The answer is always one thing – they have not practised the critical essence: meditation. They have not sought inner silence. Instead they have done some of the practices, but rarely the 'un-doing' practices. Those also lead to Death. Instead they have practised the activities which enhance status in their eyes and, they fervently demand, in the eyes of others.

Status-enhancing practices include skills at the associated enterprises. Skills at words, dreaming, dancing, music, tarot, oracles, interpreting dreams. Skills at accumulating truck-loads of information about obscure religious or shamanic concepts, or they read all kinds of new-age material which is mind-knowledge from the past. They practise these skills enough to provide them with a kind of power, giving them a sense of ascendancy.

In the worst cases they actually succeed in gaining real power over others, not just a fantasy. That is a serious disadvantage, because then they have a considerable investment in not losing that power. Which is what happens in Death. Luckily those cases are mostly rare in Western countries, as our lifestyle lacks the hardships necessary to acquire such powers. Most 'delayers' are trapped in a fantasy of their own status, their place along the Path. That fantasy is as dearly held to, as if it were real – just that the world never seems to validate it for them. Denial is a wonder drug.

Then, they give up their practices. They pride themselves on knowing all about, but no longer practising. Oh, they try their hand occasionally, just to fill out the role, but any serious effort – no, they lack the will for that.

These people become *trapped between the steps*. They can't go back – once they have committed themselves to the Path, there is never any turning back. They can't move forward either, because they have lost the way. And yet the way is so simple – inner silence. Practise sitting on your bottom doing nothing for long periods of time and not wasting that time – striving for inner calm and silence. It never fails to work.

That is the last thing they wish to do, and they soon construct vast bodies of arguments about why meditation is unnecessary. About why they are already doing it in other things, about how their whole life is a meditation, and on and on.

These people become sad ghosts of no-man's-land. Caught between the stepping stones, caught in the fog. Those who have passed through look back at these 'delayers' with disquiet and concern – puzzled as to why they have stalled. Some who are advanced upon the Path, and have the thread of teaching, make forays back into the soul-desert-land, to attempt retrievals of the stalled ones – occasionally successful, mostly failures.

The wandering of these delayers can continue for lifetimes, never happy, never knowing why. The world constantly rejecting them, but they have no place to rest, no friends.

In the end, they will run out of energy to keep this up. The first choice is the thing of real power, and once the bid is cast, its consequence cannot be thwarted. Eventually, they fall to their knees and surrender. The effort of sustaining their parody at last overwhelms them like a tidal wave, and they crumple in a heap of tears. Right where they stood! Which could be absolutely anywhere.

It is a beautiful moment, and one when all those who had given up hope, look back with love at another who has passed the gates, and joined the *hollow* people.

Chapter 18

Spiritual Development the Hard Way

In past times, for those pursuing the ultimate goal, it has been preferred to remove to a remote location and dedicate to practice, unfettered and unassailed by the concerns of the world. In environments conducive to tranquillity and meditation, fast progress was made while the outside world appreciated the place in their culture for the important work renunciants undertook. It was acknowledged their intent and dedication energetically benefited everyone.

A luxury of the past. Times have changed and we now face a new paradigm of the spiritual life, not without its advantages. Today we have to conduct inner intent alongside the outer pursuit of survival and participation in a dynamic and consuming world. A world which no longer comprehends, let alone values, the work of inner evolution, except in superficial ways.

This means we have to operate on two levels in every activity of life. It also means we have to transform outer-world activities into inner-world practices. The casual observer will see you engaged just like everyone else. But you will be mining for personal power, realisation and progress along your spiritual path, in the very same actions those all around you are doing with no intent other than that of daily, mundane living. That is the difference.

We take each action, examine it and transform it into *practice*. No one around should ever be the wiser for walking alongside us. Oh, they may feel you are a 'good person' or not, depending on your style and their mood. They may feel there is something a little different about you and that you display a degree of focus and application to tasks not normal for the general populace. But they should have no idea whatsoever that your entire inner being is perennially dedicated to the task of spiritual freedom with the most acute intensity. They don't need to know.

If you do find yourself desiring others to know your real game, then you have some reflection to do in the chapter on Pride. Even your family or spouse should never see any difference between you and the world. Naturally, you will be somewhat different – unique, and they will know you hold quite different views, but that is only when they stop and recall your responses or words. In the midst of worldly activity, you should display no indication whatsoever, that you are applying an inner attention to each task which is diametrically opposed to everyone else.

It is all on the inside!

That is what *spiritual development the hard way* means. We don't crap on about spiritual clichés and self-aggrandising postulations. There is space for this in the early stages – we are all human and tend to get excited, plus it can be useful to repeat outwardly what we are striving to embed internally. But after a time, we have to get down to the hard work of transforming every item of our life and world into alignment with our deepest intent. Either that, or toss it out. This is a mammoth task, and going to a few meditation classes, or reading the latest new-age guru's book, is not the *hard way*. Application and struggle with changing all the inner and outer furniture of your existence, is what this Path is about.

Spiritual development the hard way is the task of examining every minute corner of our world-life, both inner and outer, to align it with our purpose. But it is more than that, and this is why it is indeed the *hard way*, because we are a composite of layers. Our task of alignment has to penetrate down through the layers of being. This is what is so often forgotten.

It is a task that requires huge amounts of energy and dedication, but also extreme cleverness, as these layers are not easily accessible. They operate beneath our awareness. We can gain influence upon them through secret pivot points, and through consistent repetition, to a degree that few are capable of sustaining. The only way to align our deeper layers is to take the hard road. The easy road looks good at first, but in reality it doesn't offer us the necessary compression to reach our destination. This is the same in life as in spiritual development. Easy and comfortable, equates to failure. Always choose the hard route and you will discover, as long as you sacrifice regret, that you are enhanced with potency, and the gift of condensing that ball of commitment in your guts. Only those gifts will serve we who seek the ultimate goal available in this precious jewel that is our short life. But what is that goal?

The Goal

I have not, until now, addressed this directly, because it is not a primary consideration for the initial phases of the Path. It is intuited by those who choose the Path, and that is all it needs to be, at first. Our initial gesture of commitment is one of direction rather than goal.

The reason is that, behind the veils of speculation and strategic manoeuvres, there is one fundamental truth about the Path. It never ends!

The overwhelming goal of the Path is to achieve the state of *indissolvable intent*. That condition of our deepest spirit which knows without a shadow of doubt that we are, for all eternity, utterly aligned with the direction of Spirit. Penetration, so absolute into our being, that we know time cannot threaten us. Our rudder is fused solid for eternity, and nothing can overcome that *face* of our ancient spirit. That is the primary goal of *spiritual development the hard way*.

Yet I should say more, as there is a further discernment for those who have practised the principles and exercises in this book, and are at that point in the road where they seek a more secret knowledge of how to participate in the Path.

I will sketch here a vision, which is only for advanced travellers. What we seek is *permanency*. Death brings with it no guarantee of the continuation of selfhood, despite what so many claim. In truth, even messages from the dead cannot be trusted. You only have to see the multitude of interpretations for any world event – there are infinite variations of reality. These variations, these 'realities', are mirrors of our being which is going to die. They are projections from the arrangement of our interpretations of life and the world. An interpretation that has been arranged from a specific selection of everything which exists.

That specific selection is our world, and what we see 'out there' are always items from 'our world'. When we die, there is no guarantee 'our world' will exist, but it may carry on in a meteor tail, just long enough to be capable of interaction with those on this side of death. And what do the dead tell us? What else but items of 'our world', which is essentially the sustaining perception of our common agreement. Like the cartoon characters who keep running beyond the cliff edge, until they realise there is nothing but clear air beneath them – then they plummet like a rock.

Death is the end of 'our world'. Everything we took as permanent. Everything! Death is the unknown. Our world is the known. At death, everything dies – people, countries, humanity and its history, nature, the sun and stars, the stock exchange, all religions, everything you can think of, everything you can name, which means everything that exists as a 'known' within you – all gone, like the mirage it always was.

Permanency means the mysterious transference of our locus of awareness, our *identity*, from the being which is going to die, to a vehicle which exists in infinity. We replicate death. Everything that death will take from us, we let go. Strip away everything we fear to lose. *Permanence* can only be achieved in the pinprick centre of *impermanence*. When all is given away, what is left?

This requires a strategic manoeuvre where we don't just throw it all away without knowledge of what we are doing. We also build a vehicle in infinity, beyond time. That is done with a special tool we are all provided with from birth – our mythical perception. But most mythical constructions are only reflections of 'our world' and so they are useless, except to exercise this sense organ.

The vehicle in infinity can only be one of pure energy – no 'image' is possible. This is beyond images. We transfer our centre of existence, or rather we awaken, to our eternal essence. Always it ends up being a process of elimination, but with intent!

Not this, not that. Bit by bit we strip away everything we cling to on all levels of our being until there is nothing left, and that is who we really are. Sans ambition, sans desire, sans love, sans expectation – what we call total, absolute darkness. The black core of blackness.

It is only those who journey to this juncture who discover that what we believed to be darkness is, in fact, light. And what we believed to be light is actually darkness. This has to be realised in the very marrow! No words will suffice.

By this method, by this unassailable intent, we learn how to store our treasure in a place that survives death, and by that we secure *permanency*. The problem with the idea of *permanency*, and the reason Buddhism is so antagonistic to this word, is because we all want permanency for our temporal self. We want to survive as we know ourselves to be. We seek permanency in so many temporal ways: we have children, we store up possessions and money to 'pass on'. Utter futility – your entire family will die when you die. Your entire edifice of meaning will vanish, and you will look back at the fog from outside to see it was all illusion.

You may wish to pass on your wealth and possessions to assist those who are still struggling on the Path to freedom, or those who are suffering in the mundane world. That is fine. But, unfortunately, so long as you are not realised in the knowledge of *impermanence*, you are secretly seeking some thread of self-permanence. You are storing up wealth on a sinking ship, building your house on a crumbling bridge, placing your trust in a mirage.

We are trapped in time. The illusion of permanency is a foundational feature of that trap. Only by relinquishing permanency, can we reach for the possibility of *permanency*. But the irony is that if we seek to salvage our permanency in this way, it will fail. *Permanency* comes only as a consequence of total renunciation, never as a desire.

Permanency as a goal is the consequence of momentum: the momentum of complete and knowledgeable walking of the Path. By 'knowledgeable', I mean penetrating insight into the secrets of existence.

If we apply ourselves with dedication and imagination to the process of seeking the eternal essence within our being, we gain a slight seismic shift in the structure of our life-consciousness. This is the secret.

A gap opens at a crucial moment, and through that gap we can walk to a sacred promise embedded in the covenant of existence.

That is what we are waiting for. The fulfilment of the eternal longing of the Source of the Universe – every being has this chance. Every being has the chance to see the jewel at the centre of their being, and grasp it! Feet and all.

You have this chance. Will you grasp it?

Do you have the courage? Do you have the audacity?

Yes?

Then don't be timid.

Stand up scream it out: "YES!!"